Lithics 'Down Under': Australian Perspectives on Lithic Reduction, Use and Classification

Edited by

Christopher Clarkson
Lara Lamb

BAR International Series 1408
2005

Published in 2016 by
BAR Publishing, Oxford

BAR International Series 1408

Lithics 'Down Under': Australian Perspectives on Lithic Reduction, Use and Classification

ISBN 978 1 84171 851 4

BAR Publishing is the trading name of British Archaeological Reports (Oxford) Ltd.
British Archaeological Reports was first incorporated in 1974 to publish the BAR
Series, International and British. In 1992 Hadrian Books Ltd became part of the BAR
group. This volume was originally published by Archaeopress in conjunction with
British Archaeological Reports (Oxford) Ltd / Hadrian Books Ltd, the Series principal
publisher, in 2005. This present volume is published by BAR Publishing, 2016.

Printed in England

BAR
PUBLISHING

BAR titles are available from:

BAR Publishing
122 Banbury Rd, Oxford, OX2 7BP, UK
EMAIL   info@barpublishing.com
PHONE   +44 (0)1865 310431
FAX   +44 (0)1865 316916
www.barpublishing.com

Contents

List of Contributors

Harry Allen
Department of Anthropology
University of Auckland
Private Bag 92019
Auckland
New Zealand

Val Attenbrow
Division of Anthropology
Australian Museum
College Street
Sydney
NSW 2006
Australia

Chris Clarkson
School of Social Science
University of Queensland
St Lucia Brisbane
Qld 4072
Australia

Patricia Fanning
Graduate School of the Environment
Macquarie University
NSW 2109
Australia

Peter Hiscock
School of Archaeology and Anthropology
Australian National University
Canberra ACT 0200
Australia

Simon Holdaway
Department of Anthropology
University of Auckland
Private Bag 92019
Auckland
New Zealand

Lara Lamb
Department of Humanities and International Studies
The University of Southern Queensland
Toowoomba
QLD 4350
Australia

Boone Law
SWCA Environmental Consultants
4407 Monterey Oaks Blvd
Building 1
Suite 10
Austin Texas 78749
USA

Oliver Macgregor
School of Archaeology and Anthropology
Australian National University
Canberra
ACT 0200
Australia

Alex Mackay
School of Archaeology and Anthropology
Australian National University
Canberra
ACT 0200
Australia

Justin Shiner
Archaeologist
Environment and Heritage Section
Sustainability Support
Comalco Aluminium Limited
Post Office, Weipa QLD 4874

Michael Shott
Department of Sociology
Anthropology and Criminology
University of Northern Iowa
Cedar Falls
IA 50614-0513
USA

1 | Introduction: Casting New Light on Old Stones

Chris Clarkson and Lara Lamb

The purpose of this monograph is to take a new look at various aspects of stone artefact analysis that reveal important and exciting new information about the past. This involes reorienting our methodological approach to stone artefacts as well as the questions asked of them. The papers making up this volume tackle a number of issues that have long been at the heart of archaeology's problematic relationship with stone artefacts, including our understanding of the dynamic nature of past stoneworking practices, the utility of traditional classificatory schemes, and ways to unlock the vast amount of information about the strategic role of lithic technology that resides in stone artefact assemblages.

The dominant theme of this monograph is the pursuit of new ways of characterising the effects of manufacturing and susbsistence behaviour on stone artefact assemblages, but three central concerns are evident throughout this volume. The first centres on exploring the effects of reduction intensity on artefact form using quantitative methods for measuring reduction and changes to implement form, with implications for the way artefacts are classified and the manufacturing process depicted more generally. The second theme concerns our understanding of the important role that morphological features created during the reduction process, whether deliberately or otherwise, can have in creating opportunities and limitations for efficient tool use and continued reworking. The third and final theme explores the potential of assemblage variability to reveal valuable information about the organisation of settlement and susbsistence in Aborignial societies of the past.

All of the studies presented in this monograph incorporate measures of artefact reduction of one sort or another to understand the time-ordering of manufacutring actions, their effects on artefact morphology, and the differential investment and husbanding of tools as a result of variable use-lives, artefact transport and raw material rationing. This unifying concern for measuring the amount of shaping, resharpending and reworking an artefact has received makes this volume unique, and hopefully draws attention to this invaluable and under-utilised analytical tool as an extremely informative means of exploring past human behaviour and the determinants of assemblage variability.

The papers presented in this volume are the product of research conducted entirely within Australia, and therefore have an unavoidably atipodean flavour in terms of their theoretical outlook and methodological bent.

Rather than representing parochial interests in Australian sites and assemblages, however, this volume intends to present the distincitive persepective developed 'down under' to a larger audience. We see this perspective as largely deriving from, first of all, a freedom from the hegemony of typological schemes that have always underlain lithic analysis in the northern hemisphere; secondly, access to a rich and variable ethnographic record that has allowed observation of stone artefact production and use in dynamic social and economic contexts; thirdly, a strongly held view that few recurring formal implement types of the kind found in Europe and North America were to be found in Australia until the mid-Holocene, and that no direct form-function relationships could be found to inhere for these types; and finally, that diverse spatial and chronological patterning made broad chronological or geographic phases and culture areas difficult to establish in the way they have been in other parts of the world (Clarkson 2004; Hayden 1977, 1979; Hiscock 1998; Holdaway 1995; Holdaway and Stern 2004). Hiscock (1998) and Holdaway and Stern (2004) provide interesting historical reviews of the reasons why a distinctive approach to stone artefact analysis developed the way it did in Australia.

In turn, such factors probably account for the numerous failed attempts to introduce universally employed typologies in Australia (Holdaway 1995; Holdaway and Stern 2004), as well as the frequent confounding of simple models of colonisation and the evolution of technology both here and elsewhere (Foley and Mirazon Lahr 2003; White 1977). Thus, although Australian archaeologists have of course been aware of, and influenced by, lithic studies and theoretical perspectives in other parts of the world, they have nevertheless developed their own distinctive perspective on the subject. Hopefully this volume successfully captures some of this flavour as we re-examine the empirical basis for some of the more pervasive Australian typologies, rethink form-function realtionships, and explore assemblage variation in regions where no commonly recurring retouched implement types are found. Although most papers employ Australian case-studies, the issues raised in this volume are of direct relevance to major themes being debated in international lithic studies today.

It would be a mistake however to suggest that only a single viewpoint exists in Australia, as a wide range of perspectives on the meaning and causes of assemblage variation exists, as do many different approaches to lithic analysis itself. What this volume has chosen to focus on as a unifying theme, therefore, is the novel ways in which a consideration of artefact reduction can shed new light on old stones. To preface these studies it is important to briefly review the rationale behind our focus on analysing artefact reduction as a relevant and enlightening facet of lithic anlaysis.

Why Measure Reduction?

As stone-working is a reductive technology, measuring the degree to which this process has progressed will profitably form the basis of many kinds of lithic analysis. Quantifying the extent of reduction allows estimations to be made of the amount of time and energy invested in the production of an artefact, the level of departure of the observed form from its original form, the amount of material likely to have been created as a product of the process, how much reduction potential remains in an artefact, the position in the sequence at which changes in manufacturing strategies took place or new fracture features appeared, as well as the effects of varying reduction intensity on artefact morphology.

At a higher interpretive level, measures of reduction can be seen as critical to the testing of behavioural models that hypothesize the place of stone artefacts in broader systems of time budgeting, mobility and land use. Consequently, measures of reduction have come to be associated, at least implicitly, with discussions of risk, cost, and efficiency in past technological systems (Bleed, 2001). These discussions build on the assumption that the differential distribution of sequential steps and stages through space and time will reflect aspects of planning, land use, ecology and settlement and subsistence patterns effecting people's daily lives (Nelson, 1991, Kuhn, 1995). Measures of reduction are consequently fast becoming a central component of lithic analyses that seek to answer questions about past land use, mobility and processes of artifact manufacture and discard, as this volume demonstrates.

A common useage of measures of reduction today is the construction of sequence models. Sequence models are theoretical constructs that attempt to time-order phenomena by positioning them at points along a temporal continuum. In lithic studies, sequence models are typically used to determine the ordering of technical actions and outcomes involved in the reduction of stone materials. Models of this sort often use measures of reduction intensity to track changes in artefact morphology throughout the reduction process, enabling the identification of common forms, or the amount of variation found at different points along the reduction continuum. Sequence models have proved particularly useful in understanding and graphically depicting the various steps and transformations that characterize a wide range of lithic reduction strategies across space and time.

As Bleed (2001) and Dibble (1995) have pointed out, however, not all reduction oriented studies share the same research goals or even the same philosophical underpinning. Some approaches, they argue, promote a normative view of reduction that focuses on revealing the predetermined stages prehistoric artisans went through to produce specific 'end-products' in accordance with a mental template. Others seek to draw out the contingent nature of technological responses to changing options and circumstances by examining the nature and frequency of artefacts at different stages of reduction across space and time. Others still have used sequence models to expose the arbitrariness of typological divisions by demonstrating the existence of underlying morphological continuums.

Bleed (2001) sees different approaches to sequence modelling as falling into one of two categories, which he calls 'teological' and 'evolutionary'. Teleological models treat sequences as "a set of internally determined actions that follow one from another and lead to a predetermined goal", whereas evolutionary models describe results that are produced "by selected interaction between conditions and variables" (Bleed 2001:121). Teleological models should therefore attempt to express the variation within a particular reduction system as much as the central tendency. Thus, while reduction sequences provide a useful means of ordering different assemblage components into various degrees of reduction, there is no reason to link this depiction to normative modes of behaviour or the existence of 'mental templates' for stone artefact production.

Ultimately, once reduction sequences are well understood in a number of regions for a number of time-periods, it is anticipated that significant variations will emerge in the way people have approached the same problem of making and mending stone tools, and this is already quite apparent from only a handful of studies comparing Middle-Paleolithic scraper reduction sequences across Europe and the Middle-East (Close 1991; Dibble 1995; Gordon 1993). In fact, if charting historical and stylistic differences between regions is a focus of investigation, then a reduction approach offers great potential to explore these issues, by providing a firm basis on which to compare similarity and difference in subtle aspects of material selection, design and execution.

Studies of reduction may also cast new light on the issue of typological richness (or even cognitive complexity) by determining whether more or less types may simply represent more or less divisions of a single continuum, the emergence of new sequences, or the convergence or divergence of multiple sequences to create novel forms.

Some will argue that use-wear or residue studies are the appropriate test of reduction sequence models, as they may determine whether each stage is 'real' in the sense of having a discrete function. Alternatively, it might be argued that reduction sequences tell us little if the production of each type is 'staged' (though theoretically linked in a chain of continuing reduction), and was thus created as a discrete 'end product' to be kept in its current form for some time, either for functional reasons or as a matter of cultural convention or aesthetic preference, before proceeding immediately to the next stage, and so on. Thus, regardless of whether a type 'could' or 'would' have been transformed into another form had it not been lost or discarded, its current form was nevertheless a 'finished' form.

Although one or both of these points could be true in certain cases, Dibble (1995) has pointed out that they need not undermine the goals or validity of a reduction sequence approach, nor would they necessarily result in incompatible interpretations. Such interpretations could easily run side by side with, or could be overlaid on top of a reduction sequence model that aims initially to describe only the nature and variability of the transformation process. To arrange artefacts in a continuum based on the amount of material removed, and to order them into likely stages through which each type may progress, does not deny the existence of ethno-taxonomies or that people may have ascribed different meanings or levels of significance to different artifacts or stages in the process. Equally, it does not rule out using artefacts in different ways as their mechanical suitability changes and they become suited to new functions. Indications that certain types were used in specific ways or in certain contexts may indeed help determine whether this is so or not.

Alternatively, use-wear analysis may instead demonstrate that a range of forms could be employed in a range of tasks (as several studies now show), and therefore, that morphology may better reflect certain design requirements, such as suitability for hafting or potential for extended resharpening, rather than a simple form-function relationship. Different viewpoints on the determinants of assemblage variability may therefore coexist, and the interpretive spin will depend on the theoretical standpoint of individual archaeologists. Reduction oriented approaches provide an analytical tool that may be grafted to many theoretical frameworks.

An example of this is to be found in two contrasting approaches that have largely emerged along continental lines, and that place differing emphasis on cultural choice and intentionality as explanatory mechanisms accounting for differences in the overall system of raw material procurement, reduction, use and discard. For example the chaîne opératoire approach now common in Europe (Bar-Yosef and Meignen 1992; Boëda 1988, 1993; Boëda et al. 1990; Karlin et al. 1991; Boëda and Pelegrin 1983; Geneste 1988, 1989, 1990; Meignen 1988; Pelegrin et al. 1988; Perlès 1987; Perlès and Binder 1990; Tixier et al. 1980; Turq 1988, 1992), and largely based on the social anthropology of Leroi-Góurhan (1964) and Lemonnier (1983, 1993), views the study of reduction behaviour and the 'technical choices' involved in knapping and tool use, as a profitable means of determining the goals, social context and intended end products of prehistoric artisans,

as well as a way of exploring the phenomenological world of the maker.

Others (Dibble 1995; Neeley and Barton 1994; Gordon 1993; Hiscock 1994b, 1996b, 1998, 2000, In Press), and particularly those that are influenced by processual and evolutionary schools of thought, prefer to see stone artefacts in the archaeological record as either broken, lost or exhausted implements, reflecting as much the undesirable characteristics that led to their discard as the intentional features of design and artifice – in other words, the by-products of their manufacture and maintenance (Dibble 1995; Bleed 2001). From this standpoint, the reduction sequence is usually portrayed as a profitable way of determining the ecological context of production and discard, with priority given to the economic relations of demand and supply, cost and benefit, in explanations of assemblage variability. Individual creativity, selection and choice are recognized, but are usually portrayed as sources of variation - the persistence of which is dependant on the operation of selection and undirected evolution (Bamforth and Bleed 1997). Explanations of change from this perspective generally focus on longer time-scales and recognize the historically contingent nature of solutions that arise to meet various problems (Barton and Clark 1997; Bleed 1997; Bamforth and Bleed 1997; Hiscock In Press; Schott 1997).

Generally speaking, neither perspective denies that aspects held central to the other standpoint are important determinants of variation. Rather, various theoretical and methodological differences arise from choices about whether to place emphasis on either social or ecological/economic relations, but naturally views part-way between these two extremes can also be found (e.g. Sellet 1993).

The explanation for changes in stone technology and intensity of reduction in this volume tend more toward the latter approach, emphasizing the operation of ecological and economic processes in operation over many millennia. However, most authors acknowledge that these changes could be interpreted in other ways. Whatever the interpretive spin, analysis of reduction allows important dimensions of stone artefact procurement, manufacture, transport and discard to be measured, compared and contrasted.

One way to review the various uses to which studies of reduction can be put is to examine the wide range of case studies presented in this volume.

Themes in this Volume
The most ubiquotous of the themes in this volume is the concern for quantifying the amount of retouch artefacts have received as well as the effects of differential reduction on artefact form. This emphasis on appropriate procedures for measuring retouch results in the compilation of a new and exciting range of techniques

with which to depict the manufacturing process and its various products. In Chapter 2, for example, Hiscock and Clarkson re-examine various measures of reduction intensity that have been proposed over the last 20 years or so. The performance of a number of measures is evaluated over the course of a reduction experiment that was designed to determine which is best suited to measuring reduction intensity on flakes that are unifacially retouched along one margin. They compare the performance of each index to the actual percentage of the original weight lost from flakes as retouching continues. Their experiment reveals some surprising results that do not bode well for a number of widely publicised retouch measures, while also revealing that a common critique of Kuhn's geometric index of reduction appears largely unfounded. Hiscock and Clarkson's study prefaces many of the case studies that follow by demonstrating the success of the retouch measure most commonly employed throughout this volume.

Building on this experimental work, Clarkson (Chapter 3) employs the recommended reduction index to explore the effects of retouch intensity on scrapers from one region of northern Australia. He finds that much of the morphological variation found in these artefacts is a product of varying levels of reduction. The study also considers how well these artifacts fit into traditional typological classes once they are ordered into different levels of reduction, and whether in fact these classes form discrete and coherent categories at all. In so doing, Clarkson introduces the second theme pervading this volume - the issue of classification – in which studies of reduction are used to challenge exisiting typologies, demonstrate continuums and explore the boundaries between various subsets of retouched assemblages. Classification is one of the most germane and arguably most important activities undertaken by archaeologists, in that it shapes the way we think about phenomena, the way we partition it into analytical units, and thus the way our data are collected and communicated. Indeed, few issues have been so persistently debated in archaeology as the way classificatory systems should be constructed and their metaphysical basis, and the studies in this volume make a valuable contribution by demonstrating the mutability of artifact form and the existence of morphological continuums. Clarkson's analysis of scraper reduction continuums, for instance, adds to a growing number of studies that call into question the value of traditional typologies as useful descriptions of artefact variability.

Lamb (Chapter 4) also employs measures of reduction to explore issues of artefact form and classification. She uses measures of retouch, size and implement form to examine whether the manufacture of backed artefacts was the sole focus of reduction activities at the South Molle Island Quarry or whether they represent a subset of a broader range of manufacturing activitites undertaken at the quarry. As backed artifacts are one of the most frequently documented retouched artefact forms found in eastern Australia, regional studies such as this enable better definition of their classificatory boundaries and contribute much to our understanding of this widespread technological tradition. Lamb's methods could be used to great effect in exploring the nature of backed artefact production in other assemblages in Australia and elsewhere.

Hiscock and Attenbrow (Chapter 5) continue with the theme of reduction continuums by looking at the scraper reduction at Capertee 3 in the Sydney Basin. Rather than explore issues of classification, however, their research highlights the eternal contradiction between the traditional presumption of strong form-function relationships in stone tool types on the one hand, and the progressive modification of tool edges and changing artifact suitability on the other. Though less pervasive in archaeological thinking until recently, this notion of dynamic change and thresholds in tool suitability has formed the flip-side of functional arguments about stone tools for at least 100 years. Hiscock and Attenbrow masterfully expose naïve and yet alarmingly pervasive ideas about artefact design and stone tool function, and urge us to consider more sophisticated models of tool maintenance and optimality in future formulations.

The importance of the gradual modification, addition and obliteration of fracture features over the reduction sequence were issues raised by Hiscock and Attenbrow. Macgregor continues with this line of enquiry by examining the potential of abrupt terminations to inhibit further reduction of a nucleus. His experimental study identifies some of the causes of abrupt terminations as well as the conditions under which they are likely to be repeated, thereby hastening the discard of the nucleus, or overcome, thereby allowing reduction to continue. Macgregor introduces us to the valuable concept of 'reduction potential', which considers both core geometry and reduction technique in assessing the potential of a nucleus to be reduced to differing degress. He proposes several strategies that knappers could use to overcome the problems caused by abrupt terminations, and suggests that these strategies will likely be employed to differing degrees depending on the costs involved in raw material procurement. Macgregor is therefore able to lead us from a rigorous study of controlled fracture processes into a discussion of the organisational benefits accruing from employing certain reduction strategies in particular environmental and behavioural contexts, making this a valuable example of the potential for experimental studies to generate new data and hypotheses of direct relevance in understanding past human behaviour.

Shiner et al's study (Chapter 7) picks up on another of the themes central to this volume - the potential of studies of reduction to reveal valuable information about the nature of past landuse practices such as mobility, occupational duration and intensity. In an analysis of two open sites and a rockshelter sequence of comparable age, they examine the complex interplay of raw material transport, occupational duration and age-span as reflected in reduction intensity and assemblage composition. Their analysis reveals complex patterns that undermine simple interpretations of assemblage variability they also challenge the common notion that rich rockshelter assemblages must represent very different technological activities and occupational intensities to those seen in open sites.

Law (Chapter 8), also armed with several measures of reduction intensity, continues the examination of settlement and subsistence behaviour by exploring changing group mobility and landuse over the course of the Holocene at Purritjarra in Central Australia. Law uses his data on changing levels of reduction to assess changes in technological provisioning that might be equated with the varying frequency and predictability of residential moves. This novel approach allows Law to weigh up competing models of Holocene arid zone settlement, arriving at a new interpretation of Holocene settlement at Purritjarra to that which had previously been proposed.

Mackay (Chapter 9), on the other hand, while also concerned with mobility and landuse, is confronted with the absence of formal types in assemblages located on and around Ngarrabullgan, a table-top mountain on Cape York Peninsula. His search for a new analytical approach leads him to explore the power of a purely attribute-based analysis of assemblages from surface sites and excavated rockshelter deposits spanning the last 5,500 years. This study is an elegant example of the way in which artefacts traditionally designated 'debitage' and usually left unanalyzed can be engaged to reveal detailed information about past settlement and subsistence practices. This chapter offers a valuable example to archaeologists struggling to incorporate whole assemblages into their research rather than limiting their analysis to the tiny subset that is constituted by formal implement types.

The final paper in this volume draws together the several themes that unite this volume and assesses the value and future directions of the reduction thesis and its discontents. It also compares and contrasts the perspective and ideas taken up by those working in Australia with research that is currently being conducted elsewhere in the world. The final chapter is not only an overview of the volume, but also a substantive and insightful contribution to this exciting branch of lithics research.

Conclusion
This volume represents a compilation of papers of a kind that have rarely been assembled in one place before. It is one of the first of its kind to explore stone artefact reduction as a central and unifying theme, and to explore its many implications and applications within the realms of lithic classification, tool function and settlement and subsistence studies. We hope that readers find the ideas and approaches contained whithin this volume stimulating and worth pursuing in their own research areas.

Acknowledgements
We would like to thank Sean Ulm, Ian Lilley and John Prangnell for the invitation to present many of the papers in this volume at the Australian Archaeology conference held in Harvey Bay in 2001. We would also like to extend our thanks to Peter Bleed, Stephen Kuhn, Harold Dibble, William Andrefsky, Margaret Nelson, Michael Barton, Mary Lou Larson, Peter Veth, Peter Thorley, Bruno David and Daniel Amick for reviewing papers in this volume. Production costs were generously funded by a publication subsidy from the Centre for the Humanities at the Australian National University. Our thanks also to BAR Publishing for agreeing to publish this monograph.

References
Bamforth, D.B. and Bleed, P. 1997 Technology, flaked stone technology, and risk. In G.A. Clark (ed.), *Rediscovering Darwin: Evolutionary Theory in Archaeology*. Pp.109-140. Archaeological Papers of the American Anthropological Association, No.7. Virginia: American Anthropological Association.

Bar-Yosef, O. and Meignen, L. 1992 Insights into Levantine Middle Paleolithic cultural variability. In Dibble, H. and Mellars, P. (eds) *The Middle Paleolithic: Adaptation, Behaviour, and Variability*. Pp.163-82. Philadelphia: University of Pennsylvania Museum.

Barton, C.M. and Clark, G.A. (eds) 1997 *Rediscovering Darwin: Evolutionary Theory and Archaeological Explanation* Virginia: Archaeological Papers of the American Anthropological Association 7.

Bleed, P. 1997 Content as variability, result as selection: toward a behavioural definition of technology. In Clark, G.A. and Barton, C.M. (eds) *Rediscovering Darwin: Evolutionary Theory and Archaeological Explanation*. Pp.95-104. Washington: Archaeological Papers of the American Anthropological Association

Bleed, P. 2001 Trees or chains, links or branches: conceptual alternatives for consideration of stone tool production and other sequential activities. *Journal of Archaeological Method and Theory* 8:101-127.

Boëda, E. 1988 Le concept levallois et evaluation de son champ d'application. In Otte, M. (ed) *L'homme de Néandertal*. Pp.13-26. Liège: Actes du Colloque International de Liège.

Boëda, E., Geneste, J.m. and Meignen, L. 1990 Identification de chaînes opératoires lithiques du Paléolithique Ancien et Moyen. *Paléo* 2:43-80.

Clarkson, C. 2004 Technological Provisioning and Assemblage Variation in the Eastern Victoria River Region, Northern Australia: A Darwinian Perspective. PhD Thesis. Australian National University, Canberra.

Close, A. 1991 On the validity of Middle Paleolithic tool types: a test case from the eastern Sahara. *Journal of Field Archaeology* 18:256-269.

Dibble, H. 1995 Middle Paleolithic scraper reduction: background, clarification, and review of evidence to date. *Journal of Archaeological Method and Theory*

2:299-368.

Foley, R. and Mirazon Lahr, M. 2003 On stony ground: lithic technology, human evolution, and the emergence of culture. *Evolutionary Anthropology* 12:108-22.

Geneste, J.M. 1988 Systems d'approvisionnement en matieres premieres au Paléolithique moyen et au Paléolithique supérieur en Aquitaine. In Otte, M. (ed) *L'homme de Néandertal*. Pp.13-26. Liège: Actes du Colloque International de Liège.

Geneste, J.M. 1989 Les industries de la Grotte Vaufrey: technologie du débitage, economie et circulation de la matiere première. In Rigaud, J.P. (ed) *La Grotte Vaufrey*. Pp.441-517: Mémoires de la Société Préhistorique Française.

Geneste, J.M. 1990 Dévelopment des systèmes de production lithique au cours de Paléolithique moyen en Aquitaine septentrionale. In Farizy, C. (ed) *Paléolithique Moyen Recent et Paléolithique Supérieur Ancien en Europe*. Pp.203-14. Nemours: Mémoirs de Musée d'Ile de France 3

Gordon, D. 1993 Mousterian tool selection, reduction, and discard at Ghar, Israel. *Journal of Field Archaeology* 20:.205-218.

Hayden, B. 1977 Stone tool function in the Western Desert. In Wright, R.V.S. (ed.) *Stone Tools as Cultural Markers: Change Evolution and Complexity*. Pp.178-88. New Jersey: Humanities Press.

Hayden, B. 1979 *Paleolithic Reflections: Lithic Technology and Ethnographic Excavations among Australian Aborigines*. Canberra: Australian Institute of Aboriginal Studies.

Hiscock, P. 1994 Technological responses to risk in Holocene Australia. *Journal of World Prehistory* 8(3):267-292.

Hiscock, P. 1998 Revitalising artefact analysis. In Murray, T. (ed.) *Archaeology of Aboriginal Australia: A Reader*. Pp.257-65. St Leonards: Allen and Unwin.

Hiscock, P. 2002 Pattern and context in the Holocene proliferation of backed artefacts in Australia. In Elston, R.G. and Kuhn, S.L. (eds) *Thinking Small: Global Perspectives on Microlithization*. Pp.163-177.

Hiscock, P. and Attenbrow, V. 2003 Morphological and reduction continuums in eastern Australia: measurement and implications at Capertee 3. *Tempus* 7:167-174.

Holdaway, S. 1995 Stone artefacts and the transition. *Antiquity* 69:784-97.

Holdaway, S. and Stern, N. 2004 *A Record in Stone: The Study of Australia's Flaked Stone Artefacts*. Melbourne: Museum Victoria and AIATSIS.

Karlin, C., Bodu, P. and Pelegrin, J. 1991 Processus, techniques et chaînes opératoires. Comment les préhistoriens s'approprient un concept elaboré par les ethnologues. In Balfet, H. (ed) *Observer l'Action Technique. Des chaînes opératiores, pourquoi faire?* Pp.101-17. Paris: Editions du CNRS.

Kuhn, S.L. 1995 *Mousterian Lithic Technology*. Princeton: Princeton University Press.

Lemonnier, P. 1983 L'Etude des systèmes techniques: une urgence en technologie culturelle. *Techniques et Culture* 1:11-34.

Lemonnier, P. (ed) 1993 *Technological Choices*. London: Routledge.

Leroi-Gourhan, A. 1964 *Le Geste et la Parole 1: Technique et Language*. Paris: Albin Michal.

Meignen, L. 1988 Variabilite technologique au Proche Orient: l'exemple de Kebara. In Rigaud, J.P. (ed) *L'homme de Néandertal*. Pp.87-95. Liège: Université de Liège.

Neeley, M.P. and Barton, C.M. 1994 A new approach to interpreting late Pleistocene microlith industries in southwest Asia. *Antiquity* 68:275-288.

Nelson, M.C. 1991 The study of technological organization. *Archaeological Method and Theory* 3:57-100.

Pelegrin, J., Karlin, C. and Bodu, P. 1988 Chaîne opératoire: un outil pour lr préhistorien. In Tixier, J. (ed) *Technologie Préhistorique*. Pp.153. Paris: CNRS

Perlès, C. 1987 *Les industries lithiques taillés de Franchthi, Argolide: présentation générale et industries Paléolithiques*. Terre Haute: Indiana University Press.

Perlès, C. and Binder, D. 1990 Stratégies de gestio des outillages lithiques au Néolithique. *Paléo*: 2:257-83.

Sellet, F. 1993 Chaîne opératoire; the concept and its applications. *Lithic Technology* 18:106-12.

Shott, M.J. 1997 Transmission theory in the study of stone tools: A midwestern north Amrican example. In Barton, C.M. and Clark, G.A. (eds) *Rediscovering Darwin: Evolutionary Theory and Archaeological Explanation* . Pp.193-206 Virginia: Archaeological Papers of the American Anthropological Association

Tixier, J. Inizan, M.L. and Roche, H. 1980 *Préhistoire de la Pierre Taillée 1: Terminologie et technologie*. Valbonne: Cercle de Recherches et d'Etudes Préhistoriques.

Turq, A. 1988 Le Moustérien de type Quina du Roc de Marsal a Campagne (Dordogne): context stratigraphique, analyse lithologique et technologique. *Documents d'Archéologie Périgourdine* 3:5-30.

Turq, A. 1992 Raw material and technological studies of the Quina Mousterian. In Dibble, H. and Mellars, P. (eds) *The Middle Paleolithic: Adaptation, Behavior and Variability*. Pp.75-86. Philadelphia: University of Pennsylvania Museum.

White, J.P. 1977 Crude, colourless and unenterprising? In Bowdler, S. (ed.) *Sunda and Sahul*. Pp.13-30.

Measuring Artefact Reduction - An Examination of Kuhn's Geometric Index of Reduction

Peter Hiscock and Chris Clarkson

Abstract

A growing number of techniques have been proposed in recent years to quantify how much retouch has been applied to flakes. This paper reviews the most prominent of these, and evaluates one in particular – Kuhn's (1990) Geometric Index of Unifacial Reduction. This involves a simple experiment designed to explore the performance of the index over a sequence of retouching events for a population of thirty flakes. The results indicate that the index performs admirably in relation to absolute measures of reduction under experimental conditions, and does so especially well in comparison to a number of common alternative techniques.

Introduction

Modern examinations of Palaeolithic artefact assemblages typically depict the complexity of reduction processes and aim to quantify the extent, nature and variability of reduction. Additionally, there is a call to explore assemblages "...without presupposing that information resides only in 'end-products'" (Hiscock and Clarkson 2000). These approaches challenge archaeologists to find quantitative measurements of the rate and nature of changes to stone artefact morphology that occur during flaking. Consequently, one of the consuming methodological questions in studies of stone artefacts is to identify robust and reliable measurements of the intensity with which stone was reduced. A large number of methods have been suggested and employed, and this paper undertakes a review of prominent quantitative approaches advocated recently. In particular our focus is on one measure, the Reduction Index proposed by Kuhn (1990); a measure which has been subject to negative comments (e.g. Dibble 1995) but which has been used extensively in Australian archaeology (e.g. Clarkson 2002a, Lamb, this volume and Law, this volume; Hiscock and Attenbrow 2002; 2003, this volume). In this paper, we use experimental data to provide a quantitative description of the relationship between the index and the rate of change to retouched flakes during reduction. This experimental evidence supplies the basis for a revised comparison of the different methods of measuring the intensity of retouching on retouched flakes.

Measures of Reduction Intensity

The measurements of reduction intensity that have been proposed are diverse. Approaches broadly fall into four categories: 1. analysis of the relative abundance of different implement classes within an assemblage, 2. description of the nature of the retouching, 3. estimation of the original blank size, and 4. quantification of the extent of retouch scars. In this section we characterize and review a number of approaches.

Relative Abundance of Different Implement Classes

One approach to examining the extent of reduction displayed by an assemblage is to compare the frequency of specimens in different implement types. By hypothesizing that some implement types result from minimal reduction while other types have been heavily reduced, it becomes possible to interpret the proportions of implement types as an indicator of the typical intensity of reduction represented in an assemblage. An outstanding example of this kind of interpretation is Dibble's (1988:189) use of a 'scraper reduction index' to express the numerical abundance of convergent, transverse scrapers and Mousterian points relative to single and double scrapers as a way of inferring the emphasis on different kinds of reduction in European sites. Similar approaches to expressing the extent of reduction have been applied to Australian assemblages. One example is Hiscock's (1994) hypothesis that north Australian bifacial points had been more heavily worked than unifacial points and that consequently the percentage of points that are bifacial (or the bifacial:unifacial ratio) could be employed as a measure of the amount of reduction in an assemblage. Of course the efficacy of such analyses is largely dependent on the accuracy of the assertions about the position of each type in the reduction process, and it is partly to this end that researchers have searched for generic and robust measures of reduction suitable for analysis of individual specimens.

A variant of this approach is the observation of the abundance of shaping and resharpening debris relative to implements. In analysing knapping technologies, in which extending reduction creates more flakes, many archaeologists have therefore employed the number of flakes per 'tool' as an expression of the extent of retouching. The flake:tool ratio should be higher when the average extent of reduction is higher. The same argument has been given in analyses contrasting Australian assemblages (e.g. Hiscock and Allen 2000). These ratios typically assume that artefacts discarded on a site were knapped there, and are reliable expressions of the average number of flakes struck. Such assertions can only be made, however, when the net loss or gain accruing from artefact transportation between sites is minimal, a proposition that is difficult to test under most conditions.

Nature of Retouching
A number of archaeologists have examined the nature of retouch scars as an indication of the extent of reduction. In the context of Palaeolithic Europe this has most often been accomplished by analysing the invasiveness of retouch scars, but the angle of retouched edges and the state of flake terminations are also traits that have been cited. These analyses have involved a comparison of the typical retouch characteristics between each implement type. For example, Dibble (1984:433) recorded specimens using a four state ordinal variable he named 'retouch intensity' (light, moderate, heavy or stepped) and argued that implement types with the highest frequency of higher retouched states were those that had been most intensively worked. Dibble (1984:434) summarised his inference by concluding:

> Assuming that the level of retouch intensity corresponds in part to the amount of material removed during retouching, then these data suggest that there is an increase in the amount of modification as one moves from the single, through double, to convergent scrapers.

Gordon (1993:209) used a similar system to that of Dibble for analysis of flake reduction at the Mousterian site of Ghar in Israel. Gordon's system comprised five ordinal rankings between 0 for no retouch and 4 for retouch formed of more than two rows with deep wide scars. The reliability of ranking systems such as these depends on a number of factors, including the consistency of the classification, the accuracy of the ordinal rankings as a measurement of the extent of reduction, and the discreteness of the typological classes. Furthermore, the directionality of changes through the retouching process in traits such as edge angle, scar size and scar termination have not been independently established, either experimentally or through inspection of archaeological materials, and the dependability of ordinal categories as a measure of retouch intensity remains unclear.

Estimating the Original Blank Size or Mass
A third and very extensively exploited approach to measuring the amount of reduction is to estimate the size or mass of the flake prior to retouching. These estimates may then be employed to calculate the amount of material that has been removed during retouch. This approach has been emphasized by several researchers as one of the better indications of the intensity of reduction (Dibble 1997; Dibble and Pelcin 1995; Holdaway 1991). Its application is based on two propositions.

Firstly, that the original size or mass of a flake can be estimated from a number of attributes. These include

using measurements of thickness and platform area as a means of calculating original flake size. Platform features are regarded as critical because they often remained intact while lateral and distal portions of the flake were retouched: hence platform features can be measured and used to estimate ventral surface area. Regression analyses between thickness or platform area and the ventral surface area of unretouched flakes in archaeological assemblages serve as the empirical basis for predictive statements. An extensive list of correlation coefficients is provided by Dibble (1995:326), for a large number of Palaeolithic assemblages. Almost all are statistically significant at the $p = 0.005$ level, giving him confidence in the predictive ability of this measure. The predictive capacity of platform dimensions (platform thickness, platform width and external platform angle) as an estimator of original flake mass, on the other hand, has been examined in a number of studies using the controlled experimental fracture of simple glass cores (Dibble and Pelcin 1995; Dibble and Whittaker 1981; Pelcin 1997a, b, c, 1998) and from archaeological and experimental assemblages (Dibble 1997; Shott *et al.* 2000).

The second proposition required to transform these attributes into measures of retouch intensity is that the estimates of original size or mass can then be used to calculate the amount of stone lost from a flake through retouching. For instance, it is argued that the ratio of platform area to ventral area (Dibble 1995), or of thickness to ventral area (Holdaway *et al.* 1996), can give an indication of the amount of surface area lost from a flake through retouching. Original size or mass estimated from platform characteristics, on the other hand, can be compared to the observed mass of a flake to express the amount of stone lost through reduction (Dibble and Pelcin 1995). While Dibble advocates undertaking these analyses at the assemblage level to give an indication of the average level of retouching intensity in that assemblage (Dibble 1987b:113; 1997, 1998), others see potential to develop predictions of original mass that will accurately measure retouch for individual specimens (Pelcin 1998; Shott *et al.* 2000).

Dibble (1995:327) argued that "because of its ability to help control for original blank size, the ratio of surface area to platform area is an important variable in demonstrating scraper reduction". The evidence Dibble cited undoubtedly shows that within individual assemblages that have been created with a limited range of technological strategies the correlation of ventral area with platform area and thickness enables estimates the typical size of each implement class before retouching began. This has been a valuable inference in his quest to understand the relationship of the Bordesian types to each other. However, the usefulness of this measure is limited by the generally low explanatory capacity of these correlations.

Other indications that predictions of original size may be

unreliable have come from more recent experimental studies. Pelcin (1997b), for example, found that for a given platform area the resulting ventral area of a flake will vary according to indentor type, and that surface area therefore cannot be accurately predicted from platform attributes when indentor type is unknown (which is usually the case in archaeological assemblages). In Shott *et al.*'s (2000:888) analysis of experimentally knapped assemblages, ventral area did not correlate to platform area as well as flake mass. They partly attribute greater variation in platform area correlations to the error introduced through the use of imprecise measures of ventral area (e.g. length x width), but acknowledge that core form may also have an effect on surface area independent of platform size. Kuhn (1990) has also observed that platform size generally accounts for no more than about 20% of the variation in surface area of unmodified flakes in Mousterian assemblages he has examined.

Davis and Shea (1998), on the other hand, attempted to evaluate the performance of Dibble and Pelcin's (1995) predictor equation of original flake mass using platform thickness and external platform angle. Not surprisingly given the shift from controlled laboratory conditions to uncontrolled knapping procedures, Davis and Shea found that predicted weight deviated from actual weight by at least ±10% in most cases, but by as much as 175% in others. They concluded that caution must be shown in applying this predictor in its current form to archaeological assemblages due its generally poor performance, and pointed to the omission of platform width as a likely source of much of this error.

In his reply to Davis and Shea, Dibble (1998) concurred on the issue of platform width, but also emphasized the added variation introduced by the greater complexity of real-life knapping situations where many variables are allowed to vary freely. In Pelcin's (1998) separate reply to Davis and Shea, he disagreed with both Dibble and Davis and Shea over the matter of platform width, arguing instead that this variable only had a threshold effect in determining flake mass. Pelcin saw modeling of knapping patterns and raw materials for individual assemblages as the best way to proceed from controlled fracture of glass cores to real assemblages. Shott *et al.*'s (2000) analysis of experimentally knapped assemblages came to a similar conclusion regarding platform width, stating that "platform width's influence on flake size seems limited". They also found that "the relationship of mass to platform dimensions is even more variable in assemblages than in individual flakes", contradicting Dibble's assertion that whole assemblages represent the most appropriate scale of analysis. They concluded that while predicting original mass for individual specimens was beyond the ability of current methods, it is still worth continuing efforts to do so.

Hence the principle of inferring the extent of reduction by employing platform features to reconstruct original flake mass is theoretically sound and remains the focus of ongoing investigations. However a great deal of uncertainty still surrounds the level of precision achievable in predictions of original flake size, the most appropriate scale of analysis, and whether accurate prediction is in fact achievable at all in archaeological contexts. These methodological complexities have encouraged some researchers to explore other approaches, particularly models measuring the dimensions of retouch scars.

Quantification of the Extent of Retouch Scars
The fourth approach to measuring reduction intensity is to observe the size and abundance of retouch scars on flakes. Perhaps the simplest variant is the measurement of the length of flake margins that were retouched (e.g. Barton 1988). While that trait will be of use for many analytical purposes, it is unclear how length of marginal retouch is associated with absolute expressions of reduction such as investment of time or effort, or the loss of original mass or volume. Hence the calibration of various scar measurements with absolute measures of reduction is critical. Furthermore, the results of these indices are not strictly comparable, between specimens or assemblages, due to variation in original flake size. Such measures could be considerably improved by calculating retouch extent as a percentage of edge length or flake width, rather than an absolute measure. Such an approach was employed by McPherron and Dibble (1999) using digital image analysis and has subsequently been employed by other researchers (e.g. Hiscock and Attenbrow 2003).

Marcy (1993) took a different approach to measuring retouch coverage, using digital image analysis to calculate the proportion of surface area covered by retouch. Yvorra (2000) also employed this technique but added measurements of retouched edge angle to differentiate between steep and marginal, and low-angled and invasive, retouching. It would appear that image analysis techniques such as these offer very accurate measures of retouch coverage; however, they tend to be slow and expensive and as yet few analysts use them on a regular basis.

A different procedure for assessing scar abundance is Clarkson's (2002b) estimation of retouch scar coverage. His 'Index of Invasiveness' calculates intensity of retouch by estimating the extent of retouching around the perimeter of a flake as well as the degree to which it encroaches onto the dorsal and ventral surfaces. The index is calculated by conceptually dividing an artefact into eight segments on each face. Each segment is then further divided into an inner 'invasive' zone, ascribed a score of 1, and an outer 'marginal' zone, ascribed a score of 0.5. Scores of 0 (no retouch), 0.5 (marginal) or 1 (invasive) are allocated to each segment according to the maximum encroachment of scars into one or other of these zones. The segment scores are then totaled and divided by 16 to give an index between 0 and 1. Clarkson

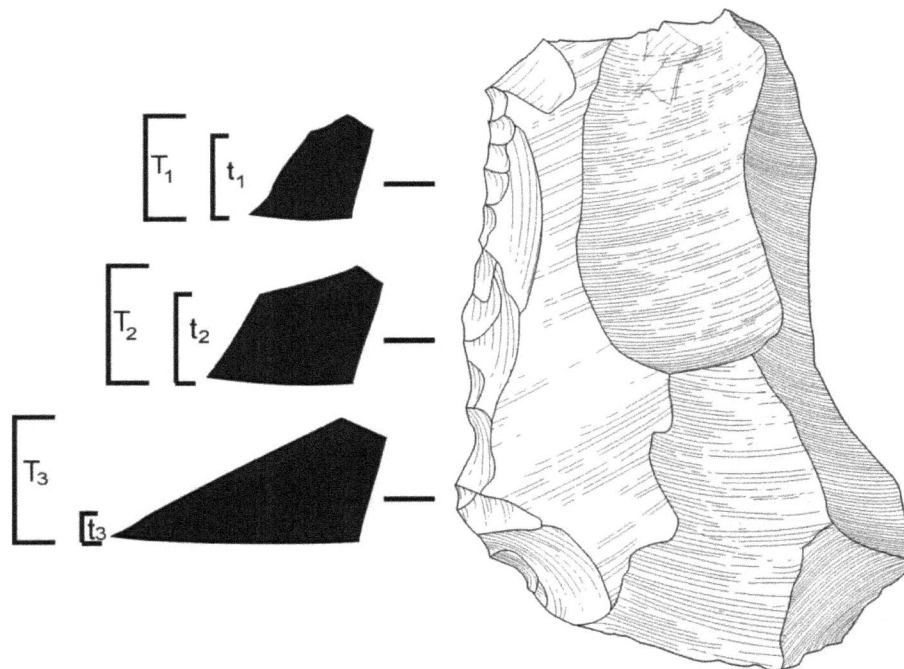

Figure 1. Illustration of the measurement of (Kuhn 1990)
Geometric Index of Unifacial Reduction on a unifacially retouched flake using Method A.

(2002a: 68-71) provided experimental evidence for a strong and significant positive relationship between the index and the number of retouch blows ($r^2 = 0.982$, p = <0.001) and the percentage of original weight lost from each specimen ($r^2 = 0.968$, p = <0.001). The rate of increase for the index of invasiveness is slightly curvilinear when plotted against both independent measures of reduction, but can be made linear using a square root transformation of index values. Little variation is evident in the rates of index increase between raw materials of varying fracture quality. The index of invasiveness has the advantage of being fast to calculate and versatile, and is well suited to the measurement of both unifacial and bifacial retouch with minimal inter-observer error (Clarkson 2002a: 71).

A limitation of techniques measuring the extent of retouch on a surface is that they are less suited to assemblages in which artefacts exhibit predominantly steep and marginal unifacial retouch, as might commonly occur on backed artifacts or steeply retouched scrapers (e.g. Quina type retouch). For instance, the index of invasiveness would not readily increase above 0.25 in such cases, no matter how much reduction takes place. In assemblages with non-invasive marginal retouch, alternative measures of reduction may be more appropriate, such as Kuhn's index of reduction.

Kuhn's Index of Reduction
A measure ideally suited to estimating the amount of reduction on marginally and unifacially retouched flakes was proposed by Kuhn (1990). The index calculates the extent of retouch by the relative 'height' (ventral-dorsal)

of retouch scars. Kuhn presented two different methods for calculating what he named the Geometric Index of Unifacial Reduction, but which we refer to here as the Kuhn Index.

The first method calculates a quantitative measure of edge attrition by dividing the height of retouch scars above the ventral face ("t") by the maximum thickness of the flake ("T"). Both measurements were taken at right angles to the ventral surface and at the same point on the retouched edge (Figure 1). Both "t" and "T" can be measured directly using calipers, a technique which we will refer to as Method A.

Kuhn suggests the use of a second, more complex method to overcome problems in accurately determining the true height of "t" given variation in the curvature of the ventral face. We term this second calculation Method B. This method arrives at "t" by multiplying the length of retouch scars ("D") by the sine of the retouch angle ("a") (Figure 2). The resulting value of "t" is then divided by "T" measured with calipers, to create the index. While Kuhn argues that Method B provides more precise and replicable results, it is difficult to see how edge angle can be measured any more accurately than the height of retouch when the ventral surface is curved.

The index calculated using either method ranges from 0 to 1. A value of 0 represents no retouch and a value of 1 indicates that retouch scars have intersected with, or crossed, the point of maximum thickness. Kuhn's index provides a straight forward and relatively simple way of measuring the amount of edge lost from a retouched flake. The nature of the index means that it is not restricted to a particular shape of retouched edge and it potentially offers a versatile measure for a wide range of assemblage types. However the index has been criticized on a number of grounds. One limitation that was acknowledged by Kuhn (1990) was that the index could only be measured on unifacially retouched flakes on which blows were applied to the ventral face and created scars on the dorsal face. Because both t and T are oriented to and measured from the ventral face, any retouching onto the ventral surface will make calculation of a Kuhn Index at that point impossible. Consequently where ventral and dorsal retouch exists on different edges of a single specimen the Kuhn Index will express the amount of retouch on only some edges. Furthermore, unifacial implements with ventral retouch and bifacially flaked specimens cannot have a Kuhn Index calculated. This restricts the proportion of an implement assemblage that can be assessed using the index, although in many parts of the world dorsally flaked unifaces are the dominant category of implement. Regions in which implements are typically bifaces may have limited use for the index.

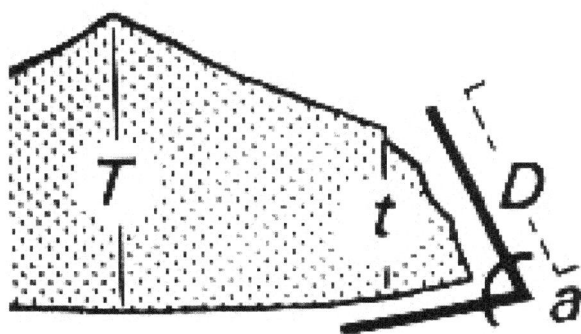

Figure 2. Illustration of the measurement of Geometric Index of Unifacial Reduction on a unifacially retouched flake using Method B
(Kuhn 1990).

An additional complexity of the Kuhn Index is that retouch located at the distal end of a flake may be less altered by reworking than retouch positioned on the lateral margins. This occurs because it may take less retouch to attain the maximum value of 1 at the distal end than on a lateral margin. For this reason some archaeologists argue that the Kuhn index is only viable on laterally retouched implements. We suggest such a position is an over-reaction to the effects of cross-sectional shape, and we will return to this issue later in the paper. For the moment the significant point is that this complication with distal end measurement is in fact a special form of what we call the 'flat-flake problem'.

The most extensively developed critique of the Kuhn Index was provided by Dibble (1995:330), who argued that while the index functioned as designed on flakes with triangular cross-sections it was unresponsive to

retouching on flakes with flat dorsal surfaces parallel to the ventral face. Using the illustration we reproduce in Figure 3, Dibble explained this 'flat-flake problem' as follows:

A problem occurs in the case of very flat flakes, however, where this ratio will approach the maximum much more quickly (i.e., after fewer resharpening episodes) than it will on more highly convex flakes... Thus, while Kuhn's Reduction Index can reflect the amount of retouch that is applied, it will also be affected by the exterior morphology of the flake. Though more objective than the previous technique, it is still not an unambiguous measure of how much material was removed.

The theoretical point that the rate at which the index changes is probably related to flake cross-sectional shape is, we argue, correct, and an appreciation of that effect should be built into interpretations of the index. However, the magnitude of this effect has not been empirically measured and its impact on the interpretation of retouch intensity using Kuhn's reduction index has not been established. While Dibble's critique is technically correct, it has not been shown to create a significant problem for interpretation of most archaeological assemblages. To assist in evaluating the robustness of the index, and examine the likely impact of the 'flat-flake problem' we proceed to a re-evaluation and experimental testing of the Kuhn index.

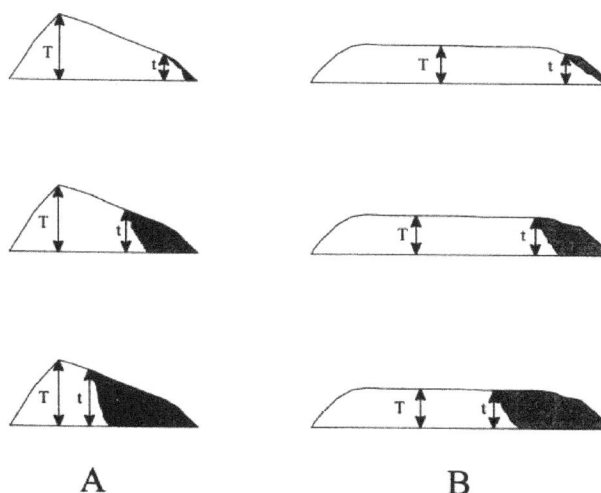

A   B

Figure 3. Dibble's (1995:329) illustration of the 'flat-flake problem'.

Evaluating Kuhn's Index
The Kuhn Index can be reliably repeated but its interpretation must be informed by a number of considerations. There are three questions that must be answered in order to interpret the index:

1. Is the index invariably positively correlated with the intensity of reduction?,

2. Is that correlation linear or non-linear?, and
3. In what conditions do those patterns vary.

Our consideration of these three questions begins with the arguments advanced by Kuhn in his initial discussion of the index.

As a way to evaluate the effectiveness of this index, Kuhn (1990) performed a series of experiments involving the retouching of 22 flakes. Each flake had an edge flaked on a number of occasions, called 'events', to simulate maintenance of a working edge. At the completion of each retouching event Kuhn measured the reduction index in two ways: by a single observation in the centre of the retouched edge (called the "centre edge" value) and by the mean of three observations along its length (called the "mean" value). On the basis of these experiments Kuhn (1990) was able to derive a number of inferences:

- Both forms of measurement reveal that the index values increase as the number of retouching events increases, so that there is a positive relationship between number of events and size of the index.
- The values of centre-edge and mean values typically differ, with the centre-edge index often being higher.
- There is considerable variation in the amount of change to the index that occurs between retouching events.
- Kuhn suggested that the relationship between retouch event and reduction index was slightly curvilinear.

A re-analysis of Kuhn's (1990) published experimental results reveals a number of further points, and a revision of his conclusions. Firstly, centre-edge measurements will often display a flatter curve with a larger range of values than mean measurements, even though the central tendencies are nearly the same for both measurement systems ($\bar{x} = 0.55$ for centre-edge and $\bar{x} = 0.53$ for

mean, N=118). This occurs because the averaging effect doesn't simply lower mean values relative to centre-edge ones it also concentrates values around the central tendency, making the distribution of mean values display more pronounced kurtosis (see Figure 4). The consequence is that in Kuhn's experiments centre-edge measure values often ranged up to 1 but low values (less than 0.1 - 0.2) were rare; whereas with the mean measure both high (0.85-1) and low values (less than 0.1 - 0.2) were rare.

This observation implies that the relationship between centre-edge and mean values is not adequately depicted simply as centre-edge values being larger. As shown in Figure 4 a linear regression between paired centre-edge and mean values shows that the two values are strongly correlated ($r^2 = 0.945$).

Figure 4 also illustrates Kuhn's observation that there is noticeable variation in the amount of change to the index that occurs between retouching events. The overlap between the reduction index values returned within retouching events 4-6 is greater than the overlap between events 1, 2, and 3. This decrease in the magnitude of change in index values per event as reduction proceeds, from about 0.14 early in the sequence to only 0.4 - 0.7 later in the sequence, was the subject of extended analysis by Kuhn (1990) and will not be elaborated here, although we return to this point in the discussion of our own experiments below.

Change in the magnitude of index increase between retouch events underlays Kuhn's conclusion that the relationship between retouch event and reduction index was slightly curvilinear. While that may be true, our reanalysis of his experimental data suggests that Kuhn may have over-emphasised the non-linearity of the relationship. Linear regressions of both mean / event and centre-edge / event pairs show impressively high

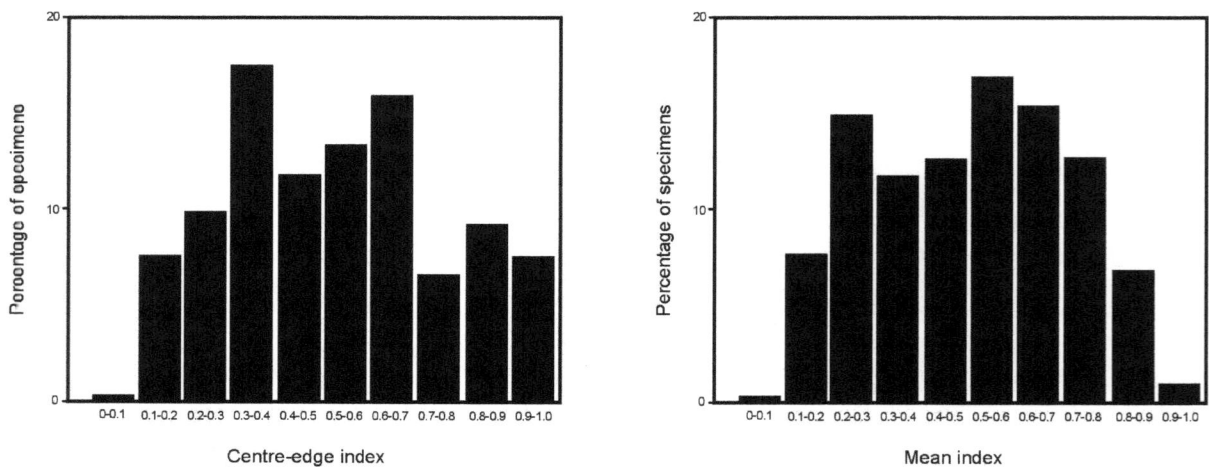

Figure 4. Histograms showing the values of the centre-edge and mean indices produced during Kuhn's (1990) experiments.

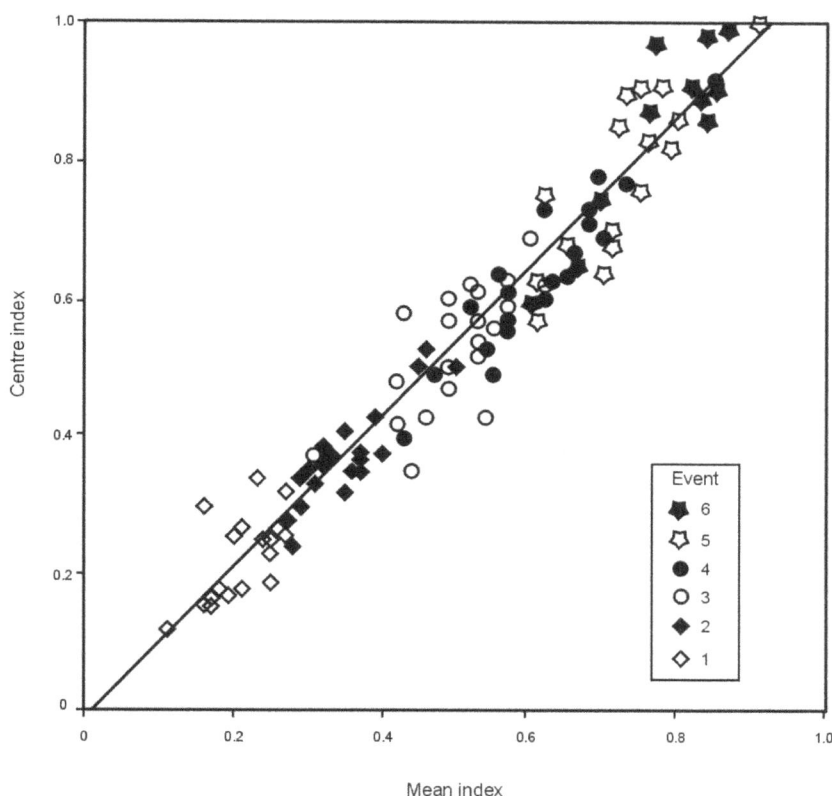

Figure 5. Scattergram comparing the values of paired centre-edge and mean measurements produced during Kuhn's (1990) experiments.

Table 1. Relationship between the variables in Kuhn's (1990) experiment as expressed by Pearson's coefficient and (Spearman's coefficient).

	Centre-edge	Mean	Event
Centre-edge	1.000 (1.000)	0.972 (0.974)	0.902 (0.909)
Mean	0.972 (0.974)	1.000 (1.000)	0.929 (0.936)
Event	0.902 (0.909)	0.929 (0.936)	1.000 (1.000)

All correlations are significant at p = 0.001 for both test statistics. N = 118 for all pairs.

coefficients using either Pearson's product-moment statistic or Spearman's (Table 1). These coefficients reveal that for Kuhn's experiments the number of retouching events explains more than 80% of the variation in centre-edge values ($r^2 = 0.814$) and more than 85% of mean values ($r^2 = 0.863$) - a conclusion almost identical with that of Kuhn (1990:591). This connection between the extent of retouch and Kuhn's reduction index is impressive and given suitable flake morphologies should give analysts confidence in inferring the relative intensity of retouching from either of the Kuhn indices - especially in contrast to the low predictive power of area/platform area indices discussed above.

Our main concern about Kuhn's experiments is his use of the 'retouching event' to measure reduction. Despite the care that he took in conducting the experiments, Kuhn's

choice of this unit of observation was a poor one since there is no reason to believe that these events were of equivalent magnitude to each other; either within or between experimental specimens. Hence, while we accept that Kuhn's experiments demonstrate that the reduction index displays a unidirectional relationship with the extent of reduction, we do not accept his experiments as an adequate demonstration of the linear or non-linear nature of the relationship. Despite the high linear correlations displayed in the experiments it is possible that the use of retouching events has either created the impression of a curvilinear relationship where a very linear one exists or, alternatively, has created the impression of a strong linear relationship while hiding the non-linear nature of the relationship. We believe that an exploration of the linearity of the relationship between the extent of reduction and Kuhn's reduction index should be conducted using weight of rock removed and/or number of flakes removed during retouching. To this end we conducted an experiment that was very similar to Kuhn's but in which we measured changes to mass as well as numbers of flakes struck.

An Experimental Re-Evaluation
Methods
The methods chosen to evaluate Kuhn's index are similar to those undertaken by Clarkson (2002b), and involved tracking changes in the rate of increase in index values against numbers of retouch blows and the percentage of weight lost from each specimen. By establishing the nature of the relationships between these variables, we hope to determine the degree of linearity, the actual as opposed to theoretical range of the index, and the limitations of this approach for measuring retouch.

The experiments involved unifacial percussion flaking of thirty flakes. Blows were applied to the ventral face of one lateral margin, removing flakes from the dorsal face to create a straight retouched edge. This was done in a number of episodes, each comprising ten flake removals more than 3mm in length positioned along the entire length of the specimen, and at the end of each retouching episode a number of attributes were recorded on each specimen. This provided a record of the progressive changes in morphology for each specimen during reduction, and gave a total of 348 data points. The approach to reduction was conservative, with the authors aiming to remove enough of the edge to effectively resharpen or rejuvenate it, but without removing unnecessary mass. To avoid judgments on functionality, retouching was continued until the specimen broke.

A summary of the experimental results is given in Table 2. The amount of reduction varied, with as little as 68 flakes and as many as 203 flakes being removed before specimens broke. This resulted in an average weight loss of approximately half the original weight of flakes,

although the percentage of weight removed varied between specimens. All specimens had attained high Kuhn reduction index values before they were broken.

This experiment held many factors constant, including raw material (mudstone), the technique of retouching (direct hand held percussion), the face retouched (dorsal), the number of margins retouched (one), the shape of the retouched edge (straight), the interval between measurement (10 blows), and the weight of hammer stones (two hammers weighing 82gm and 55gm were used throughout). The main factor that was varied was the flake blank, as a way of evaluating the effect of flake morphology on the development of high values of the Kuhn reduction index. We created a number of flakes that were broadly similar in size to those retouched in prehistoric Australian assemblages. As summarized in Table 3, these flakes were quite varied in weight (27-344g), width (29-89mm), thickness (8-33mm), cross-section (steep triangle to flattish trapeze, see Figure 6), number of ridges (1-4), and edge angles (32°-104°). We intend to explore the relationship of these aspects of flake morphology to changing values of the Kuhn reduction index on another occasion; here our only purpose is to evaluate those trends in the Kuhn index that are so robust they exist despite this massive variation in blank morphology.

Results
In this experiment the number of blows has a complex relationship with the Kuhn reduction index. As shown in Figure 7, the experimental data points display a wedge-like pattern with low reduction index values having been reached in only a few blows but high index values being associated with both large and small numbers of flakes, reflecting wide differences in the number of flake removals required to achieve large Kuhn values. While the correlation is statistically significant the coefficient reveals that the relationship is only moderately strong ($r = 0.716$, $r^2 = 0.513$, $r_s = 0.748$, N=348, p<0.001). The

Table 2. Summary of experimental results

	N	Minimum	Maximum	Mean	$\pm$	Std. Dev.
Number of flakes	30	68	203	111.90	$\pm$	31.73
Kuhn reduction index	30	0.79	1.00	0.95	$\pm$	0.06
Percentage weight loss	30	15.0	82.3	51.73	$\pm$	16.65

Table 3. Summary of experimental flake blanks

	N	Minimum	Maximum	Mean	$\pm$	Std. Dev.
Weight	30	27.3	344.2	75.11	$\pm$	67.37
Length	30	49.2	119.7	72.45	$\pm$	15.82
Width	30	28.9	88.5	45.74	$\pm$	13.82
Thickness	30	8.0	32.7	16.11	$\pm$	6.46
Number of ridges	30	1	4	1.93	$\pm$	0.58
Average edge angle	30	32.3	103.7	51.5	$\pm$	15.6

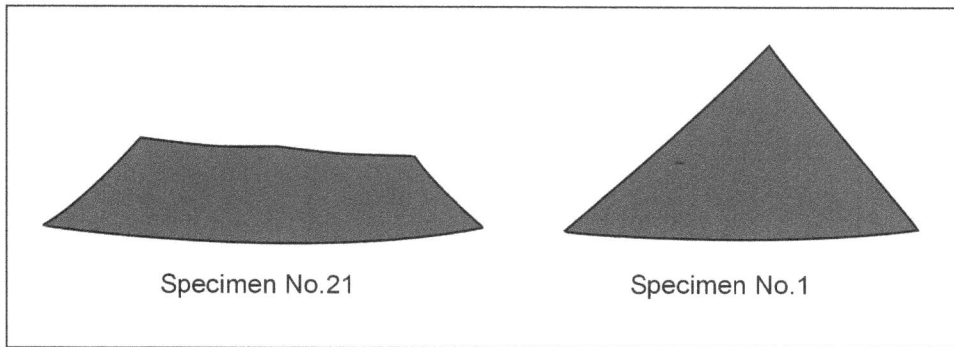

Figure 6: Examples of the range of flake cross-sections used in the reduction experiment. Specimen No.21 has a flattish trapezoidal-like cross-section similar to Dibble's 'flat flakes', while Specimen No.1 has a steep triangular cross-section.

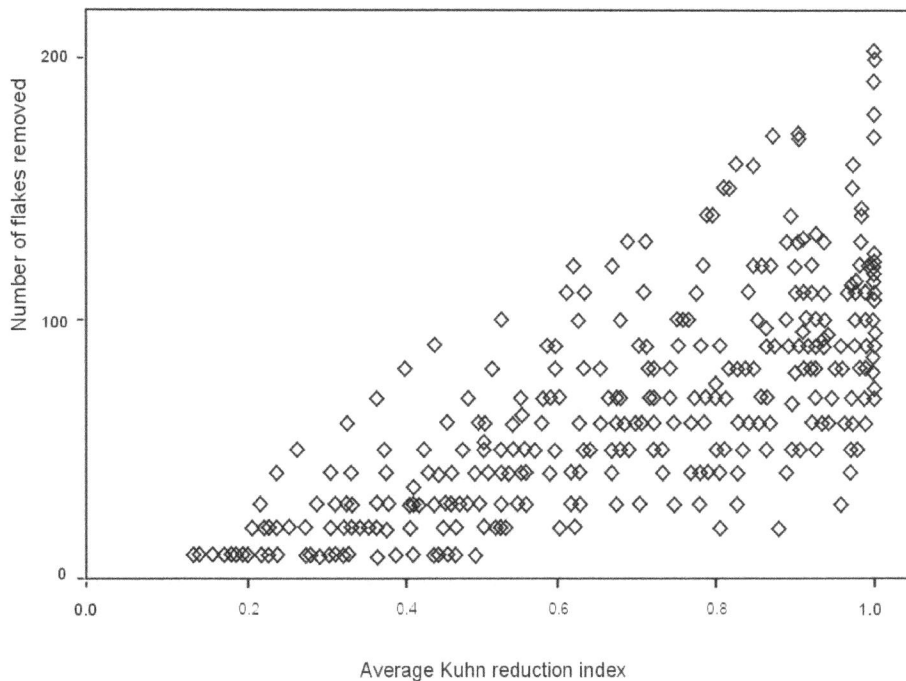

Figure 7. Scattergram depicting the relationship between the number of flakes removed and Kuhn's Index of reduction in our experiments.

primary cause of this pattern is the variation between flakes in mass removed. A more robust description of the relationship of reduction and the Kuhn index is achievable by focusing on mass removed.

A different depiction of the relationship between the extent of reduction and the Kuhn index is found when the percentage of weight of the original flake that has been lost during retouching is used as the measure of reduction. Figure 8a plots percentage of weight lost against the Kuhn index for our experimental specimens. The datum points show that there is a discernable and strong positive relationship between the mass removed during retouching and the Kuhn index values generated

by that retouch. This graph of experimental data also reveals that weight loss is related to the Kuhn index in a distinctly non-linear manner. The covariation is approximately log-linear in nature; a pattern that is clear in Figure 8b, which reduces the data to a series of bars displaying the 95% confidence interval for the mean of each 0.1 unit of the Kuhn index. It is worth noting that every bar is separated from and lies entirely above the preceding one – revealing the strength of positive covariation. This depiction of the trend makes the log-linear relationship between the variables apparent: low Kuhn index values are attained by removing a small amount of material whereas on extensively retouched specimens the removal of a proportionally large amount of material produces only small changes in the Kuhn index.

There are a number of reasons for the non-linear nature of this association. Flake geometry is partly responsible. On many flakes the increase in thickness away from the lateral margin means that similar blows will remove less mass from the margins of the flake, early in the retouching process, than from the centre of the flake, later in the process. The nature of reduction also changes as retouching continues, with the creation of steep angles and step terminated scars compelling the knapper to rejuvenate the edge by striking bigger and more invasive flakes, creating longer scars. Furthermore, since the Kuhn index, by definition, has a maximum value of 1 and reduction can continue after that value is reached, the relationship must become non-linear as retouching continues, because on heavily retouched specimens mass is lost without altering the Kuhn index.

The curvilinear relationship of the Kuhn index to mass reduction is significant for interpretations of the index. Since relatively more weight is lost later in the flaking sequence than early in the retouching process, not all increments in the Kuhn index are equivalent. For example, in terms of mass lost the interval between 0.8 and 0.9 is substantially greater than between 0.2 and 0.3. Consequently, comparisons between assemblages and sections of assemblages that have different values of the Kuhn index should be couched in terms of relative rather than absolute differences in the extent of retouch, unless a relevant calibration is available.

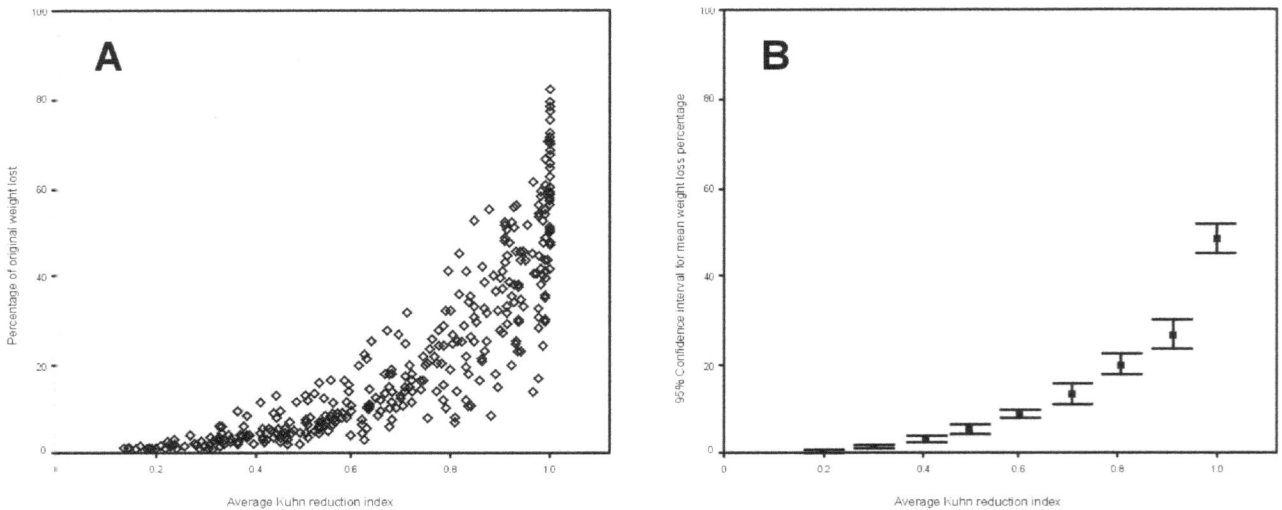

Figure 8. Illustrations of the relationship between the percentage of original mass lost and Kuhn's Index of reduction for our experimental specimens. A is a scattergram of the raw data. B shows bars displaying the 95% confidence interval for the mean of each 0.1 of the Kuhn index.

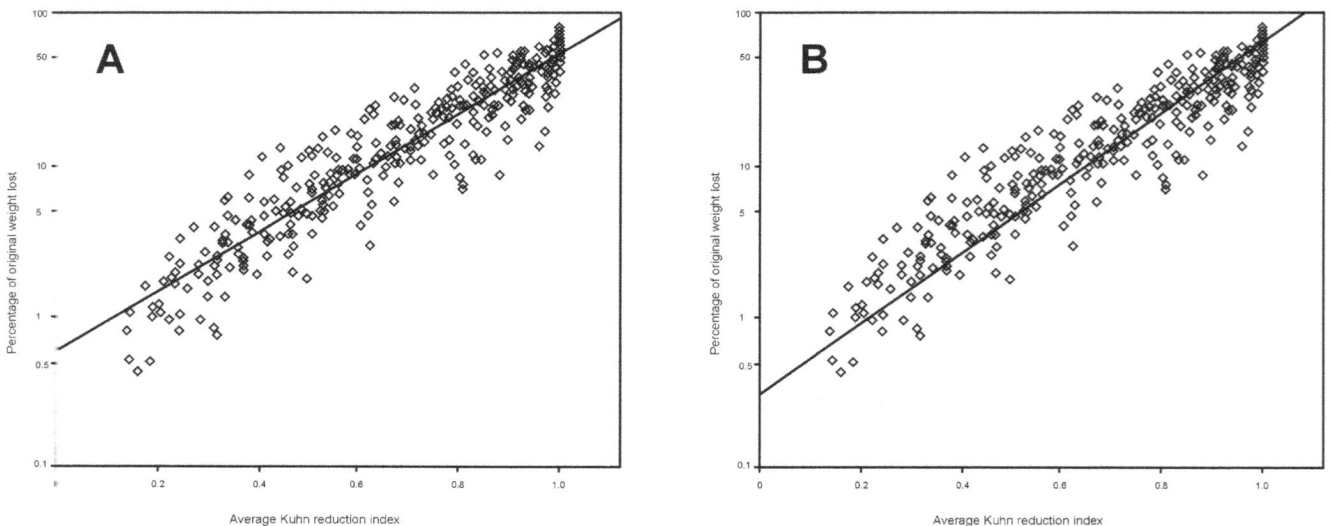

Figure 9. Illustrations of the relationship between the percentage of original mass lost expressed on a log scale and Kuhn's Index of reduction for our experimental specimens. A Shows the regression line calculated with a constant ($r^2 = 0.871$), while B shows the line of best fit constructed without a constant ($r^2 = 0.985$).

Depictions of the data provided in Figure 8 reveal several further patterns. Firstly, the minimum value recorded for the Kuhn reduction index, on specimens with minimal retouch, was 0.14. This demonstrates that even in the initial phase of retouching values less than 0.2 may be rare, and depending on the definition of retouch employed, values less than 0.1 may not be found in many assemblages; a pattern congruent with the results of Kuhn's (1990) own experiments.

A second observation is the continued loss of mass through retouching on some specimens after a value of 1 has been reached. Twelve specimens, 40% of the experiments, reached Kuhn values of 1 before breaking. Those specimens reaching values of 1 did so when weight loss was 57.1 $\pm$ 8.3 percent of the original flake (N=12). For those specimens 13.1 $\pm$ 7.7 % of the original flake weight was removed after values of 1 were recorded. It should be emphasized that the conditions of our experiments exaggerate this effect, because all specimens were reduced until they were broken.

The implications of these findings are:

1. Although in theory the index is scaled from 0, in practice the range of values will usually be less, starting between 0.1 and 0.2,
2. While the maximum value of Kuhn index is typically reached when 50-65% of original mass has been removed, specimens with values of 1 represent varying levels of reduction and should not necessarily be interpreted as a maximum or near maximum amount of retouch, and
3. In relation to the change in the relative mass of each flake produced by retouching the Kuhn reduction index is not linearly scaled and should not be interpreted as though it was. The reduction index can reliably be used as a relative measure of the amount of mass removed, but a further analytical step is required to 'calibrate' it and allow it to be used as an absolute measure.

Our experiments indicate that in some instances the transformation of variables may be sufficient to create a strong linear relationship, thereby providing a basis for absolute statements of different levels of reduction. For our experimental data it is a simple matter to re-express the percentage of original flake weight lost through retouch on a logarithmic scale, thereby transforming the relationship of mass loss and the Kuhn index into a linear one. The scatterplot resulting from this transformation is illustrated in Figure 9. A linear regression of these data, calculated with a constant, gives a correlation coefficient of 0.933 (N=348, p<0.001), which can be interpreted as 87% of the variation in mass loss being expressed by values of the Kuhn index ($r^2 = 0.871$). A similar analysis, without constant, gives a coefficient of 0.993 (N=348, p<0.001), a remarkably high value that indicates that approximately 98% of mass loss is explicable in terms of the Kuhn reduction index ($r^2 = 0.985$). With correlation

coefficients of these strengths it is reasonable to assert that, at least in single margin reduction of the type experimentally tested, the percentage of weight lost could be reliably predicted from the value of the Kuhn reduction index that can be measured on specimens.

Kuhn as a Predictor of Extent of Reduction
The experiments we have described here indicate that the Kuhn reduction index is a poor predictor of the number of flakes removed, but is a robust indicator of the progressive loss of weight from a retouched flake worked on a single lateral margin. The relationship between loss of mass and the reduction index is non-linear, with relatively more weight lost later in the retouching process per measured interval. This pattern must be considered in deriving interpretations based on the Kuhn reduction index, and we suggest that inferences can be based on the principle that the value of the index measures log(%weight loss). Treated in this way the Kuhn index is a reliable description of the amount of flake retouching. We particularly note that the flakes we retouched were selected to represent a large variety of cross-sections, ranging from very flat to steeply triangular. The strong non-linear correlation displayed by our experimental data therefore provide grounds for concluding that the flat-flake problem discussed by Dibble may exist but need not create an obstacle to employing the Kuhn reduction index as a powerful way of measuring the extent of flake reduction.

It remains to be seen how well the Kuhn index performs as a measure of extent of reduction outside of the parameters set for this experiment. Retouching one, two or three additional margins, for instance, or adopting patterns of retouch that begin on one margin and expand outwards versus those that begin on separate margins and converge toward a point may perhaps create quite different index to mass relationships to those documented here. It is for future experimentation to resolve this issue.

A further consideration is how well the index performs in the measurement of distal retouch. A theoretical expectation at least is that the measurement of distal retouch should present difficulties for the consistent measurement of reduction due to variation in cross-section shape found along the percussion axis of flakes. Flakes that taper little over their length for instance would lead to very little increase in the index in the same way that Dibble predicted for flat flakes. However, we believe that the suitability of the Kuhn index to the measurement of distal retouch is not out of the question, but merely involves careful attention to determining the types of blanks that might be suited to this kind of analysis, enhanced by experimental studies designed to evaluate various cross-sectional shapes similar to those conducted here.

For instance, a common form of retouched flake found in arid regions of Australia is known as the *tula*. Specimens of this type exhibit a very large bulb of force with the point of maximum thickness often near the proximal end and retouching is unifacial and typically only at the distal end. Because the thickest part of a tula is normally at or near the platform the Kuhn Index may only approach or attain a value of 1 when retouch scars began to remove the platform edge. It is therefore possible to find examples of distally retouched flakes that might be suited to measurement of the Kuhn index, at least once appropriate calibrations for various retouch patterns are devised. Future experiments might well resolve such issues, and ideally such studies should endeavor to produce a list of criteria for suitable flake blanks and accompanying calibrations that enable the use of the Kuhn index as a measure of extent of reduction in a wide variety of situations.

Comparing the Methods

An evaluation of Kuhn's index would not be complete without a comparison of its performance to alternative measures. To provide a basis for comparing different kinds of measurements we have calculated from our experimental data a number of the different reduction measures discussed in this paper (see Table 4). For each measure we have calculated its linear correlation with changing weight loss. Table 4 provides regression coefficients for five measures of reduction, including the Kuhn Index, determined using the percentage of weight lost from each specimen as the independent absolute measure of reduction. Where appropriate we have corrected for non-linear relationships by applying a data transformation; the last column in Table 4 indicates the type of transformation that obtains the highest coefficient for each measure. Due to the design restrictions embedded in our experimental methods, we have excluded several indices that, while no doubt of great interest to archaeologists, are inappropriate in this context. Measures of retouch distribution (i.e. the index of invasiveness, % scar coverage and % perimeter of retouch), for instance do not change during the course of reduction in our experiments because we held them constant. Those measures are therefore excluded from analysis.

To develop a ranking system that in some ways approximates those used by Dibble (1995) and Gordon (1998), but excludes any measure of retouch distribution, we have used a ranking system that incorporates only the relevant attributes of those ranking systems; that is, edge angle, scar length and frequency of step terminated retouch. To calculate this index, the range of values recorded in each variable over the sequence of reduction was divided into four equal intervals (ranks) and assigned to each specimen for each retouching event. The mean of these three rankings was calculated for each specimen, providing an overall ranking that was regressed against log percentage of original weight lost to determine the performance of these attributes as a measure of reduction over the experimental sequence.

Calculated in this way the coefficients provided in Table 4 allow a comparative judgement of the effectiveness of different measures of reduction in the circumstances of our experiment: highly variable blank forms reduced in a standard way by unifacial retouching one lateral margin. Note that because of the large number of observations available, all tests show a decidedly non-random pattern, as measured by $p<0.001$ in every case. These significance values cannot be employed as an indication of the relative differences in predictive strength of the different measures, and we therefore adopt the simple practice of emphasising the coefficient as the apposite means of comparing the predictive power of each measure. We have ordered the various measurements by the size of the calculated coefficients, making the order in Table 4 a rank-order list of the effectiveness of the different measures in describing the proportion of original flake weight that had been lost. The Kuhn index performs extremely well compared to other indices, and explains at least 35% more variation than other measures (as revealed in an r^2 calculation). In contrast, some indices performed very badly, such as Dibble's (1995) surface area to platform area index which explains as little as 6.7% of variation. In the kind of situation represented by our experiment, such as assemblages of side scrapers, we would strongly recommend abandoning the use of a surface area to platform area index in favour of other more powerful measures. Interestingly, the variant of this index devised by Holdaway *et al* (1996) that uses thickness rather than platform area as the estimator of original flake size is far superior, explaining 47% more of

Table 4. Comparison of regression correlation coefficients for various measures of reduction.

Measure	Coefficient (r)	Probability	Transformation
Kuhn Index: Method A	0.933	<0.001	Log(% weight lost)
Kuhn Index: Method B	0.912	<0.001	Log(% weight lost)
Surface Area/Thickness	0.727	<0.001	None
Retouch Scar Length	0.697	<0.001	Log(% weight lost)
Ranked scar characteristics	0.674	<0.001	Log(% weight lost)
Surface Area/Platform Area	0.259	<0.001	None

the variation. That conclusion is also consistent with the correlation analyses presented by Dibble (1995). Close's (1991) retouch scar length and the retouch ranking system also achieve only moderate success with both explaining less that 50% of variation.

Our conclusion is that in these circumstances the Kuhn Index is the most powerful of the measures, and should be employed as a robust indicator of the extent of reduction when retouching patterns are suited to the calculation of the index.

Note that while both of the methods used to calculate the Kuhn Index gave high correlation coefficients Kuhn's preferred method of calculating the index - Method B which employs edge angle – provides a marginally lower coefficient than the simpler ratio of t/T used throughout this paper. This is an interesting result, and suggests that user-error may be compounded by the introduction of a third measurement, especially one that is notorious for its inaccuracy (Odell 1989). The difficulty of accurately measuring edge angle from a curved ventral surface would likely make edge angle measurements particularly prone to error. We therefore recommend the use of Method A in making Kuhn index calculations.

While it could be argued that the experimental techniques adopted here constrain retouching techniques beyond what might reasonably be expected in archaeological assemblages, we see the use of rigid retouching patterns as providing an opportunity for each index to perform to the best of its ability without interference from complicating factors such as variation in flaking patterns. That they have been judged and found wanting suggests that Kuhn's index is likely the most robust measure of marginal unifacial reduction currently available, both for individual specimens and assemblage-wide comparisons.

Conclusion
All reduction indices are likely to have a number of strengths and weaknesses, and while it is worthwhile considering these on purely theoretical grounds, experimental evaluations are ultimately our most effective means of determining the relative merits and operational limits of each one. Our experimental evaluation of Kuhn's geometric index of unifacial reduction indicates a level of performance that appears to be well above any of its current competitors, at least within the stringent experimental procedures we adopted. Our results suggest that Kuhn's index approximates an absolute measure of reduction once index values are recalibrated.

As the experiments were necessarily limited to the repetitive reduction of a single straight margin, however, further experiments are required to evaluate the performance of the index under a wider range of knapping situations (e.g. when more margins are included, for distal retouch etc). It is highly encouraging, however, that within such a narrow experimental framework in which all measures should be able to achieve their best results, Kuhn's index performs well above all the other measures evaluated. We therefore see no reason to reject the use of this index in archaeological analysis.

Our experiments have also raised issues, at least in our own minds, concerning the potential of experiments such as these to understand the morphological transformations that commonly take place on retouched flakes over the course of reduction. These include changes to edge angle, the frequency of step terminations, effects of edge rejuvenation, and breakage thresholds that result from continued reduction on a single margin. It is our intention to further explore such issues in future work.

References
Barton, C.M. 1988 *Lithic Variability and Middle Paleolithic Behaviour: New evidence from the Iberian Peninsula*. Oxford: British Archaeological Reports.

Clarkson, C. 2002a Holocene scraper reduction, technological organization and landuse at Ingaladdi Rockshelter, Northern Australia. *Archaeology in Oceania* 37:79-86.

Clarkson, C. 2002b An index of invasiveness for the measurement of unifacial and bifacial retouch: a theoretical, experimental and archaeological verification. *Journal of Archaeological Science* 1:65-75.

Davis, Z.J. and Shea, J.J. 1998 Quantifying lithic curation: an experimental test of Dibble and Pelcin's original flake-tool mass predictor. *Journal of Archaeological Science* 25:603-610.

Dibble, H. 1984 Interpreting typological variation of Middle Paleolithic scrapers: function, style, or sequence of reduction? *Journal of Field Archaeology* 11:431-436.

Dibble, H. 1987 Reduction sequences in the manufacture of Mousterian implements of France. In Soffer, O (ed.) *The Pleistocene Old World Regional Perspectives*. New York: Plenum Press.

Dibble, H. 1988 Typological aspects of reduction and intensity of utilization of lithic resources in the French Mousterian. In Dibble, H. and Montet-White, A (eds) *Upper Pleistocene Prehistory of Western Eurasia*. Pp.181-198. Philadelphia: University of Pennsylvania.

Dibble, H. 1995 Middle Paleolithic scraper reduction: background, clarification, and review of evidence to date. *Journal of Archaeological Method and Theory* 2:299-368.

Dibble, H. 1997 Platform variability and flake morphology: a comparison of experimental and archaeological data and implications for interpreting prehistoric lithic technological strategies. *Lithic Technology* 22:150-170.

Dibble, H. 1998 Comment on "Quantifying lithic curation: An experimental test of Dibble and Pelcin's original flake-tool mass predictor", by Zachary J. Davis and John J. Shea. *Journal of Archaeological Science* 25:611-613.

Dibble, H. and Pelcin, A. 1995 The effect of hammer mass and velocity on flake mass. *Journal of Archaeological Science* 22:429-439.

Dibble, H. and Whittaker, J. 1981 New experimental evidence on the relation between percussion flaking and flake variation. *Journal of Archaeological Science* 8:283-296.

Gordon, D. 1993 Mousterian tool selection, reduction, and discard at Ghar, Israel. *Journal of Field Archaeology* 20.205-218.

Hiscock, P. 1994 The end of points. In Sullivan, M., Brockwell, S. and Webb, A. (eds) *Archaeology in the North*. Pp.72-83. Darwin: Australian National University (NARU).

Hiscock, P. and Allen, H. 2000 Assemblage variability in the Willandra Lakes. *Archaeology in Oceania* 35:97-103.

Hiscock, P. and Attenbrow, V. 2002 Early Australian implement variation: a reduction model. *Journal of Archaeological Science* 30:239-249.

Hiscock, P. and Attenbrow, V. 2003 Morphological and reduction continuums in eastern Australia: measurement and implications at Capertee 3. *Tempus* 7:167-174.

Hiscock, P. and Attenbrow, V. This Volume, Reduction continuums and tool use.

Hiscock, P. and Clarkson, C. 2000 Analysing Australian stone artefacts: an agenda for the Twenty First Century. *Australian Archaeology* 50:98-108.

Holdaway, S. 1991 Resharpening Reduction and Lithic Assemblage Variability Across the Middle to Upper Paleolithic Transition. PhD Thesis, University of Pennsylvania.

Holdaway, S., McPherron, S. and Roth, B. 1996 Notched tool reuse and raw material availability in French Middle Paleolithic sites. *American Antiquity* 61:377-387.

Kuhn, S. 1990 A geometric index of reduction for unifacial stone tools. *Journal of Archaeological Science* 17:585-593.

Lamb, L. This volume Backed and forth: an assessment of typological categories and technological continuums.

Law, B. This volume Chipping away in the past: stone artefact reduction and mobility at Puritjarra Rockshelter.

Marcy, J.L. 1993 Aperçu sur les stratégies de producion des raclois du niveau. In *Riencourt-lés-Baupaume (Pas-de-Calais):Un Gisement du Paléolithique Moyen*. Documents d'Achéologie Français, No. 37.

McFherron, S. and Dibble, H. 1999 Stone tool analysis using digitized images: examples from the Lower and Middle Paleolithic. *Lithic Technology* 24:38-52.

Odell, G.H. 1989 Experiments in lithic reduction. In Amick, D.S. and Mauldin, R.P. (eds) *Experiments in Lithic Technology*. Pp.163-198. Oxford: British Archaeological Reports.

Pelcin, A. 1997 The effect of core surface morphology on flake attributes: evidence from a controlled experiment. *Journal of Archaeological Science* 24:749-756.

Pelcin, A. 1997 The effect of indentor type on flake attributes: evidence from a controlled experiment. *Journal of Archaeological Science* 24:1107-1113.

Pelcin, A. 1997 The formation of flakes: the role of platform thickness and exterior platform angle in the production of flake initiations and terminations. *Journal of Archaeological Science* 24:1107-1113.

Pelcin, A. 1998 The threshold effect of platform width: a reply to Davis and Shea. *Journal of Archaeological Science* 25:615-620.

Shott, M.J., Bradbury, A.P., Carr, P.J. and Odell, H.O. 2000 Flake size from platform attributes: predictive and empirical approaches. *Journal of Archaeological Science* 27:877-894.

Yvorra, P. 2000 *Exploitation de l'analyse quantitative des retouches pour la caracterisation des industries lithiques du Mousterien: application au facies Quina de la vallee du Rhone* Oxford: British Archaeological Reports.

3 Tenuous Types: Scraper Reduction Continuums in the Eastern Victoria River Region, Northern Territory

Chris Clarkson

Abstract

To better understand the relationship between changing retouched implement morphology and intensity of reduction, archaeologists must develop measures of morphological change that work outside of, and challenge, existing typologies. This paper attempts such an approach by exploring changes in four aspects of implement morphology as retouch increases, using a population of 'scrapers' - or non-formally retouched flakes - from four rockshelters in northern Australia. The results allow the formulation of a reduction model that accounts for many of the differences in implement morphology that underlie most traditional scraper typologies. The results provide the basis for a critique of an early but influential scraper typology that underlies most Australian classifications in use today.

Introduction

The relationship between implement form and intensity of reduction is emerging as a key issue in international debates concerning the factors contributing to assemblage variation in a wide range of archaeological contexts. Recent studies demonstrate that in many cases a great deal of variation in implement form can be explained in terms of the amount of retouch an artefact has received, rather than simply stylistic or functional differences *per se* (Clarkson 2002a; Dibble 1984, 1987a, b, 1988, 1989, 1995; Gordon 1993; Hiscock 1994, 1996, 2002; Hiscock and Attenbrow In Press-b; Holdaway *et al.* 1996; McPherron 1994; Morrow 1997; Neeley and Barton 1994). These studies strike at the heart of traditional essentialist/typological thinking and challenge the notion that certain common stone artefact morphologies are real, discontinuous and immutable kinds that directly reflect mental templates or the desired end-products of the manufacturer (Dibble 1995; Dunnell 1986; Hiscock 2001, 2002; Lyman *et al.* 1997; O'Brien 1996). In place of those typologies, archaeologists have begun considering ways in which the effects of sequential reduction processes on implement variation might best be depicted (e.g. staged or continuous (Bleed 2002)), as well as the ways in which these processes may expose the non-reality of rigid typologies.

One approach to teasing out the continuums that underlie and connect various implement forms has been to develop sequence models that order individual artefacts according to the amount of reduction they have received, as measured in a variety of ways (see Hiscock and Clarkson, this volume). Somewhat ironically, many of these studies remain locked within the normative typological schemes they effectively undermine. This is best seen in the analyses of changing implement morphology that are undertaken through comparison of measures of central tendency between the type classes themselves, rather than using individual specimens removed from a typological framework.

While these type-based approaches nevertheless go some way toward demonstrating the mutability of implement forms, they are neither the most powerful nor useful means of depicting reduction continuums. This is because the type classes employed are not specifically designed to investigate reduction issues, and hence are unlikely to reveal sequential patterns to maximum effect. As Kuhn (1992b) states, type classes are "created to describe formal variation as observed in the archaeological record, and not to measure the results of some specific prehistoric phenomenon or process. As such [they are] likely to embody the effects of *many* independent influences on artefact form".

An alternative approach to depicting reduction continuums is adopted in this paper. This explores the presence or absence of reduction continuums through the analysis of a series of changes to a number of important aspects of flake morphology as reduction intensity increases. Reduction intensity is here measured using Kuhn's (1990) Geometric Index of Unifacial Reduction. This index has been demonstrated by Hiscock and Clarkson (this volume) to be a robust measure of unifacial reduction for non-invasively retouched artefacts that is relatively unaffected by blank size and shape. The results of this analysis also serve as a spring board from which to evaluate the reality and utility of an influential Australian scraper typology that has served as the basis for many current Australian classificatory systems. The study employs a sample of 338 retouched flakes from four stratified rockshelter sites in the study region, located around 120km southwest of Katherine in the Northern Territory (Figure 1). The principle site, Ingaladdi, has played a key role in defining the industrial sequence for this part of northern Australia (Cundy 1990; Mulvaney 1969; Mulvaney and Kamminga 1999; Sanders 1975).

The need for sequence models in Australia has reached new heights in recent times. At present, most Australian classifications fail to incorporate any understanding of

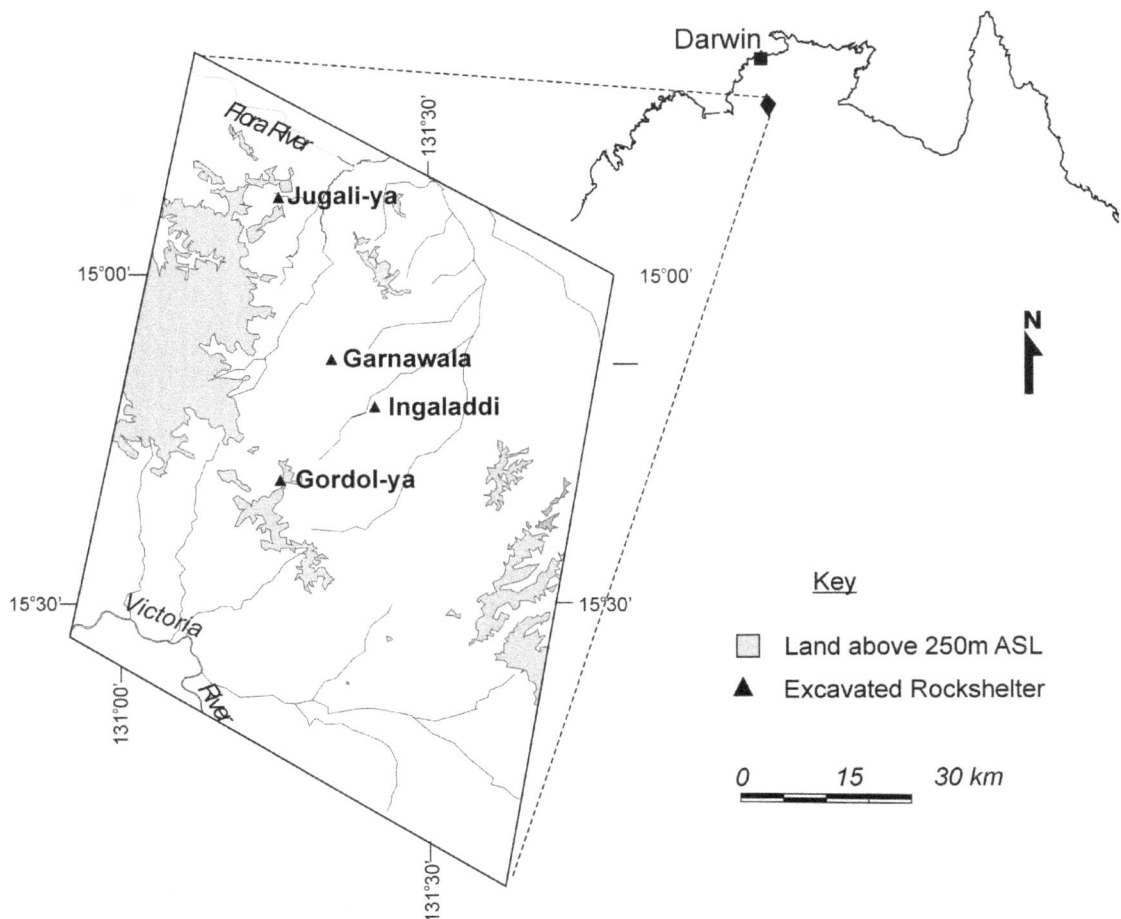

Figure 1. Map showing the location of the study region and the four stratified rockshelters
from which the scraper sample is derived.

manufacturing technology, and most take little or no account of the effects that differential reduction may have on assemblage variability despite the growing number of studies that draw attention to this fact (Clarkson 2002a; Hiscock 1994; Hiscock and Attenbrow 2002, 2003, In Press-a, This Volume; Hiscock and Veth 1991). This is particularly alarming since Australian prehistory is largely built on the record of changes in assemblage content over space and time. Consequently, Australian prehistory is fast reaching a point at which it must either tackle the vast gaps in empirical knowledge that surround the causes of assemblage variability in different spatial and temporal contexts, or face stagnation as far as its ability to use stone artefacts to provide meaningful statements about the past. A starting point in redressing this problem lies in the formulation and testing of reduction sequence models at regional scales. This would allow determination of the nature and number of reduction sequences present across space and time, the ways in which knappers responded to situational demands by modifying sequences or switching strategies, as well as the relatedness of individual sequences found in different parts of the continent. This paper offers a step

in this direction and contributes to a small but growing corpus of studies that present sequence models for a variety of implement forms from different parts of the country (e.g. Hiscock and Attenbrow 2002, 2003, In Press-a, This Volume; Lamb This Volume; Law This Volume)

Australian Approaches to Scraper Classification
Archaeologists have grappled with the interpretation and classification of scraper variability, or the 'amorphous' dorsally retouched flakes found in many assemblages, since archaeology began. This is best seen in Australia in the multitude of largely incompatible scraper typologies that found their most elaborate form in the period spanning the 1940s to 1970s. At this time scrapers were typically classified and named according to the location of retouch (e.g. side, end, side and end, double side and end etc), the nature of retouch (e.g. nosed, notched, denticulate), assumed function (e.g. knives, drills, piercers, adzes, choppers, planes, scrapers, spokeshaves), the curvature of the retouched portion (e.g. straight, round, convex, concave) overall shape and size (thumbnail, horsehoof, flat) and the steepness of the edge

A

B

C

D

E

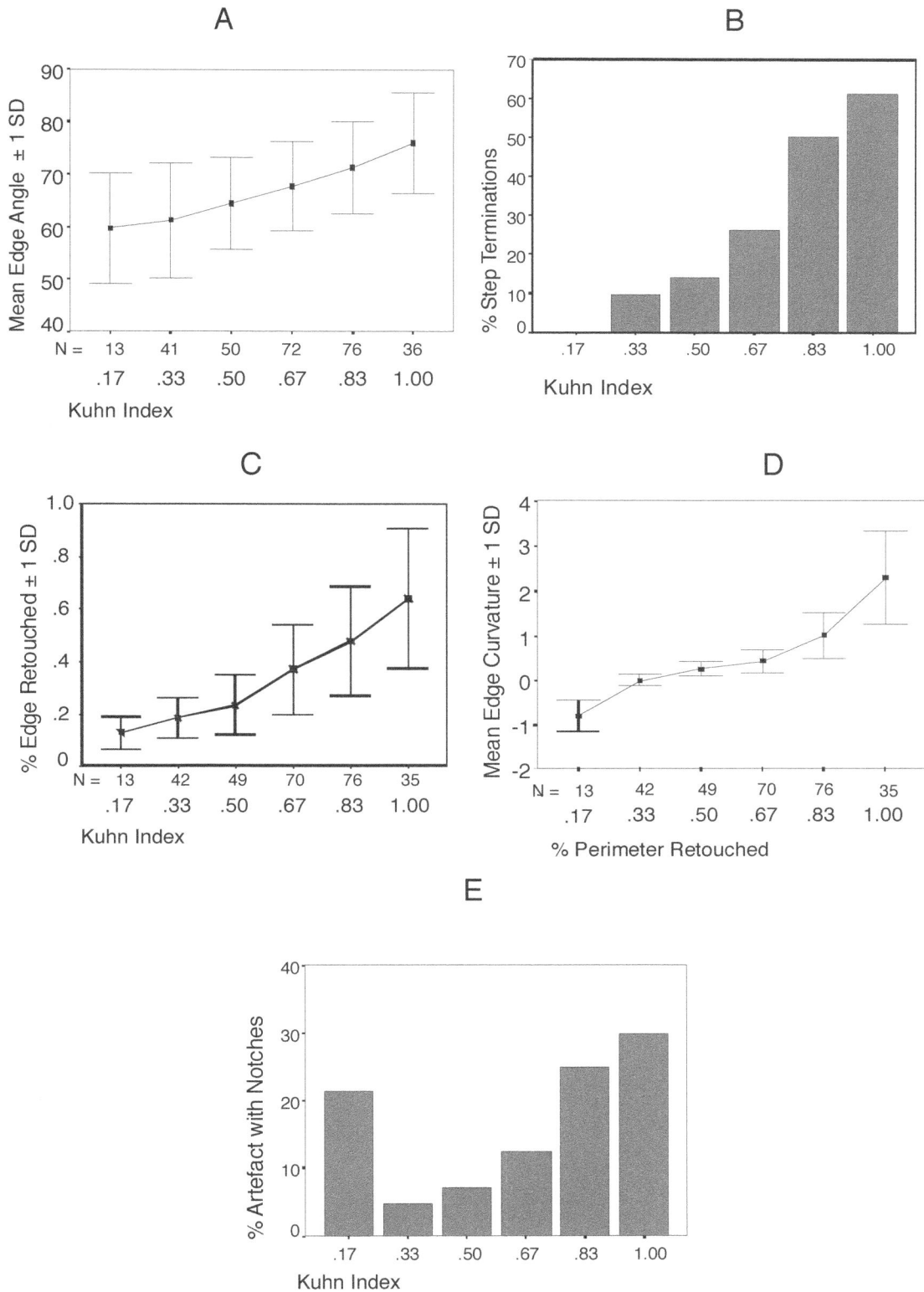

Figure 2. Graphs showing mean changes to scraper morphology as reduction increases.
Intervals of the Kuhn Index are rounded up from 0.166.

(e.g. low angled, steep edged) (Allen 1972; Bowler *et al.* 1970; Clegg 1977; Flood 1973, 1974; Jones 1971; McCarthy *et al.* 1946; Mulvaney and Kamminga 1999; Sanders 1975; White 1969). Combinations of these attributes and names were also employed at various times, usually in unsystematic ways, and often ending in large and confusing taxonomies. Mirroring global trends, Australian archaeologists have tended to attribute the diversity of retouched forms to stylistic or ethnic variation (Bowdler 1981; McCarthy 1948; McCarthy 1949, 1958; Mitchell 1949; Tindale 1957; White and O'Connell 1982), the functional efficiency of tool edges (usually tied to edge angle and edge shape) (Sanders 1975; White 1969), seasonal constraints on toolkit design (White 1971; White and Peterson 1969), efficiency of raw material use (Hiscock 1993; Morwood and Hobbs 1995):183), or design requirements related to hafting (Mulvaney and Joyce 1965).

Characterising Scraper Reduction
The first section of this paper illustrates the possibility of developing a reduction sequence model for north Australian scrapers that accounts for much of the observed variation in implement morphology, by building on past observations of the interplay between various aspects of flake shape and fracture mechanics. This is achieved by observing changes in four aspects of flake morphology as retouch increases, measured using Kuhn's (1990) Reduction Index. These are edge angle, edge shape, retouch perimeter, and retouch termination type - the same four variables that are frequently used to classify scrapers into types (Clarkson 2002). Demonstrating a consistent progression of changes in each of these variables allows flakes to be ordered into a relative position in a single reduction continuum.

Edge Angle
A number of researchers (Dibble 1995; Hiscock 1982; Morrow 1997; Wilmsen 1968:60) have drawn attention to the likely relationship that exists between retouched edge angle and the amount of unifacial retouch a flake has received. In many cases, unifacial retouching reduces the width of a flake without reducing its thickness. This in effect moves the margins closer to the thickest (often central) section of the artefact, causing an overall increase in the angle of the retouched edge.

To examine whether such a relationship holds for the sample of scrapers, edge angle was recorded at the same three locations where retouch height and flake thickness were taken for measurement of Kuhn's Index (see Hiscock and Clarkson, this volume). Figure 2a plots the mean edge angle and standard deviation of scrapers for six intervals along the Kuhn index, and indicates that mean edge angle increases appreciably over the reduction sequence, with all means showing an increase relative to the previous Kuhn interval. The standard deviations, on the other hand, overlap to some degree, indicating that a single morphological continuum underlies these sequential changes.

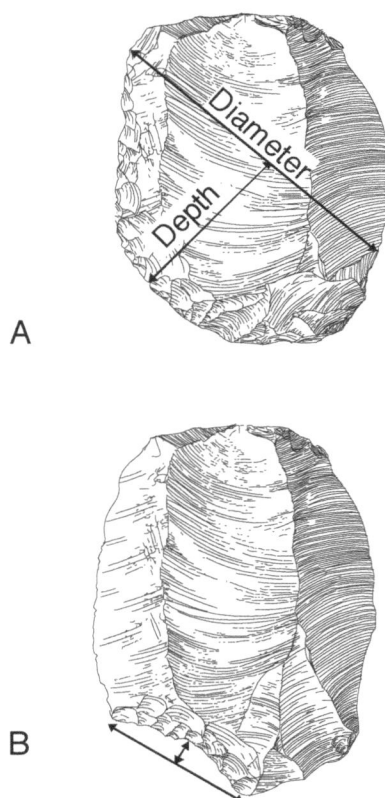

A

B

Figure 3. Procedures for calculating the index of edge curvature (retouch depth / retouch diameter). The index of edge curvature for A = 0.5, and B = -0.16.

Step Terminated Retouch
As the angle of the retouched edge is shown to increase with retouch, it is expected that step terminations should accrue with increasing frequency as force requirements change, inertia thresholds are reached, and terminations become more difficult to control (Dibble and Pelcin 1995; Pelcin 1997a, 1998). To explore this relationship, the frequency of scrapers with pronounced stepped retouching is again plotted at six intervals on the reduction index in Figure 2b. This graph reveals a gradual increase in the frequency with which areas of step terminated retouch build up on the edges of flakes as reduction continues.

Perimeter of Retouch
The proportion of the artefact perimeter that is worked might also be expected to increase if new and adjacent edges are used and resharpened as existing ones become exhausted. Figure 2c plots this relationship and reveals a strong trend toward use of more of the perimeter as Kuhn's Index increases. Standard deviations also reveal the existence of continuous variation that underlies and unites the observed changes in central tendency.

Edge Curvature
As retouch perimeter is observed to increase with retouch intensity, it might also be expected that the retouched

edge would become increasingly curved as more of the perimeter is worked. Edge curvature is here calculated by dividing the depth of retouch by its diameter (Figure 3). Using this technique, concave edges give a negative result while convex edges give a positive one. Figure 2d indicates that edge curvature, which begins as a slightly concave edge, becomes highly convex as the Kuhn Index increases.

Notching
Notches, or deep retouched concavities on an otherwise straight or curved margin, are found on a small number of scrapers (N=55, 16%). In her study of the function of scrapers from Ingaladdi, Sanders (1975:44) noted that notches were most often represented by a single deep retouch flake scar, with a total absence of use-wear within these edge concavities, despite noting its occurrence along portions of the adjacent margins. In these cases it seems more likely that notches either represent early stages in the retouching process, and/or early stage edge rejuvenation, rather than a functionally specific feature.

White (1969:23) and Lenoir (1986) have both noted that heavily retouched and stepped edges can at times be rejuvenated by removing deep retouch flakes from the edge. The incidence of deep and adjacent notches on the margins of flakes could then also represent an attempt to return a heavily stepped edge to its pristine state. It might also be expected that deep rejuvenating blows of this kind would have a significant subsidiary effect of reducing the average edge angle as well as the number of step terminations remaining on the margin.

Examining the incidence of notching throughout the sequence of reduction reveals that edge concavities are most common in the earliest and the latest stages of

reduction (Figure 2e). This trend appears to confirm the operation of two separate reduction processes that may both create concavities on scraper edges: single deep flake scars added to the edge at the outset of retouching, and deep rejuvenating blows delivered to remove stepped and exhausted sections of margins from more heavily reduced scrapers.

Retouch Location
In Figure 4, the changing frequency and distribution of retouch found around the perimeter of flakes is shown as Kuhn's Index increases. For this test, flakes were divided into eight segments of equal length, with the central three segments divided into 'left' and 'right' cells. The light and dark shading is used in this diagram to illustrate the evenness with which retouch is distributed across each of the eight segments. The number in each cell indicates the frequency (expressed as a percentage of all retouched segments) with which that segment is retouched for that interval of the Kuhn Index. The results show a trend from an earlier uneven distribution of retouch that is centred on the distal end and left margin, to a later and more even distribution of retouch around the entire perimeter of the flake.

A Reduction Model for Non-Formal Retouched Flakes
From the preceding tests it is clear that retouch intensity constitutes an important determinant of scraper morphology in the study region. To test the significance of the observed changes in implement morphology, t-tests were performed on adjacent Kuhn Index categories for mean retouched edge angle, the percentage retouched perimeter and the index of edge curvature. The results are presented in Table 1 and indicate that almost all comparisons return significant results. The two comparisons that do not yield significant results are those between 0.17 and 0.33, and 0.33 and 0.5 for mean

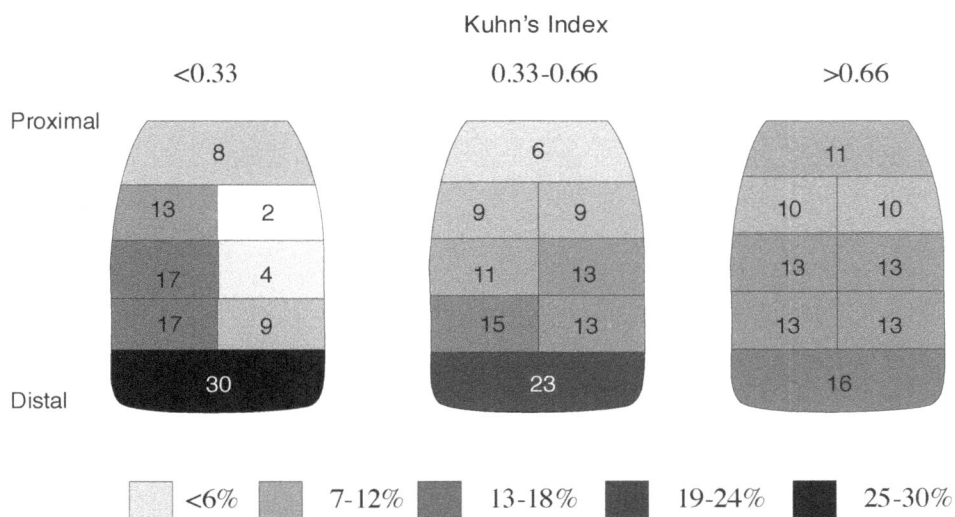

Figure 4. Graphic depiction of changes to the frequency and evenness with which retouch is distributed across eight segments as retouch increases.

retouched edge angle. This result is understandable given that some flakes are steep edged even before retouching begins, and these will naturally overlap to some degree with flakes at later stages of reduction. This problem appears to have disappeared, however, once flakes reach values of >0.5 on the Kuhn Index, and all comparisons return significant results thereafter.

Chi-Square tests were also performed to measure the significance of changes in the frequency of step terminations, notches and the evenness of retouch distribution over the sequence of reduction. The results are shown in Table 2 and indicate the changes over the reduction sequence are highly significant. The correlation between Kuhn's Index and all measures of morphological change also give Spearman's r and Kendell's tau results of 1, and are significant to the 0.01 level.

Thus the morphological changes described above appear to take place in a consistent sequence that reflects the steady increase in reduction from relatively unworked through to relatively 'exhausted' forms. This sequence is illustrated in the reduction diagram shown in Figure 5, and depicts the changes to the extent, angle, shape, and location of retouch demonstrated to occur as reduction increases.

A typical sequence might therefore begin with the removal of a single deep flake scar on the left distal, or distal end of the flake, creating a small concavity or 'notch' (Figure 5a). This concavity is subsequently removed as retouch expands around more of the margin, creating a convex edge with a steeper edge angle (Figure 5b). By the time retouch spans around 50% of the perimeter, edge curvature and edge angle have both increased dramatically (Figure 5c). Towards the end of the sequence, retouch has increased to span the entire margin, become very steep and exhibits areas of overlapping stepped scars in several places (Figure 5d). At this stage, edge rejuvenation may be attempted to remove accumulations of step terminations by delivering deep and forceful blows to the edge. This often creates a number of adjacent concavities that can give the implement a distinctive 'nosed' appearance (Figure 5e).

Typological Distinctions and Reduction Continuums
The preceding analysis has allowed the construction of a reduction model that explains much of the variation found in retouched implement morphology. Yet this morphological continuum demonstrated in this case to be causally linked to reduction intensity, is traditionally broken up into a number of discrete scraper types, commonly held to represent real, discontinuous and internally consistent kinds. This can be seen for instance in an early Australian scraper typology devised by McCarthy *et al* (1946), that still forms the basis of many typologies in use today.

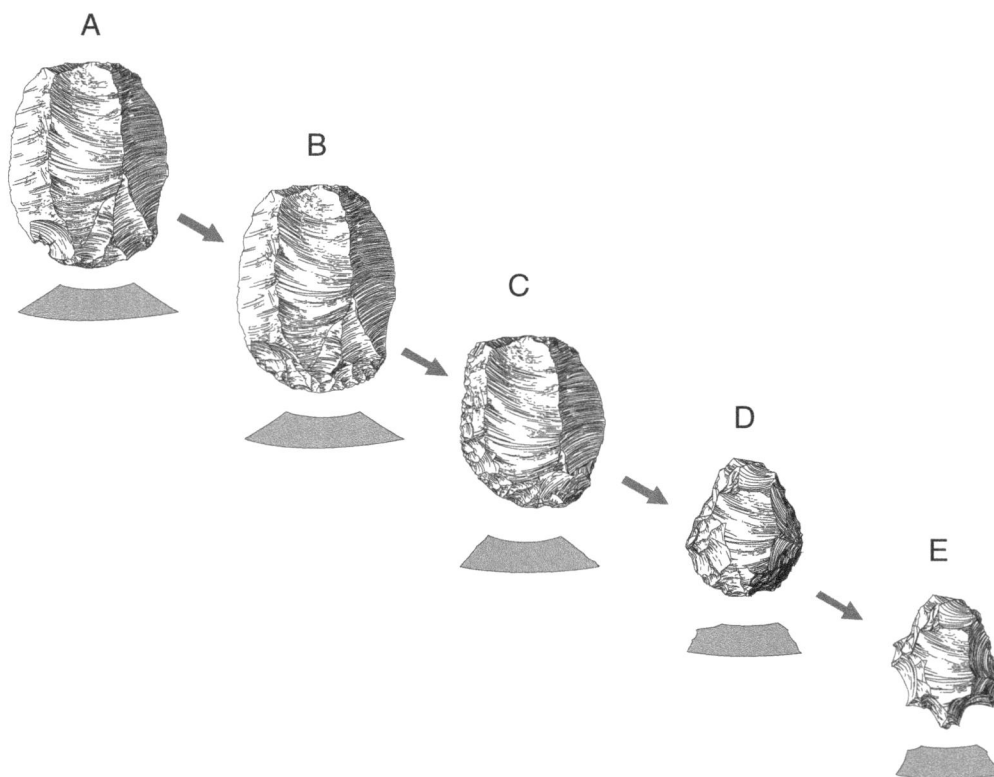

Figure 5. A reduction model for scrapers from the study region.

McCarthy *et al.'s* (1946) typology was primarily constructed around the location of retouch on one or more margins of an artefact, resulting in the creation of eight classes: *Side, End, Side and End, Double Side, Double End, Double Side and End, Double End and Side,* and *Double Side and Double End.* McCarthy *et al.* (1946) also employed five categories to describe the nature and degree of curvature in the plan-shape of retouched edges: straight, convex (slightly curved), semi-discoidal (quite curved), discoidal (very curved), and concave. Combining these two classificatory principles gave classes with labels such as *Semi-Discoidal Double Side and End* scrapers, or *Straight-Edged End* scrapers.

As one of the first comprehensive typologies developed in Australia, McCarthy *et al.'s* system has had a profound influence on later typologies, with many types imported wholesale into later schemes, while the concern for location and shape of the retouched portion also continues to pervade most recent typologies. Size and edge angle are often added to later typologies, however, due to the importance placed on these features as presumed measures of tool function.

Testing the Typology
By plotting each of McCarthy *et al.'s* type classes against measures of both reduction intensity and morphological change, it is possible to evaluate the utility of the typology as an analytical tool in three respects. First, whether type classes provide an accurate depiction of the nature of implement variation as previously demonstrated from individual specimens; second, whether types can justifiably be treated as discrete and tightly bounded entities; and finally, whether typologies focussed on the location and number of retouched margins can provide an effective measure of reduction intensity, as they have been used in the recent literature (Close 1991; Dibble 1987a, 1995; Gordon 1993; Kuhn 1992a; Rolland and Dibble 1990). To address these questions, the same population of 338 retouched flakes was assigned to one of McCarthy *et al.'s* eight scraper classes, using the principles outlined above. As only two *Double End* scrapers were identified in the sample this class was omitted from the following analysis. The mean and standard deviations for Kuhn's Index, percentage perimeter of retouch and the index of edge curvature were then calculated for each class and plotted in Figures 6 and 7.

Both figures reveal that the type classes reflect to some degree the relationships between Kuhn's Index, percentage edge retouched and edge curvature found for individual specimens in the previous section. It is also clear, however, that it is the number of retouched margins rather than retouch location that is driving this trend, as all types with the same number of retouched margins share similar means and even standard deviations in some cases. McCarthy *et al.'s* use of retouch location as a primary classificatory variable therefore serves to split the sample into a number of sets of overlapping

groupings that obscure the underlying reduction continuum.

Table 1. t-test results for changes in measures of implement morphology for adjacent Kuhn intervals. Asterisks indicate results are significant at the .05 level. t-test results are calculated using separate variance.

Kuhn Interval	df	t	F	p
Mean Retouched Edge Angle				
0.17 - 0.33	49	-.504	.194	.551
0.33 – 0.50	89	-1.527	.657	.139
0.50 – 0.67	120	-2.022	.036	.047*
0.67 – 0.83	146	-2.497	.002	.014*
0.83 – 1.00	110	-2.588	.022	.015*
% Perimeter Retouched				
0.17 - 0.33	53	-3.228	2.087	.003*
0.33 – 0.50	89	-2.425	3.477	.018*
0.50 – 0.67	117	-5.169	10.281	<.0005*
0.67 – 0.83	144	-3.435	2.702	.001*
0.83 – 1.00	109	-3.487	3.967	.002*
Index of Edge Curvature				
0.17 - 0.33	51	-4.269	5.977	<.0005*
0.33 – 0.50	85	-2.249	.111	.028*
0.50 – 0.67	109	-4.178	7.596	<.0005*
0.67 – 0.83	135	-3.404	16.529	.001*
0.83 – 1.00	103	-2.635	8.031	.03*

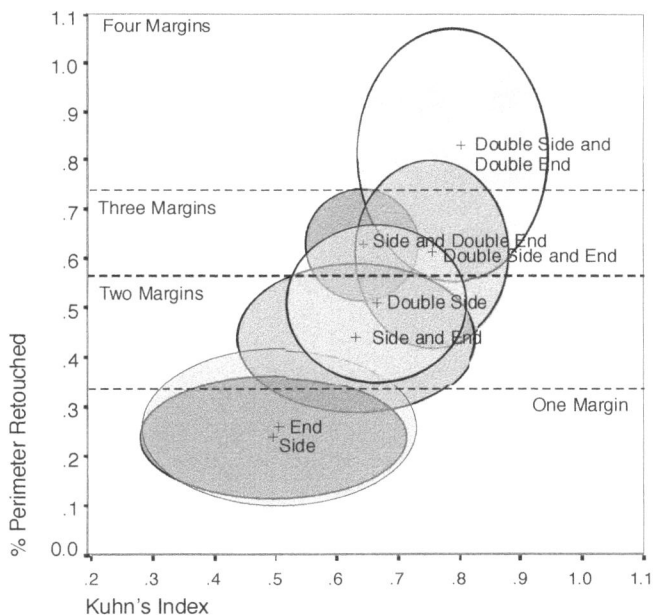

Figure 6. Scattergram showing the relationship between Kuhn's Index and the percentage perimeter of flake margins that have been retouched for each of McCarthy *et al.'s* scraper types. Crosses indicate the mean while circles enclose the standard deviation for that group. The broken lines approximate the point at which new margins are retouched.

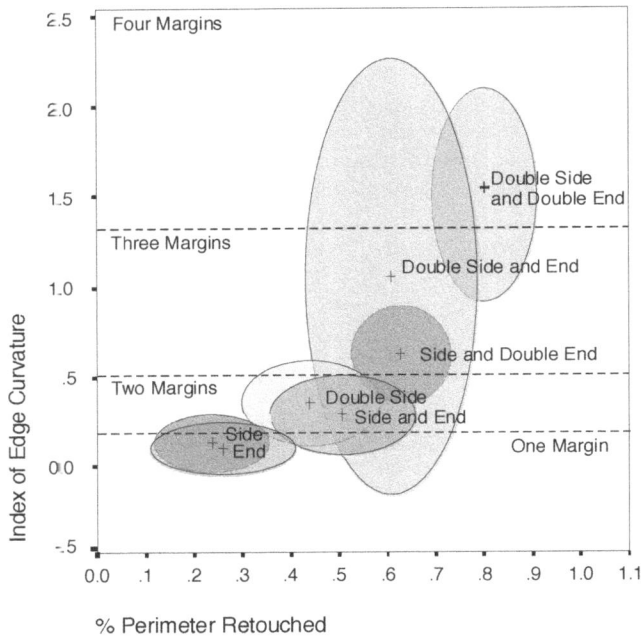

Figure 7. Scattergram showing the relationship between Kuhn's Index and the index of edge curvature for each of McCarthy et al.'s scraper types. Crosses indicate the mean while circles enclose the standard deviation for that group. The broken lines approximate the point at which new margins are retouched.

Table 3. t-test results for comparisons of morphological changes between adjacent types ranked according to their mean Kuhn Index. Asterisks indicate results are significant to the .05 level. t-test results calculated using separate variance.

Type Comparison	df	t	F	p
Index of Edge Curvature				
End vs Side	158	-2.12	1.30	0.036*
Side vs Side and End	118	-6.16	6.60	0.001*
Side and End vs Double Side	65	0.79	0.05	0.430
Double Side vs Side and Doule End	11	-2.40	0.18	0.035*
Side and Double End vs Double Side and End	28	-0.76	1.90	0.452
Double Side and End vs Double Side and Double End	41	-1.42	1.55	0.165
Kuhn Index				
End vs Side	171	-0.33	0.09	0.740
Side vs Side and End	123	-3.93	2.87	0.001*
Side and End vs Double Side	68	-5.67	1.30	0.573
Double Side vs Side and Doule End	13	0.34	1.48	0.738
Side and Double End vs Double Side and End	30	-2.06	0.58	0.049*
Double Side and End vs Double Side and Double End	44	-1.05	2.13	0.322
Mean Retouched Edge Angle				
End vs Side	167	1.16	0.01	0.250
Side vs Side and End	122	-3.12	0.21	0.020*
Side and End vs Double Side	68	2.02	0.09	0.070*
Double Side vs Side and Doule End	13	-1.64	0.04	0.130
Side and Double End vs Double Side and End	30	-0.56	0.29	0.646
Double Side and End vs Double Side and Double End	44	-2.08	0.12	0.047
% Perimeter Retouched				
End vs Side	167	0.47	0.76	0.640
Side vs Side and End	123	-8.77	3.80	0.001*
Side and End vs Double Side	68	-1.38	0.14	0.209
Double Side vs Side and Doule End	13	-1.59	1.49	0.136
Side and Double End vs Double Side and End	30	0.21	1.62	0.836
Double Side and End vs Double Side and Double End	44	-3.16	1.19	0.005*

Comparing *t*-test results for morphological changes in adjacent types (ranked according to their mean Kuhn Index) (Table 3) also shows typological divisions to be poorly separated in comparison with those obtained for divisions of the Kuhn Index, with only 37.5% of type comparisons proving significant, as opposed to 87% for Kuhn's Index.

It follows that McCarthy *et al.*'s typology cannot provide an effective measure of reduction intensity, as the criteria employed in the classification (number and location of retouched margins) result in types that directly overlap one another, subsume artefacts from quite different parts of the reduction continuum, and contain vast amounts of variation. In combination, these tests serve to demonstrate that McCarthy *et al.*'s types provide a clouded depiction of the reduction continuum and constitute an unreliable set of categories with which to measure reduction intensity.

Furthermore, standard deviations for all of McCarthy *et al.*'s types in Figure 6 overlap with at least one other class, and in the case of *Double Side* scrapers, overlap the means of five surrounding classes (*End, Side and Double End, Double Side and End, Side and Double End* and *Side and End* scrapers). The same trend can be seen in Figure 7, where *Double Side and End* scrapers overlap the standard deviations of four of its surrounding classes, as well as the means of two adjacent ones. The level of overlap between types can also be illustrated by plotting the distribution of artefacts making up both the least and most heavily reduced classes (*End* and *Double Side and Double End*) against Kuhn's Index and the percentage perimeter retouched. Both types overlap by nearly 50% and contain artefacts that are widely separated from the mean. The extent of overlap in the means and standard deviations of types therefore indicates that the notion that types represent real, discrete and discontinuous 'kinds' that are tightly bounded and internally consistent must be rejected.

That the typology reveals any relationship between reduction intensity and morphological change is not entirely surprising given it is constructed around the number of retouched margins, and this is itself a crude measure of reduction intensity. However, it is also clear that its apparent success in depicting gross changes in implement morphology is only revealed by having independent and quantitative measures of morphology and reduction in the first place.

It may also be the case that far better correlations between the typical (mean) characteristics of types and levels of reduction have been obtained in this study than might be expected in the majority of cases. This is because, in practice, typologists commonly classify artefacts according to 'the most significant' portion of retouch, usually determined according to how 'deliberate' each area of retouch appears, and typically with a view to identifying the 'working edge'. In such cases, it is

entirely conceivable that a flake with more than one retouched margin might be classified as a side scraper due to the presence of heavy retouch on a single margin only. Hence, the level of success that any typology will hold as a measure of reduction intensity is also dependent on the degree to which its theory is consistently applied, and the degree to which subjective judgments about tool function or the knapper's intentions are avoided.

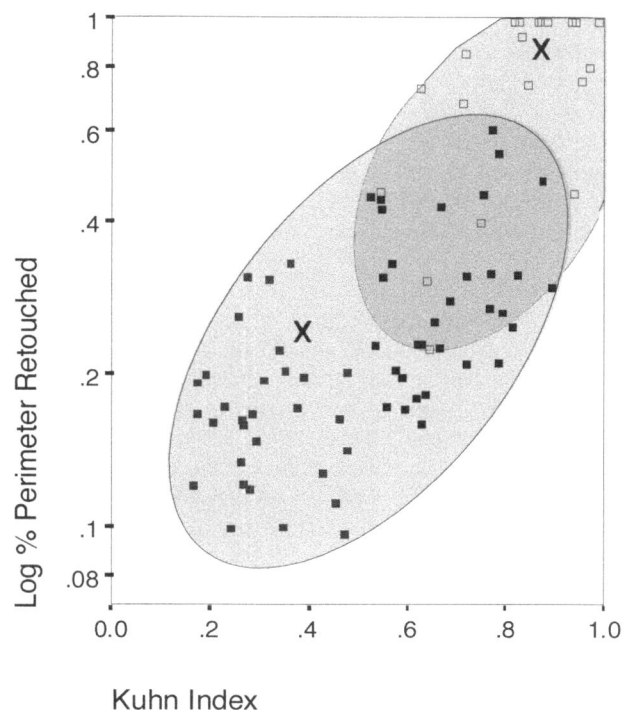

Figure 8. Scatter plot showing the overlap in two of McCarthy et al.'s scraper types (End and Double Side and Double End) that sit at opposite ends of the reduction continuum. Crosses indicate the mean for each type.

Discussion

The conclusion that may be drawn from both the technological and typological analyses presented in this paper is that reduction intensity provides a parsimonious explanation of scraper form, and that tool function or stylistic convention need not be invoked to explain much of this variation. Revealing the continuum that underlies individual typologies illustrates not only that types are not real kinds in and of themselves, but that typologies are unlikely to be effective tools for measuring reduction intensity in most cases.

Taking this point a step further, this study suggests it is unlikely that typologies built primarily around the location of retouch (such as Bordes' (1961; 1972) scheme that includes such classes as side, double side, convergent and transverse scrapers) will provide accurate depictions of the reduction process, particularly compared to analyses that examine continuous morphological variation for individual specimens removed from a typological framework. This suggests, for instance, that a better understanding of Middle Paleolithic scraper reduction sequences could be obtained from technological analyses that explore morphological variation in retouched flakes in relation to a number of independent and quantitative measures of retouch intensity, rather than retaining traditional categories that obscure these processes, as Dibble's (1995) recent analysis of the scrapers from Biache demonstrates.

Turning to the overall significance of reduction continuums as interpretive tools, an important question inevitably arises from studies of this kind; that is, if common implement morphologies are not real and immutable kinds manufactured to predetermined mental templates, or to meet specific functional requirements, but more simply reflect the amount of retouching they have received, then what can this tell us about past human behaviour?

Bleed (2001) points out that in many cases sequence models have come to be associated, at least implicitly, with discussions of risk (Bamforth 1986; Bamforth and Bleed 1997; Myers 1989; Torrence 1989), cost (Bleed 1996), and efficiency (Jeske 1992) in past technological systems. These discussions build on the assumption that the differential distribution of sequential steps and stages through space and time will reflect aspects of planning, land use, ecology and settlement and subsistence patterns effecting people's daily lives (Kuhn 1995; Nelson 1991). It may be then that the recurrence of specific forms in certain times and places tells us more about the degree to which people have had to conserve and extend the reduction of the materials to hand in order to meet novel circumstances or anticipate future needs, than it does about people's cultural preferences or even the functions for which tools are optimally suited.

The growing number of use-related studies that demonstrate poor form-function relationships certainly suggests the need to search for explanations of morphological variability that look beyond tool function alone (Anderson-Gerfaud 1990; Beyries 1988; Bienenfeld 1985; Cantwell 1979; Moss 1983; Salls 1985; Siegel 1984; Spenneman 1986). Furthermore, sequential models provide good reason to consider what effect changes in artefact morphology over the use-life of an implement might have on functional efficiency (see also Hiscock and Attenbrow, this volume).

The ability to document specific reduction sequences also raises the question of whether patterns of technological actions in time and space might encode information about degrees of contact, similarity and distance between the peoples that created different assemblages. This does seem a profitable avenue to explore in future, and particularly since studies of interregional contact and differentiation have recently become popular in Australian archaeology (David and Chant 1995; McNiven 1999). After all, the notion that prehistoric artisans often received ideas about the techniques and range of products

they intended to use through some form of social transmission is surely not difficult to accept. As Bleed (2001:122) states:

it is inconceivable that patterned actions of technology – even those that seem essentially ad hoc and responsive to immediate conditions – can proceed without some kind of "plan" even if that plan is nothing more than a vocabulary of known alternatives.

Despite its potential for investigating social and ecological questions, however, it should be emphasized that a reduction approach to stone implement morphology need make no assumptions regarding the cognitive or social aspects of technology that may underlie perceived patterns, and indeed, nor is it possible for sequence modeling, or any other approach to stone artefact analysis for that matter (including typology), to empirically investigate issues pertaining to the 'intentions' of prehistoric knappers. Moreover, understanding why people used certain techniques and made certain implements and not others also requires that we first develop a thorough understanding of the various constraints placed on technology by the availability and quality of raw materials and the various provisioning systems people employed to cope with different environments, before we may progress to comparisons of variation and central tendency in regional reduction sequences.

Conclusion

The purpose of this paper has been to illustrate that a reduction sequence approach to describing the transformative nature of flake morphology is effective, and that much of the variation in scraper forms seen, at least in northern Australia, can probably be explained by differing degrees of retouch intensity. By drawing attention to the problems that exist with typology as a means of understanding the reduction process, or as measures of reduction intensity, it is hoped that archaeologists will begin exploring techniques that emphasize materialist/technological approaches to the description of assemblage variation over essentialist/typological ones.

In conclusion, it can be argued that reduction approaches offer archaeologists a chance to begin exploring what assemblage-level variation in reduction intensity might mean in terms of mobility patterns, uncertainty in the scheduling and location of activities, and its effects on settlement and subsistence systems, and perhaps even the nature of inter-regional contacts and connections. Such an approach offers a chance to significantly advance Australian lithic studies, and allows exploration of the implications of technological and typological changes free from the stylistic and functional straightjacket of traditional archaeological thought.

Acknowledgements
I would like to thank all my colleagues at the ANU from

whose advice and encouragement I have benefited enormously over the years. I would also like to thank Bill Harney, July Blutja, Lilly Gin.ginna, Oliver Raymond and the rest of the Wardaman Community for their encouragement, assistance in the field and permission to conduct archaeological research at important sites.

References

Allen, H. 1972 Where the Crow Flies Backwards: Man and land in the Darling Basin. Ph.D. Thesis. Australian National University.

Anderson-Gerfaud, P. 1990 Aspects of behaviour in the Middle Paleolithic: functional analysis of stone tools from Southwest France. In P. Mellars (ed.), *The Emergence of Modern Humans: An Archaeological Perspective*. Pp.389-418. Edinburgh: Edinburgh University Press.

Bamforth, D.B. 1986 Technological efficiency and tool curation. *American Antiquity* 51:38-50.

Bamforth, D.B. and Bleed, P. 1997 Technology, flaked stone technology, and risk. In G.A. Clark (ed.), *Rediscovering Darwin: Evolutionary Theory in Archaeology*. Pp.109-140. Archaeological Papers of the American Anthropological Association, No.7. Washington: American Anthropological Association.

Barton, C.M. 1988 *Lithic Variability and Middle Paleolithic Behaviour: New evidence from the Iberian Peninsula*. Oxford: British Archaeological Reports.

Beyries, S. 1988 Functional variability of lithic sets in the Middle Paleolithic. In A.M. Montet-White (ed.), *Upper Pleistocene Prehistory of Western Eurasia*. Pp.213-223. Pennsylvania: University of Pennsylvania Museum.

Bienenfeld. 1985 Preliminary Results from a Lithic Use-wear Study of the Swifterbant Sites, S-51, S-4 and S-2. *Helinium* XXV:194-211.

Bleed, P. 1996 Risk and cost in Japanese microcore technology. *Lithic Technology* 21.

Bleed, P. 2001 Trees or chains, links or branches: conceptual alternatives for consideration of stone tool production and other sequential activities. *Journal of Archaeological Method and Theory* 8:101-127.

Bleed, P. 2002 Obviously sequential, but continuous or staged? Refits and cognition in three late paleolithic assemblages from Japan. *Journal of Anthropological Archaeology* 21:329-343.

Bordes, F. 1961 Mousterian cultures in France. *Science* 1961:803-810.

Bordes, F. 1972 *A Tale of Two Caves*. New York: Harper and Row.

Bowdler, S. 1981 Stone tools, style and function: evidence from the Stockyard Site, Hunter Island. *Archaeology in Oceania*:64-69.

Bowler, J.M., Jones, R., Allen, H. and Thorne, A. 1970 Pleistocene Human remains from Australia: a living site and human cremation from Lake Mungo, western New South Wales. *World Archaeology* 2:39-60.

Cantwell, A.-M. 1979 The Functional Analysis of Scrapers: Problems, New Techniques and Cautions. *Lithic Technology* 8:5-11.

Clarkson, C. 2002a Holocene scraper reduction, technological organization and landuse at Ingaladdi Rockshelter, Northern Australia. *Archaeology in Oceania* 37:79-86.

Clarkson, C. 2002b An index of invasiveness for the measurement of unifacial and bifacial retouch: a theoretical, experimental and archaeological verification. *Journal of Archaeological Science* 1:65-75.

Clegg, J.K. 1977 The four Dimensions of Artificial Variation. In R.V.S. Wright (ed.), *Stone Tools as Cultural Markers: Change, Evolution and Complexity*. Pp.60-66. New Jersey: Humanities Press.

Close, A. 1991 On the validity of Middle Paleolithic tool types: a test case from the eastern Sahara. *Journal of Field Archaeology* 18:256-269.

Cundy, B.J. 1990 An Analysis of the Ingaladdi Assemblage: critique of the understanding of lithic technology. Ph.D. Thesis. Australian National University.

David, B. and Chant, D. 1995 Rock art regionalisation in North Queensland prehistory. *Memoirs of the Queensland Museum* 37:357-528.

Davis, Z.J. and Shea, J.J. 1998 Quantifying lithic curation: an experimental test of Dibble and Pelcin's original flake-tool mass predictor. *Journal of Archaeological Science* 25:603-610.

Dibble, H. 1984 Interpreting typological variation of Middle Paleolithic scrapers: function, style, or sequence of reduction? *Journal of Field Archaeology* 11:431-436.

Dibble, H. 1987a The interpretation of Middle Paleolithic scraper morphology. *American Antiquity* 52:109-117.

Dibble, H. 1987b Reduction sequences in the manufacture of Mousterian implements of France. In O. Soffer (ed.), *The Pleistocene Old World Regional Perspectives*. Pp.33-45. New York: Plenum Press.

Dibble, H. 1988 Typological aspects of reduction and intensity of utilization of lithic resources in the French Mousterian. In A. Montet-White (ed.), *Upper Pleistocene Prehistory of Western Eurasia*. Pp.181-198. Philadelphia: University of Pennsylvania.

Dibble, H. 1989 The implications of stone tool types for the presence of language during the Lower and Middle Paleolithic. In C. Stringler (ed.), *The Human Revolution: Behavioural and Biological Perspectives on the Origins of Modern Humans*. Pp.415-432. Edinburgh: Edinburgh University Press.

Dibble, H. 1995 Middle Paleolithic scraper reduction: background, clarification, and review of evidence to date. *Journal of Archaeological Method and Theory* 2:299-368.

Dibble, H. 1997 Platform variability and flake morphology: a comparison of experimental and archaeological data and implications for interpreting prehistoric lithic technological strategies. *Lithic Technology* 22:150-170.

Dibble, H. 1998 Comment on "Quantifying lithic curation: An experimental test of Dibble and Pelcin's original flake-tool mass predictor", by Zachary J.

Davis and John J. Shea. *Journal of Archaeological Science* 25:611-613.

Dibble, H. and Pelcin, A. 1995 The effect of hammer mass and velocity on flake mass. *Journal of Archaeological Science* 22:429-439.

Dibble, H. and Whittaker, J. 1981 New experimental evidence on the relation between percussion flaking and flake variation. *Journal of Archaeological Science* 6.

Dunnell, R.C. 1986 Methodological issues in Americanist artifact classification. In M.B. Schiffer (ed.), *Advances in Archaeological Method and Theory*. Pp.35-99. New York: Academic Press.

Flood, J.M. 1973 The Moth-Hunters. Ph.D. Thesis. Australian National University.

Flood, J.M. 1974 Pleistocene man at Clogg's Cave: his tool kit and environment. *Mankind* 9:175-178.

Gordon, D. 1993 Mousterian tool selection, reduction, and discard at Ghar, Israel. *Journal of Field Archaeology* 20:.205-218.

Hiscock, P. 1982 The meaning of edge angles. *Australian Archaeology*.

Hiscock, P. 1993 Bondaian technology in the Hunter Valley, New South Wales. *Archaeology in Oceania* 28:64-75.

Hiscock, P. 1994 The end of points. In A. Webb (ed.), *Archaeology in the North*. Darwin: Australian National University (NARU).

Hiscock, P. 1996 Transformations of Upper Palaeolithic implements in the Dabba industry from Haua Fteah (Libya). *Antiquity* 70:657-664.

Hiscock, P. 2001 Looking the other way: a materialist/technological approach to classifying tools and implements, cores and retouched flakes, with examples from Australia. In J. Lindley (ed.), *Tools or Cores? The Identification and Study of Alternative Core Technology in Lithic Assemblages*. Pennsylvania: University of Pennsylvania Museum.

Hiscock, P. 2002 Quantifying the Size of Artefact Assemblages. *Journal of Archaeological Science* 29:251-258.

Hiscock, P. and Allen, H. 2000 Assemblage Variability in the Willandra Lakes. *Archaeology in Oceania* 35:97-103.

Hiscock, P. and Attenbrow, V. 2002 Early Australian implement variation: a reduction model. *Journal of Archaeological Science* 30:239-249.

Hiscock, P. and Attenbrow, V. 2003 Morphological and reduction continuums in eastern Australia: measurement and implications at Capertee 3. *Tempus* 7:167-174.

Hiscock, P. and Attenbrow, V. In Press *Australia's Eastern Regional Sequence Revisited: Technology and Change at Capertee 3*. Oxford: British Archaeological Reports.

Hiscock, P. and Attenbrow, V. This volume Reduction continuums and tool use.

Hiscock, P. and Clarkson, C. 2000 Analysing Australian stone artefacts: an agenda for the Twenty First Century. *Australian Archaeology* 50:98-108.

Hiscock, P. and Veth, P. 1991 Change in the Australian Desert Culture: a reanalysis of tulas from Puntutjarpa. *World Archaeology* 22:332-345.

Holdaway, S. 1991 Resharpening Reduction and Lithic Assemblage Variability Across the Middle to Upper Paleolithic Transition University of Pennsylvania. Philadelphia

Holdaway, S., McPherron, S. and Roth, B. 1996 Notched tool reuse and raw material availability in French Middle Paleolithic sites. *American Antiquity* 61:377-387.

Jeske, R.J. 1992 Energetic efficiency and lithic technology. *American Antiquity* 57.

Jones, R. 1971 Rocky Cape and the problem of the Tasmanians. Ph.D. Thesis. Sydney University.

Kuhn, S. 1990 A geometric index of reduction for unifacial stone tools. *Journal of Archaeological Science* 17:585-593.

Kuhn, S.L. 1992a Blank form and reduction as determinants of Mousterian scraper morphology. *American Antiquity* 57:115-128.

Kuhn, S.L. 1992b On planning and curated technologies in the Middle Paleolithic. *Journal of Anthropological Research* 48:185-207.

Kuhn, S.L. 1995 *Mousterian Lithic Technology*. Princeton: Princeton University Press.

Lamb, L. This volume Backed and forth: an exploration of variation in retouched implement production on the South Molle Island Quarry, Central Queensland.

Law, W.B. This volume Chipping away in the past: stone artefact reduction and mobility at Purritjarra Rockshelter.

Lenoir, M. 1986 Un mode d'obtention de la retouche "Quina" dans la Moustérian de Combe Grenal (Domme, Dordogne). *Bulletin de la Société Anthropologique de la Sud Ouest* 21:153-160

Lyman, R.L., O'Brien, M.J. and Dunnell, R.C. 1997 *The Rise and Fall of Culture History*. New York: Plenum Press.

Marcy, J.L. 1993 Aperçu sur les stratégies de producion des raclois du niveau, *Riencourt-lés-Baupaume (Pas-de-Calais):Un Gisement du Paléolithique Moyen*. Pp.87-94. Documents d'Achéologie Français, No. 37.

McCarthy, F. 1948 The Lapstone Creek Excavation: two culture periods revealed in eastern New South Wales. *Records of the Australian Museum* 22:1-34.

McCarthy, F.D. 1949 The prehistoric cultures of Australia. *Oceania* 19:305-19.

McCarthy, F.D. 1958 Culture succession in south eastern Australia. *Mankind* 5:177-190.

McCarthy, F.D., Brammell, E. and Noone, H.V.V. 1946 The Stone Implements of Australia. *Memoirs of the Australian Museum* 9:1-94.

McNiven, I. 1999 Fissioning and regionalisation: The social dimensions of change in Aboriginal use of the Great Sandy region, southeast Queensland. In I. McNiven (ed.), *Australian Coastal Archaeology*. Pp.157-168. Resarch Papers in Archaeology and Natural History 31. Canberra: Archaeology and Natural History Publications.

McPherron, S. and Dibble, H. 1999 Stone tool analysis using digitized images: examples from the Lower and Middle Palaeolithic. *Lithic Technology* 24:38-52.

McPherron, S.P. 1994 A reduction model for variability in Acheulian biface morphology. Unpublished PhD Thesis, University of Pennsylvania.

Mitchell, S.R. 1949 *Stone-Age Craftsmen. Stone Tools and Camping Places of Australian Aborigines.* Melbourne: Tait Book Company.

Morrow, T.A. 1997 End scraper morphology and use-life: an approach for studying paleoindian lithic technology and mobility. *Lithic Technology* 22:51-69.

Morwood, M. and Hobbs, D.R. 1995 Quinkan Prehistory: the archaeology of Aboriginal art in S.E. Cape York Peninsula, Australia. *Tempus* 3.

Moss, E.H. 1983 *The Functional Analysis of Flint Implements: Pincevent and Pont d'Ambon: Two Case Studies from the French Final Palaeolithic* (British Archaeological Report International Series 177).

Mulvaney, D.J. 1969 *The Prehistory of Australia.* London: Thames and Hudson.

Mulvaney, D.J. and Joyce, E.B. 1965 Archaeological and Geomorphological Investigations on Mt. Moffatt Station, Queensland, Australia. *Proceedings of the Prehistoric Society* 31:147-212.

Mulvaney, D.J. and Kamminga, J. 1999 *Prehistory of Australia*: Allen and Unwin.

Myers, A. 1989 Reliable and maintainable technological strategies in the Mesolithic of mainland Britain. In R. Torrence (ed.), *Time, Energy and Stone Tools*. Pp.78-91. Cambridge: Cambridge University Press.

Neeley, M.P. and Barton, C.M. 1994 A new approach to interpreting late Pleistocene microlith industries in southwest Asia. *Antiquity* 68:275-288.

Nelson, M.C. 1991 The study of technological organization. *Archaeological Method and Theory* 3:57-100.

O'Brien, M.J. 1996 Evolutionary archaeology: an introduction. In M.J. O'Brien (ed.), *Evolutionary Archaeology: Theory and Application*. Salt Lake City: University of Utah Press.

Odell, G.H. 1989 Experiments in lithic reduction. In R.P. Mauldin (ed.), *Experiments in Lithic Technology*. Pp.163-198. Oxford: British Archaeological Reports.

Pelcin, A. 1997a The effect of core surface morphology on flake attributes: evidence from a controlled experiment. *Journal of Archaeological Science* 24:749-756.

Pelcin, A. 1997b The effect of indentor type on flake attributes: evidence from a controlled experiment. *Journal of Archaeological Science* 24:1107-1113.

Pelcin, A. 1997c The formation of flakes: the role of platform thickness and exterior platform angle in the production of flake initiations and terminations. *Journal of Archaeological Science* 24:1107-1113.

Pelcin, A. 1998 The threshold effect of platform width: a reply to Davis and Shea. *Journal of Archaeological Science* 25:615-620.

Rolland, N. and Dibble, H. 1990 A new synthesis of Middle Paleolithic Variability. *American Antiquity* 55:480-499.

Salls, R.A. 1985 The Scraper Plane: a Functional Interpretation. *Journal of Field Archaeology* 12:99-106.

Sanders, B. 1975 Scrapers from Ingaladdi. MA Thesis. Australian National University.

Shott, M.J., Bradbury, A.P., Carr, P.J. and Odell, H.O. 2000 Flake size from platform attributes: predictive and empirical approaches. *Journal of Archaeological Science* 27:877-894.

Siegel, P.E. 1984 Functional Variability Within an Assemblage of Endscrapers. *Lithic Technology* 13:35-51.

Spenneman, D.H.R. 1986 On the Use-Wear of Stone Adzes and Axes and Its Implication for the Assessment of Humans Handedness. *Lithic Technology* 16:22-27.

Tindale, N.B. 1957 Cultural succession in South-Eastern Australia from Late Pleistocene to the Present. *Records of the South Australian Museum* 13.

Torrence, R. 1989 Re-tooling: towards a behavioral theory of stone tools. In R. Torrence (ed.), *Time, Energy and Stone Tools*. Pp.57-66. Cambridge: University of Cambridge.

White, C. 1971 Man and Environment in Northwest Arnhem Land. In J. Golson (ed.), *Aboriginal Man and Environment in Australia*. Pp.141-157. Canberra: ANU Press.

White, C. and Peterson, N. 1969 Ethnographic Interpretation of the Prehistory of Western Arnhem Land. *Southwestern journal of Anthropology* 25:45-67.

White, J.P. 1969 Typologies for some prehistoric flaked stone artefacts of the Australian New Guinea Highlands. *Archaeology and Physical Anthropology in Oceania* 4:18-46.

White, J.P. and O'Connell, J.F. 1982 *A Prehistory of Australia, New Guinea and Sahul*. Sydney: Academic Press.

Wilmsen, E.N. 1968 Functional analysis of flaked stone artefacts. *American Antiquity* 33:156-161.

Yvorra, P. 2000 *Exploitation de l'analyse quantitative des retouches pour la caracterisation des industries lithiques du Mousterien : application au facies Quina de la vallee du Rhone* (BAR International Series, No.869.) Oxford.

4 | Backed and Forth: An Exploration of Variation in Retouched Implement Production on the South Molle Island Quarry, Central Queensland

Lara Lamb

Abstract

The South Molle Island Quarry is unique in Australia because it is situated on a reasonably remote island off the east coast of Australia, and is formed from a rare and distinctive type of extremely high quality stone. The isolation and distinctive nature of the stone provides an opportunity to examine procurement costs and distribution patterns at a regional scale, while also possessing a large number of retouched flakes at various stages of production. The aim of this paper is to describe the origins, properties and form of outcrop of the distinctive stone found at this quarry, and to determine whether retouch on the South Molle Island Quarry is directed exclusively at the production of large backed artifacts (i.e. "Juan Knives"), or whether additional retouch strategies were practiced at the site. This is achieved through the use of metric and non-metric analyses which determine both the extent and degree of variability within the retouched flakes found at the quarry.

Introduction

Descriptions of prehistoric Aboriginal stone quarries are rare in Australian archaeological literature, yet they remain an important source of information. This is because they allow us to understand the variation, range of strategies and frequency of production failures that underlie the procurement and production of stone implements and raw materials that are transported away from quarries, and therefore form a highly informative subset of Australian archaeological sites. The South Molle Island Quarry, located in the Whitsunday Islands, is unique in Australia because it is situated on an island, some 2km from the mainland, and is formed from a rare and distinctive stone raw material type. The quarry thus presents a unique opportunity to examine, not only procurement costs and distribution patterns at a regional scale (the subject of future studies), but it also possesses a large number of retouched artefacts of both informal and formal (backed) design, and therefore lends itself to the description of early stage implement production and the level of variation within techniques in this region. The South Molle Island Quarry is also significant as there is now evidence that it was utilized for at least the last 9,000 years for the production of stone artefacts found throughout the Whitsunday region (Lamb 2005).

Backed artefacts in Australia continue to be defined by a wide range of typological categories, determined by morphological differences, the use of which is often supported by distinct spatial and temporal boundaries between 'types' (McCarthy 1976; Mulvaney and Kamminga 1999; White and O'Connell 1982). In recent years there has been a growing body of evidence that deconstructs these boundaries – temporal, spatial and typological – as being less clearly defined than previously thought (Hiscock 1994; Hiscock and Attenbrow 1998; McNiven 2000). This throws into doubt the validity of

such classificatory systems across the spectrum of types, not only, but including backed artefacts. This has led to a range of fresh approaches to the study of stone artefacts in Australia, with an increasing tendency to turn away from typologies and focus instead on technology and processes of artefact reduction and manufacture (Clarkson 2002; Clarkson this volume; Hiscock and Attenbrow 2002; Hiscock and Attenbrow this volume; Hiscock and Clarkson this volume). Exploring variation in artefact morphology in this manner, with the expectation of clinal patterning, and using measurements drawn from an understanding of manufacturing technology, opens the way for inclusion in the analysis of a larger number of artefacts that would not normally meet the requirements of formal typologies, and does so without making arbitrary judgments about prehistoric knappers' intentions.

This type of analysis is meaningful in the South Molle Island context because the quarry contains formal implements (backed artefacts) from initial stages of raw material procurement through to final stages of retouch (Lamb 1996). The identification of these systems requires the separation of distinct technological groupings, which requires measurement of variation and overlap, as well as the identification of strategies involved in their manufacture. Typological systems are not well suited to addressing these issues because they are often constructed without reference to technology or process, and thus suppress variation within the boundaries between types.

In this paper, I examine a sample of 445 retouched artefacts from the South Molle Island Quarry on the central Queensland coast. As backed artefacts were manufactured at this locale, it is expected that a portion of the retouched artefact sample will represent stages in the manufacturing process. The aim of this analysis is to

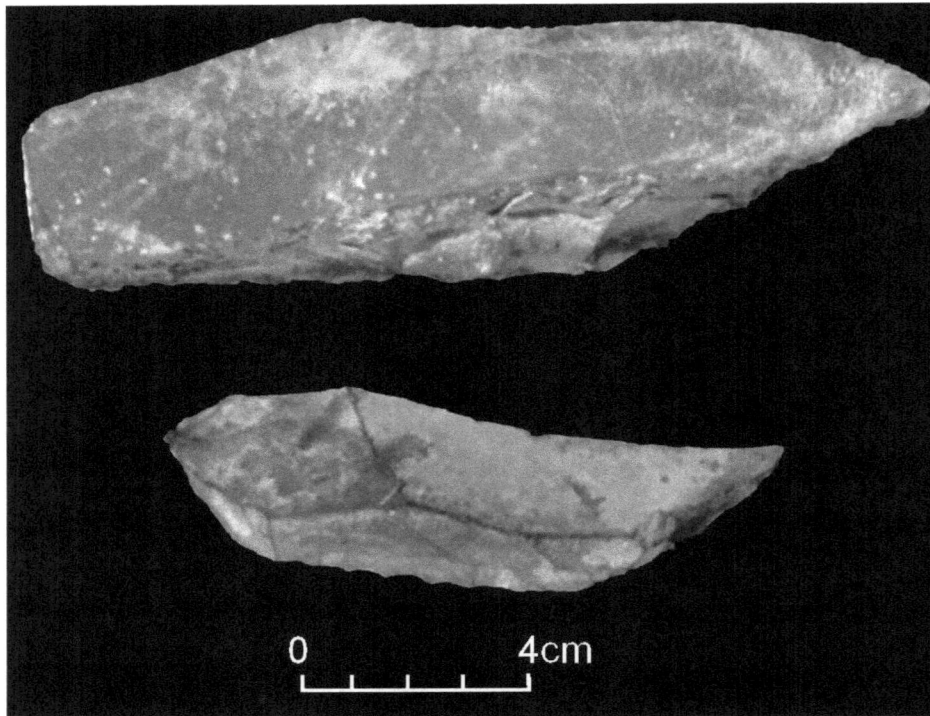

Figure 1: Examples of backed artefacts from the South Molle Island quarry.

determine whether retouch on the South Molle Island Quarry is directed exclusively at the production of backed artefacts, or whether there are other retouch strategies being practiced in addition to backing (see Figure 1 for some examples of backed artefact specimens). This is achieved through the use of metric and non-metric analyses which determine both the extent and degree of variability within the retouch located on the quarry.

South Molle Island Quarry, Whitsundays

South Molle Island is a small offshore island, located on the central Queensland coast, approximately 2km from the mainland. The South Molle Island Quarry (SMIQ) occupies a steep rocky ridge on the north-eastern side of South Molle Island and the site complex as a whole, including quarrying and reduction sites. The quarry and associated artefact scatters cover an area of at least 42,000m². Areas of high-density artefact scatter extend along the ridge top for 400m in a north-south orientation, extend down the eastern face of the ridge for 75m, and extend intermittently down the western slope to the beach 300 meters away. Surface artefact densities typically range from between 100-500/m² (Figure 2).

The SMIQ source is characterized as a pyroclastic surge deposit and is the only source of this material known to be exploited on the central Queensland coast (Barker and Schon 1994). A complex interaction between basaltic magma and ground water produced a base-surge deposit, which has been classified as a silicious volcanic tuff with a flint-like habit (Brian 1991:56). These deposits typically produce unidirectional bed forms which can

include dune forms, low angle cross stratification, pitch and swell structures and wavy lamination. Unweathered, base surges range in colour from gray to black, and demonstrate a 'flint-like' habit which is the result of secondary silicification (Brian 1991:55-56). Grain size, colour, and texture of the SMIQ raw material varies substantially across the site. This is in keeping with the overall characteristics of pyroclastic base surge deposits, which typically become finer grained further away from the source.

The SMIQ source ranges in colour from black, through to dark gray, gray and olive gray. The further from black the colour becomes, the larger the grain size. This pattern extends in a clear north/south orientation in line with the quarry ridge top. The black, fine-grained material occurs at the northern (or beach end) of the quarry, and grades into gray courser grained material, in a southerly direction along the ridge. The material's limited glassy quality combined with the fine-grained matrix gives it remarkably homogenous flaking properties, and thus makes it a versatile raw material for the purposes of stone artefact manufacture.

On the SMIQ, the siliceous volcanic tuff occurs in several different forms and the extraction techniques differ accordingly, as outlined below. The two main distinguishable forms of raw material are the vertically bedded nodules which occur primarily towards the southern end of the quarry, and the much larger horizontally bedded slabs that range in size up to several meters in diameter and are found toward the northern end.

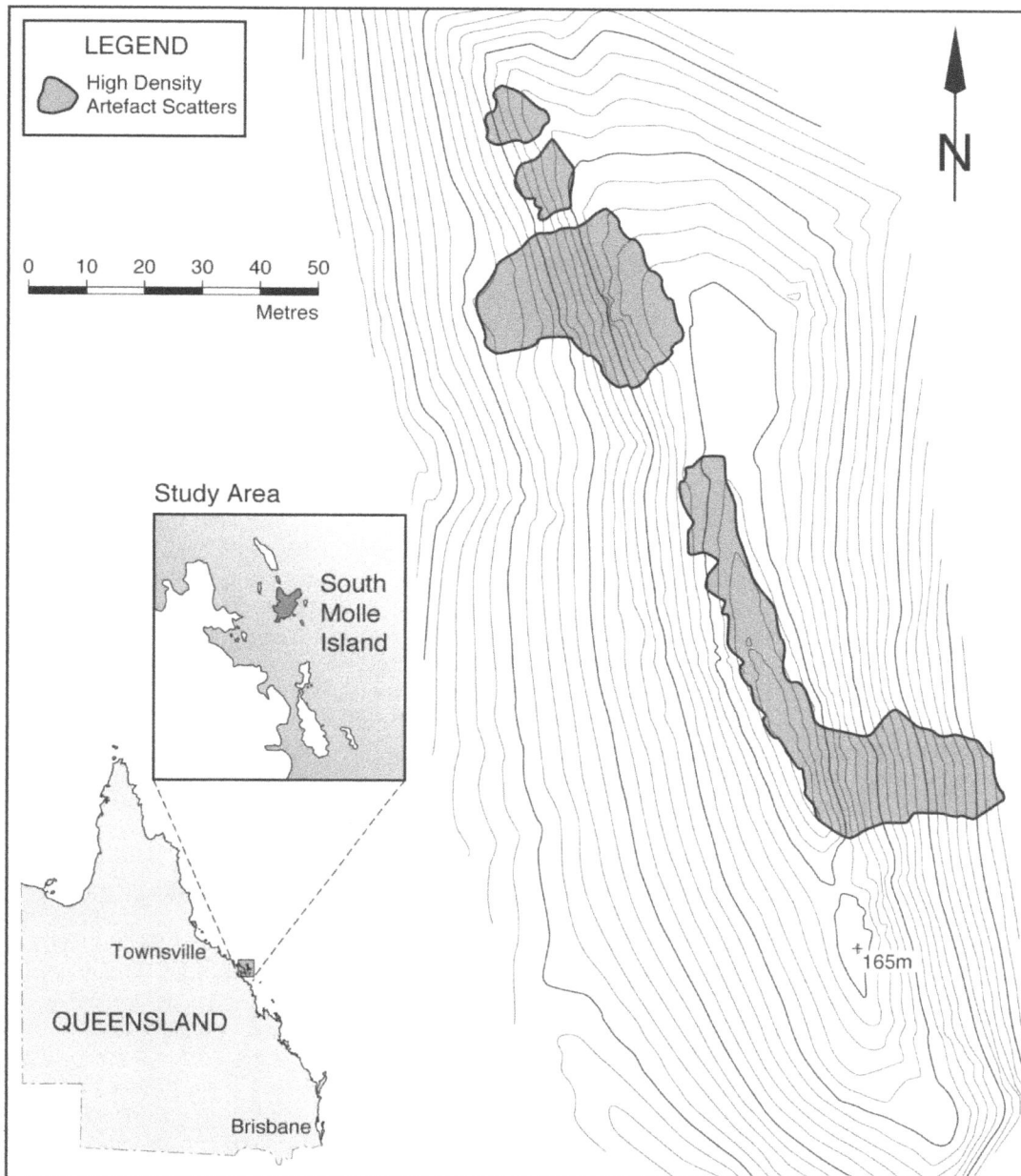

Figure 2. Map of the South Molle Island Quarry, Whitsundays

Base surge deposits result from a ground-level, horizontal surge of pyroclastic materials, mixed with water vapour and ash. These are frequently interspersed or overlain by pyroclastic fall deposits (Brian 1991:55). In these instances, cross-bedding can occur, with one type of material overlaying another. With differing capacity to withstand weathering, one material weathers faster than another, leaving discrete, unidirectional bedded nodules. These vary in size from several centimetres to several metres in diameter, and remain bedded in the soil matrix of the local sedimentary environment. Whether they are exposed or not, depends on local erosional conditions. There is evidence for the extensive procurement of these vertically bedded nodules using several methods, and

these are also reflected in various core morphologies found at the SMIQ.

Characterising Variability in Flake Retouch
The SMIQ is both a quarry site and a reduction site (Hiscock and Mitchell 1993). The reduction of the raw material ranges from early stages of core reduction to late-stage retouch of backed artefact forms (Lamb 1996). Fieldwork conducted on the quarry as part of a broader doctoral research project has yielded a sample of 445 retouched artefacts (of which 329 are backed). The following analysis presents a series of tests which together attempt to characterise the nature of retouch in the SMIQ. These tests aim at determining retouch

Table 1. Direction of retouch on all retouched artefacts.

	Bi-directional	Unidirectional	
Backed Artefacts (N=146)	90 (62%)	53 (36%)	
		From dorsal only	From ventral only
		12 (8%)	41 (28%)
Other Retouch (N=63)	17 (27%)	46 (73%)	
		From dorsal only	From ventral only
		22 (35%)	21 (33%)

direction, retouch location, percentage of length retouched, extent of retouching and size of retouched artefacts.

In order to determine the variability of retouch practiced on the SMIQ, a range of variables are examined on two classes of artefacts: backed and non-backed. For the purpose of this study, the term *backed artefact* refers to those artefacts with steep retouch along one margin, at near 90 degree angles to the dorsal and/or ventral plain (Hiscock and Attenbrow 1996; Hiscock 2002a). The pattern of retouch can take bidirectional or unidirectional form, and is not restricted to the lateral margins (Lamb 1995). As the process of backing is already clearly identified and defined in the Australian stone artefact literature (Hiscock 1998, 2002b; Lamb 1996; McNiven 2000), and variation among the backed sample from the SMIQ is the subject of a separate study, I wish to further examine the sample of non-backed artefacts, with a view to characterising the reduction process, and highlighting the nature and variation of retouched artefact manufacture on the SMIQ.

Retouch Direction
During analysis, two directional categories were identified in order to determine retouch direction: bi-directional and unidirectional (with subsets of *unidirectional from dorsal surface only* and *unidirectional from ventral surface only*). Table 1 illustrates a polarity between backed artefacts and non-backed artefacts in terms of retouch direction, with the majority of backed artefacts exhibiting bidirectional

retouch, while the opposite is true of non-backed artefacts. The differences in the proportion of bidirectional retouch between categories also proves significant (Chi Square = 100.771; P=<.0005). This result is of particular note and will be discussed in more detail below.

Retouch Location
The location of retouch was recorded as right, left, proximal or distal margins, oriented according to the ventral surface. Adjacent margins are defined as distinct from one another according to the orientation of the retouch to its opposite margin (right being opposite to left, and proximal being opposite to distal). For example, if a line extending out perpendicular to the proximal margin locates retouch on the opposite margin, then that retouch is said to be located on the distal end. If a line extending out perpendicular to the left margin also encounters retouch, then it would be classed as occupying two margins: distal and right.

Generally, the majority of implements were retouched on one margin only (this is in keeping with the generally low curvature index for backed artefacts – see below). However, of note is the fact that non-backed artefacts exhibit significantly higher rates of retouch on *multiple* margins than do backed artefacts (Chi Square = 100.771; P=<.0005), suggestive perhaps of a sub-grouping exhibiting generalised retouch on a range of margins, and not exclusively devoted to early-stage backing of a single margin (Table 2). However, the retouching of multiple margins could instead suggest that this group represents

Table 2. Number of margins retouched.

	1 Retouched Margin	2 Retouched Margins	3 Retouched Margins	4 Retouched Margins	Missing Data
Backed (N=146)	103 (71%)	17 (12%)	2 (1%)	-	24 (16%)
Non-backed (N=63)	35 (56%)	15 (24%)	7 (11%)	1 (1.5%)	5 (8%)

Table 3. Average weight of artefacts, according to number of margins retouched.

	1 Retouched Margin	2 Retouched Margins	3 Retouched Margins	4 Retouched Margins
Backed Mean Weight (N=146)	160g	214g	136g	-
Non-backed Mean Weight (N=63)	724g	1111g	1527g	3259g
t-test	p=.000	p=.004	p=.006	-

Table 4. Mean maximum length of retouched artefacts.

	N	Mean percent of maximum length retouched (mm)	Std. Dev.
Backed	146	89.55	17.7
Non-backed	59	70	25.9

Table 5. Kuhn's reduction index, curvature index and retouched edge angle.

	N	Backed Artefacts	Non-backed Artefacts
Kuhn Reduction Index (mean, std. dev.)	232	0.97 ± 0.07	0.96 ± 0.06
Curvature Index (mean, std. dev.)	233	0.17 ± 0.08	0.2 ± 0.09
Retouched Edge Angle (mean, std. dev.)	372	87.5 ± 11.2	71.7 ± 17.4

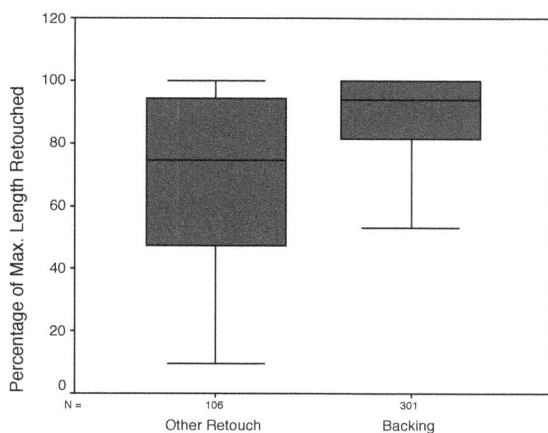

Figure 3. Percentage of maximum length retouched.

the reworking of backed artefacts. If this were the case,we might expect to see similar but not lower mean weights for such a 'reworked' (non-backed) sample. In fact, the opposite is observed (Table 3). A *t*-test indicates that non-backed artefacts are significantly heavier than backed artefacts (Table 3).

Extent of Retouching
In order to determine extent of retouching, three tests were conducted on the South Molle Island Quarry sample: Kuhn's Reduction Index (Kuhn 1992), the Edge Curvature Index (Hiscock and Attenbrow 2002), and the measurement of retouch edge angle as an indicator of retouch intensity (e.g. Clarkson, this volume; Dibble 1995; Hiscock 1982) (Table 5). The use of the Kuhn Index as a tool for measuring reduction intensity has been discussed extensively by Clarkson and Hiscock (this volume). Essentially the test provides a relative measure of reduction by establishing a ratio of retouch height to artefact thickness. This is measured on a scale of 0 (no reduction) to 1 (complete reduction). The edge curvature index is determined by dividing the depth of retouch by the retouch span (Hiscock and Attenbrow this volume). A negative value indicates a concave edge, while a value of >0 indicates a convex edge. A higher positive value represents a greater convex edge. The results are presented in Table 5 for backed and non-backed artefacts.

Two observations can be made from Table 5. Firstly,

according to the Kuhn reduction index and the curvature index, the majority of implements in the sample are reduced to a uniform extent and exhibit no significant differences in shape between backed and non-backed categories. Secondly, there is a highly significant difference (*t*-test, p=.000) in retouched edge angle between the two retouch categories, with non-backed artefacts recording lower retouched edges than the remainder of the sample, while maintaining a near-maximum Kuhn reduction index.

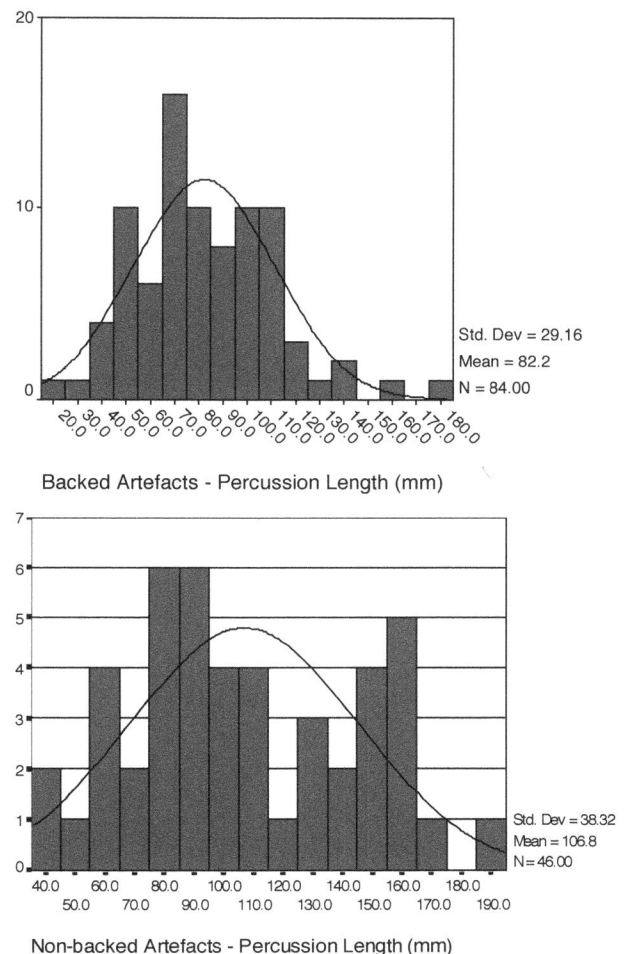

Backed Artefacts - Percussion Length (mm)

Non-backed Artefacts - Percussion Length (mm)

Figure 4. Percussion length of retouched artefacts, illustrating a bimodal pattern within the sample of non-backed artefacts.

Size of Retouched Artefacts

The majority (83.5%) of backed artefacts show a unimodal distribution for percussion length of between 50mm and 105mm, and centred on around 70mm (Figure 4). The non-backed artefacts on the other hand show a bimodal distribution. The lower mode overlaps almost exactly with that of backed artefacts, but the upper mode (37% of non-backed specimens) indicates the existence of a group of much larger artefacts with a percussion length centred on around 160mm. These larger non-backed artefacts are also more often retouched on multiple margins (59%). Thus, while both backed and non-backed artefacts are common up to around 110mm, only non-backed artefacts retouched on multiple margins are common above this size.

Edge Angle and Scar Size

Both the Kuhn Reduction Index and the Curvature Index results indicate that the sample of retouched artefacts has been reduced to a reasonably uniform extent (Table 5). Yet despite the fact that both groups show extensive retouching, there is a significant difference in the mean retouched edge angle of each group, with non-backed artefacts showing much lower edge angles than backed artefacts.

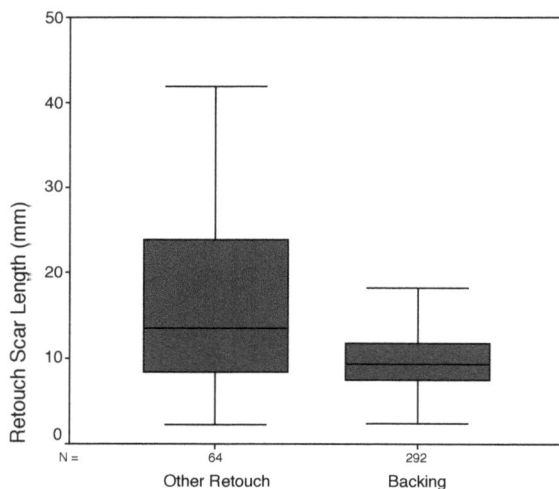

Figure 5. Mean length of retouch scars.

We might typically expect edge angles either to increase as unifacial reduction increases and step terminations build up, as found by Clarkson (this volume), or to increase and then decrease as these areas of steeply retouched edge are removed by deep blows, as found by Hiscock and Attenbrow (this volume). Which of these models best explains the differences in edge angles noted between the backed and non-backed implements found at the SMIQ might be investigated by considering the size of retouch flake scars themselves. Very large and invasive flake scars could conceivably succeed in producing very high Kuhn index values while also maintaining edges at fairly low angles. Figure 5

demonstrates that this in fact seems to be the case, and that a greater range and mean length of retouch scars is found for the non-backed category than for backed artefacts. The conclusion that can be drawn from this test is that some artefacts received relatively short, steep-edged retouch, while others had long flakes removed from their margins that did not overly increase edge angle.

Discussion: The Nature of SMIQ Reduction Strategies

Together, the results of the tests presented above suggest that two quite distinctive reduction processes were in operation at the SMIQ in the past. The first focussed on the production of backed artefacts ranging in size up to around 110mm in length that were steeply and bidirectionally retouched along a single margin. The second strategy was focussed on the production of flakes from numerous margins of other large flakes (i.e. those greater than 110mm in length). While the size distinction seems important in separating these two populations, the overlap between backed artefact and the lower mode in non-backed artefact length is still to be explained. It is suggested here that the smaller mode may represent early-stage backed artefacts that had not yet progressed from single margin unidirectional retouching to the single margin bi-directional flaking that typifies backing.

For example, in backing an edge it is conceivable that the length of the edge might first be unifacially flaked in its entirety before turning the artefact over and working it from the other side, giving it is bidirectional form. Thus, the higher rate of unidirectional retouch on smaller (i.e. <110mm), unimarginal, non-backed artefacts might indicate that many of these specimens belong to an early stage in the backing process. This smaller group is also characterised by a corresponding *percentage of length retouched* which falls within the range for backed artefacts (Figure 3).

In contrast, the differences in retouch location provide an indication that the larger grouping of artefacts within the non-backed category (i.e. >110mm) can be distinguished from both backed artefacts and early-stage backed artefacts. Artefacts within this group have multiple margins retouched - suggestive of a more generalised retouching around the perimeter of the flake. This group also exhibits large flake scars and low edge angles indicative of a very different reduction strategy. I propose that this subgroup of non-backed retouched artefacts was used to produce flakes from their margins of comparable size to those produced from cores. To support this assertion, two further lines of evidence can be presented. Firstly, retouch scars found on the larger non-backed artefact group average 53.5mm in length, compared with an average of 21.4mm for those found on the smaller non-backed artefact group, and for the sample of *backed artefacts* longer than 110mm (*t*-test, p=.000). Secondly, the mean length for flake scars measured on a sample of 424 cores from the SMIQ, is 50.1mm. Thus the length of flake scars on the large non-backed artefact group compares very favourably with that of cores. There is therefore strong evidence to support the existence of two very different strategies of flake retouch having been practised at the SMIQ over the last 9,000 years.

A recent study (Lamb and Barker 2001) has refined the temporal sequence for the stratified rockshelter site Nara Inlet 1, on Hook Island, some 3km from South Molle Island. Among other things, they demonstrate a decline in stone artefact discard from c.7,000BP. In a forthcoming study (Lamb in prep), it is argued that this decline reflected changing patterns of access to the quarry, influenced by rising sea-levels, which saw less stone transported away from the site, and a greater degree of late stage reduction occurring on the site; including the production of backed implements. Thus, while still a topic of future investigation, it seems likely that the backing industry on the South Molle Island Quarry had its origins some 7,000 years ago during a time of changing mobility and provisioning patterns across an altering landscape.

Conclusion

The South Molle Island Quarry was utilised for a period of at least 9,000 years for the production of stone artefacts in the Whitsunday region. A systematic survey of the quarry identified a sample of 443 retouched artefacts, including 329 backed artefacts. The current study has attempted to utilise technological tests to comprehensively characterise the nature of the retouch occurring on the quarry. Analysis of the sample as a whole has identified attributes which suggest that quarry production was aimed at the manufacture of backed artefacts (including early-stage backed artefacts) and larger retouched flakes that appear broadly similar to cores in terms of the size of flakes being removed. Analysis of the variation within the production of the sample of backed artefacts, and the implications for the regional economic tempero-spatial trends is the topic of further study.

Acknowledgements

I would like to thank Peter Hiscock and Bryce Barker for reading drafts of this paper. Particularly, I wish to acknowledge Chris Clarkson for his editorial contribution and his friendship throughout. I also wish to acknowledge the Ngaro people as the traditional owners of the Whitsunday region, and thank Irene Butterworth for her continuing support of my work.

References

Barker, B. 1991 Nara Inlet 1: Coastal resource use and the Holocene marine transgression in the Whitsunday Islands, central Queensland. *Archaeology in Oceania* 26(3):102-109.

Barker, B. and R. Schon 1994 A preliminary assessment of the spatial distribution of stone artefacts from the South Molle Island Aboriginal quarry, Whitsunday Islands, central Queensland coast. *Memoirs of the Queensland Museum* 37:5-12.

Barker, B. 1996 Maritime hunter-gatherers on the tropical coast: a social model for change. In S. Ulm, I. Lilley and A. Ross (eds) Australian Archaeology 95, Proceedings of the 1995 Australian Archaeological Association Annual Conference. *Tempus* 6:31-43.

Barker, B. 2004 The Sea People: Late Holocene Maritime Specialisation in the Whitsunday Islands, Central Queensland. Pandanas Press, Australian National University, Canberra.

Brian, S.E. 1991 Geology and Geochemistry of the Southern Molle Group, the Whitsundays, Northeast Queensland. Unpublished B.A.Hons Thesis, Department of Geology and mineralogy, University of Queensland, Brisbane.

Clarkson, C. 2002 An index of invasiveness for the measurement of unifacial and bifacial retouch: a theoretical, experimental and archaeological verification. *Journal of Archaeological Science* 29:65-76.

Clarkson, C. This volume Tenuous types: 'scraper' reduction continuums in Wardaman country, northern Australia.

Dibble, H. 1995. Middle Palaeolithic scraper reduction: background, clarification and review of evidence to date. *Journal of Archaeological Method and Theory* 2:229-368.

Hiscock, P. 1982 The meaning of edge angles. *Australian Archaeology* 14:79-85.

Hiscock, P. 1994 Technological responses to risk in Holocene Australia. *Journal of World Prehistory* 8(3):267-292.

Hiscock, P. 1998 Revitalising artefact analysis. In (T. Murrey, Ed) *Archaeology of Aboriginal Australia*. Allen and Unwin.

Hiscock, P. 2002a Looking the other way: a materialist/technological approach to classifying tools and implements, cores and retouched flakes. In S. McPherron and J. Lindley (Eds) *Tools or Cores? The Identification and Study of Alternative Core Technology in Lithic Assemblages*. University of Pennsylvania Museum.

Hiscock, P. 2002b Pattern and context in the Holocene proliferation of backed artefacts in Australia. In R.G. Elston and S.L. Kuhn (eds) *Thinking Small: Global Perspectives on Microlithization*. Pp.163-177. Archaeological Papers of the American Anthropological Association (AP3A), Number 12.

Hiscock, P. and V. Attenbrow 1998 Early Holocene backed artefacts from Australia. *Archaeology in Oceania*, 33:49-63.

Hiscock, P. and V. Attenbrow 2002. Early Australian implement variation: a reduction model. *Journal of Archaeological Science* 30:239-249

Hiscock, P. and V. Attenbrow This volume Reduction continuums and tool use.

Hiscock, P. and C. Clarkson This volume Measuring artefact reduction – an examination of Kuhn's geometric index of reduction.

Hiscock, P. and Mitchell, S. 1993 *Stone Artefact Quarries and Reduction Sites in Australia: Towards a*

Type Profile. Canberra: Australian Heritage Commission.

Kuhn, S. 1992 Blank form and reduction as determinants of Mousterian scraper morphology. *American Antiquity*, 57:115-128.

Lamb, L. 1996 A methodology for the analysis of backed artefact production on the South Molle Island Quarry, Whitsunday Islands. *Tempus* 6:151-159.

Lamb, L.D. 2005 Rock of Ages: Use of the South Molle Island Quarry, Whitsunday Islands, and the Implications for Holocene Technological Change in Australia. Unpublished PhD Thesis, School of Archaeology and Anthropology, Australian National University, Canberra.

Lamb, L. and B. Barker 2001 Evidence for early Holocene change in the Whitsunday Islands: a new radiocarbon determination, Nara Inlet 1. *Australian Archaeology* 53:42-43.

McCarthy, F.D. 1976 *Australian Aboriginal Stone Impliments*. Sydney: Australian Museum Trust.

McNiven, I. 2000 Backed to the Pleistocene. *Archaeology in Oceania* 35:48-52.

Mulvaney, J. and J. Kamminga 1999 *Prehistory of Australia*. Allen and Unwin.

White, J.P. and J.F. O'connell 1982 *A Prehistory of Australia, New Guinea and Sahul*. Academic Press.

5 | Reduction Continuums and Tool Use

Peter Hiscock and Val Attenbrow

Abstract

This paper focuses on a contradiction between two central principles frequently embedded in lithic studies: the notion that implement form often reflects intended function because prehistoric artisans designed specimens to be functionally specific and proficient, and the notion that there is often a progressive alteration of implement form during its use-life. Tension between these two seemingly incompatible propositions creates an interpretative paradox that we have expressed with the question: "how can implements be designed for, and be efficient in, a specific use if their morphology is continuously changing?" We illustrate the interpretive difficulties arising from this question through an analysis of a classic Australian site, Capertee 3, at which we document a pattern of change in edge characteristics of retouched flakes (often called 'scrapers') during the reduction of each specimen. Drawing on this case study we explore the implications of this contradiction for interpretations of Palaeolithic assemblages. Our conclusion is that further studies and theorising are required to help archaeologists move beyond the naïve presumption that conventionally recognized implement types have a simple association with particular uses and that by implication those types must be designed to be efficient in the particular use to which it was constructed.

Introduction

One of the persistent myths of Palaeolithic research is that stone implements are always, or at least dominantly, designed to efficiently carry out a specific function. This notion has pervaded analyses of stone artefacts on all continents since the beginnings of modern archaeology, and is embedded in the interpretation and even the names applied to many implement types. Examples of this view can be plucked from published works decades apart, revealing the robust and ingrained nature of this functional perspective on stone implement variability. From Binford's (1973) famous conclusion that for the European Middle Palaeolithic "A reasonable suggestion as to what Bordes' taxonomy is measuring is the character of differentiation in the design of tools as such" to Bisson's (2001:167) recent statement that "The primary constraint on tool form is, of course, function", the view that stone implements are designed to be functionally efficient is explicit.

Elements of these functional propositions have been challenged by arguments that implements do not have stable morphologies but actually display progressively changing sizes and shapes until they were discarded. In particular there is a plethora of studies showing that in many sites unifacially retouched flakes form a pattern of continuous morphological variation, reflecting the continuous reduction to which some specimens are subjected. This paper investigates some of the implications of these reduction continuums for our understanding of the use of these implements as tools. In particular we pose the obvious but little discussed question: *"how can implements be designed for, and be efficient in, a specific use if their morphology is continuously changing?"* An Australian case study is employed to explore the magnitude of the problem contained within this question, to evaluate alternative explanations for variation in implement morphology, and illustrate potential methods by which these issues can be examined. However, the appropriate starting place for this exploration is the foundation principles that have long been recognized by researchers arguing that form follows function in the production of variability in assemblages of stone artefacts. Explicit statements of these principles can be exemplified, not with Australian publications, but by using two celebrated papers from North American researchers.

The idea that tool form reflects functional constraints or intentions is often manifested in arguments about the characteristics of the retouched edge. Most notably researchers often associate the plan shape/position and cross-sectional angle of retouched edges with the nature of intended use. Such an argument was contained in two seminal papers published in a single volume of *American Antiquity* 35 years ago (Frison 1968; Wilmsen 1968). In the first of these papers Frison (1968:152) framed the key theoretical statement that "working edges must be right for the task at hand". This proposition, held by many archaeologists then and since, was explored by the second of these papers in which Wilmsen (1968:156) hypothesized that frequency modes of implement edge angles within assemblages reveal broad categories of functional operations, claiming that "...the different angle sizes are related to different function" (Wilmsen 1968:159). For example, Wilmsen suggested that very low retouched edges (<40°) were functionally efficient for cutting soft materials; while medium angled edges (45-60°) were efficient for skinning, scraping and cutting of hard materials; and even steeper retouched edges

(>65°) were best employed for uses that required more robust edges such as woodworking and bone working. Existence of a covariation between the type of use activity and the edge characteristics that were prepared in anticipation of that activity was considered to be a primary explanation of the morphology of retouched flakes recovered by archaeologists. Discussing the posited form-function relationship Wilmsen (1968:160) concluded:

> An attempt has been made to account for formal variation in stone-tool inventories. A functional foundation has been postulated for most of this variation. While the technical basis of tool modification is recognized, it is clear that modification was directed toward improving the functional qualities of tools and that, therefore, the specific character of this modification should provide insights into the actual functional role of any set of tools.

This principle has a long history in archaeological inference, and although the Wilmsen article in particular stimulated research projects that deduced the use of both individual implements and implement types on the basis of edge angle (e.g. Fergusson 1980), the presumption that intended function was the central cause of implement morphology has been independently employed by many researchers. Indeed, the quintessential historical debate in Palaeolithic variability focused on the sparring between Bordes (1961, 1972, 1973; Bordes and de Sonneville-Bordes 1970) and Binford (1973; Binford and Binford 1966) concerning the explanation for Mousterian assemblages, and involved assertions about the extent and manner in which implements could be interpreted in terms of their design for particular uses. Even when Dibble (1984, 1987) reshaped this debate by introducing the notion that the technology of manufacture was a significant factor in the construction of variation he advocated that this technology was principally involved in resharpening edges being used. Even in recent reviews we continue to receive statements about the primacy of design for use in creating implements, such as the

statement that "...the morphology of Middle Palaeolithic scrapers is generated by functional contingencies, including intended use..." (Bisson 2001:180).

Underlying the presumption that implement types appear different because their makers shaped each in accordance with design rules relevant for their intended uses is the view that implement types are morphologically distinct from one another, with not only a strong tendency to similarity of specimens within each type but also clear morphological/size discontinuities between types. These principles typify typological approaches to stone artefacts, presupposing that perceived types reveal designed tools that are morphologically distinct (see Hiscock in press a; Whallon and Brown 1982). We label this viewpoint a 'segmented' model of implement variation, reflecting its advocacy of discontinuous implement morphology, as illustrated in Figure 1. In typological analyses of Palaeolithic assemblages it is commonly implied that each segment of the discontinuous morphological variation, supposedly recognized as a 'type', represents a functional category for which that morphology is efficient. Such a model represents one way that a technology could create archaeological implements.

An alternative structure for archaeological assemblages is a pattern of continuous rather than discontinuous morphological variation; a pattern we label the 'continuum' model of artefact variation. As illustrated in Figure 1 this structure is in theory distinguished from segmented patterns simply by the absence of any significant breaks in the morphological range visible in large assemblages. This continuum model has occasionally been invoked for Australian artefacts (see Hiscock and Attenbrow 2002, 2003), but has been more consistently emphasised by northern hemisphere researchers studying variation within assemblages of bifaces. Continuum models of this kind have often been used to argue that morphological variation primarily reflects differences in the extent to which specimens have

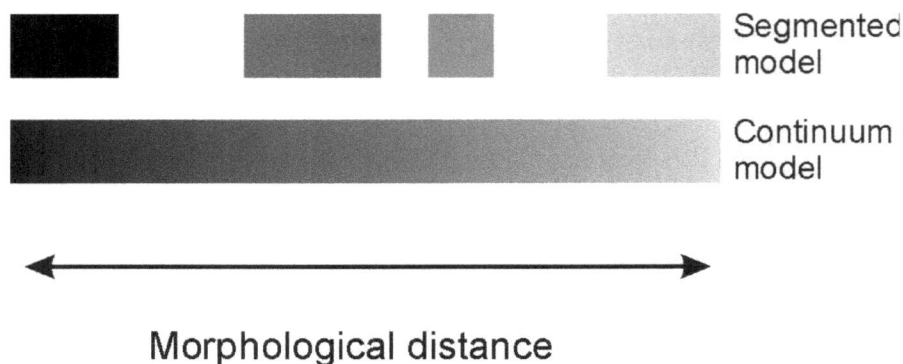

Morphological distance

Figure 1. Graphical representation of the difference between segmented and continuum models of morphological variation.

been reduced. The linking of continuum models with explanations invoking differential degrees of reduction has now been shown to be a powerful depiction of implement variation in the Old World (e.g. Dibble 1984, 1987, 1995; Gordon 1993; Hiscock 1996; Holdaway *et al.* 1996; Kuhn 1992, 1995; McPherron 2000; Neeley and Barton 1994; Rolland and Dibble 1990).

The recognition that artefact morphology is modified during reduction has been explicit for more than a century (e.g. Holmes 1893), and those classic discussions of form and function cited above acknowledged this mechanism in their considerations. For instance, Wilmsen (1968:159) suggested that as resharpening proceeded the angle of retouched edges would increase. This posed a problem for the purported existence of a simple correspondence between angle and intended use, a predicament that Wilmsen (1968:160) recognised in the context of an illustration of form-function associations in hide-working tools:

> It may be, for example, that distal angles of approximately 50°-55° were useful for hide-working; that resharpening progressively steepened some of these angles to a point where they were no longer functional in their original task; and that these more steeply-bitted tools were then used for different purposes such as bone and wood shaping.

The perception of continuous modification of tool morphology in response to edge blunting was an issue that Frison (1968) focussed on in his highly cited paper. His central point was the proposition that discarded tools were probably dysfunctional. Frison (1968:149) framed this idea in the following way:

> Tools such as side scrapers, end scrapers, knives, and drills were continually modified throughout their lifetime of functional utility, and at the time when they were discarded or became non-functional, they were usually quite different than when originally completed.

By targeting the conditions leading to abandonment of a specimen Frison's statement was not meant to deny a form-function association during much of the use-life of a tool, but is primarily concerned with the failure of discarded tools to retain morphological features that are indicative of their function. The implications of a morphological change immediately prior to, and perhaps provoking, discard of a tool is undoubtedly an important one for typological investigations into site function. However, that process is not as challenging for claims of form-function associations as Wilmsen's suggestion that the use of a specimen may change sequentially in proportion to the extent of resharpening it has undergone.

Progressive change in the characteristics of retouched edges has been interpreted as a consequence of resharpening in many studies over the past two decades, a perspective to which Jelinek (1976) and Dibble (1984,

1987, 1995) attached the label the "Frison effect" in reference to Frison's (1968) discussion of the process of reuse and remodification of tool forms. In fact the term "Frison effect" might be better restricted to the process of radical morphological change towards the end of the use-life of a specimen and immediately prior to discard or recycling; since that is the sense of Frison's (1968) own discussion. A process of gradual morphological change throughout the entire existence of an implement, perhaps with minimal alteration in the rate or direction of morphological change prior to discard, is the pattern actually being referred to by Dibble (1984, 1987) and other recent researchers, and this is notionally different from what we recommend should be referred to as the "Frison effect". For gradual morphological change throughout the existence of an implement we propose the term "Holmes effect", named for the remarkable William Holmes (1890, 1891, 1892, 1893) who most powerfully asserted continuing reshaping of complex stone artefacts. It is this gradual change in implement morphology that has been the focus of many discussions of Palaeolithic variation in recent decades.

Although this mechanism has been widely discussed the implications for interpretations of use and use-form relationships have been little explored. For example, in the context of debates about Middle Palaeolithic implement variation a frequent assertion is that continuous change in implement morphology implies only a small number of functionally distinct categories, each displaying a range of morphological varieties created by different levels of reduction (e.g. Kuhn 1992:125). Another depiction of the changing implement morphology is that these were generalised tools, not standardised for a specific task (Kuhn and Stiner 1998). The questions: how many tasks were carried out by such tools and how a generalised tool would be employed have not been comprehensively examined. The imperative to explore these questions has grown as the diversity of Middle and Upper Palaeolithic typological forms recognised as representing phases of resharpening has grown to incorporate not only lateral and transversely retouched scrapers but also points, notches and denticulates (e.g. Dibble 1984, 1987, 1995; Gordon 1993; Hiscock 1996; Holdaway et al. 1996; Rolland and Dibble 1990). It is also common to note the absence of a simple form-function correspondence, such as the statement by Holdaway et al. (1996:377) that "...edge-wear analysis has demonstrated that there is no simple one-to-one correlation between tool form and function." Dibble (1995:343) has concluded that the lack of association between morphological differences and functional differences is to be expected of, and is consistent with, reduction models of implement variation. However, in reaching that conclusion Dibble notes the importance of Beyries' (1988) study suggesting use-wear differences between implement categories, but dismisses it because of the extremely small sample sizes involved in that study. Of course Dibble is correct to doubt the robustness of form-function discussions developed from small sample use-wear investigations, but we argue that in view of the small number of wear studies examining this issue and their inconsistent sampling and results it would be better to conclude that the nature and strength of correspondence between morphology and use is not as yet established. Furthermore, Dibble's (1995) implied dichotomy, between a poor form-function correspondence when reduction continuums exist and a strong relationship when they don't, may not be a generalisation that will operate in all assemblages and industries. The possible relationship of form and function in a reduction continuum is a complex issue, and one to which more consideration should be given.

We believe these various discussions reveal a number of aspects of the multifaceted association between Palaeolithic implements and the uses to which they may have been put. However, we also argue that in the archaeological literature the contradiction that exists between an expectation of a distinct form-function relationship and the demonstration of progressively altering implement form has been inadequately recognized and discussed. Consequently we advocate that assemblage analyses should regularly pursue the question we posed earlier: "*how can implements be designed for, and be efficient in, a specific use if their morphology is continuously changing?*" To begin the investigation of this question we present a study of the nature of morphological change on an assemblage of unifacially flaked stone implements from Australia. These 'scrapers' and 'scraper-like' artefacts have been chosen as a case study because of their similarity with one class of implements that have often been the subject of debates about both reduction continuums and function.

The Example of Capertee
This example is concerned with the large collection of implements from Capertee 3, a rockshelter in the Blue Mountains west of Sydney. Artefacts from this site were employed by pioneer archaeologist Fred McCarthy (1964) in his description of the prehistoric sequence in eastern Australia. His typological analysis of the assemblages from Capertee 3 examined the dorsally retouched flakes, which he treated as discrete types, describing them variously as 'scrapers', 'knifes', burins, and 'saws'. McCarthy additionally noted the presence of notches and 'noses' on working edges. These categories and features were clearly regarded by McCarthy as having functional significance. This is indicated by McCarthy's repeated use of the term "working edge" in describing the retouched portions of flake margins, and it is obvious that he thought the shape of the retouched margin was indicative of the nature of the use to which the specimen had been put. In some instances the inferred function was explicitly identified, such as when McCarthy (1964:238) concluded that "Simple knives...probably served as flesh cutters"; but in most instances the presumed function was merely implied by the name of the implement. The purported correspondence between typological groupings and function which McCarthy presented was influential in Australian archaeology and has survived until today in the work of conservative typologists (see Hiscock and Attenbrow 2003). For example, in their review of Pleistocene Australian implements Mulvaney and Kamminga (1999:217-219, 227) recognized categories such as 'end scraper', 'straight-edged scrapers', 'notched scrapers' 'concave scrapers', and 'nosed scrapers', attributing a different function to each.

The original typological description of the Capertee 3 assemblage, with its functional implication, involved the categorisation of different implement types on the presumption that a segmented model was an appropriate depiction of assemblage patterning. Our concern in this paper is to summarise the evidence for continuous scraper reduction in this assemblage, as detailed by Hiscock and Attenbrow (2002, 2003), and to then explore the implications of the assemblage pattern for functional statements.

A first question we ask is whether McCarthy's depiction of separate, morphologically discrete types is an accurate representation of the assemblage. The alternative hypothesis is that differences between the various scraper-like implement types are arbitrary divisions of morphological continuums and may be explained in terms of the extent of knapping each specimen has undergone (see Hiscock and Attenbrow 2002, 2003). This model predicts a positive relationship between morphological changes and the amount of retouching that has been applied to a flake, irrespective of whether that retouching was maintaining edges and/or generating flakes. Specimens that have received little retouch will have relatively straight retouched edges, with small retouch scars restricted to a short portion of the flake margin. In contrast specimens that have been extensively retouched will have longer more curving retouched edges, with larger retouch scars spread along much of the flake margins. This reduction model can be tested by making a number of observations about each specimen.

We use a number of quantitative measures to evaluate the relationship between retouch characteristics and extent of reduction on the scraper-like implements from Capertee 3. Our analysis does not incorporate flakes that have been backed, but deals with all of the measurable, complete, dorsally-retouched chert specimens in this scraper-like category in the Capertee assemblages. To this end we have excluded specimens that are technically cores, unretouched flakes or unmeasurable heat shattered fragments, and specimens made on materials other than chert; yielding a sample of 168 complete non-backed dorsally retouched flakes on which our measurements could be made. This sample includes specimens from all levels in Capertee 3 and is larger than the one used in our previous publications (see Hiscock and Attenbrow 2002, 2003). Although more than one third of the objects do not retain any information of McCarthy's original classification, we know how he classed the majority of

Table 1. Tabulation of the typological categories of specimens in our sample of retouched flakes.

McCarthy's type	Bondaian	Capertian	Total
Burin	1	0	1
Core	8	0	8
Elouera	1	0	1
Knife	6	2	8
Saw	3	8	11
Scrapers	46	26	72
Unlabelled	47	20	67
Total	112	56	168

these specimens (see Table 1). McCarthy had classified most of these specimens as scrapers or saws, with the remainder being called knives, burins, elouera and even cores.

Dorsal retouch on these specimens is both marginal and steep. For this reason we consider that Kuhn's (1990) index of reduction is an appropriate measure of the extent of retouching. This index expresses retouch height (designated 't') as a fraction of the possible height that could be obtained on that specimen (designated 'T'). We applied Kuhn's measurement at three places, evenly spaced, along the longest retouched edge of each specimen (see Figure 2), and calculated the average as $(t_3/T_3 + t_2/T_2 + t_1/T_1)/3$, a value we refer to as the 'Average Kuhn reduction index'. In this procedure our calculation is identical with that made by Hiscock and Clarkson (this volume). For the sample from Capertee 3 defined above this index varied between 0.12 and 1.00 ($\bar{x}$ =0.49, s.d=0.23). Since Kuhn's index has the benefit of ranging between 0 and 1, it is clear that the specimens at Capertee 3 include those that had been minimally reduced as well as those that were far more highly reduced. Furthermore, as Hiscock and Attenbrow (2002, 2003) have demonstrated, the Capertee 3 assemblage displays a continuous, unimodal distribution of Kuhn reduction index values, consistent with a single form reduced by varying amounts, and without multiple modes that could hint of several overlapping but discrete classes.

We take values of this index to be positively related to the amount or extent of retouching for reasons explained by Kuhn (1990) and by Hiscock and Clarkson (this volume). Furthermore, in the Capertee 3 assemblage there is a strong positive association between the Average Kuhn reduction index and other characteristics of retouching that could also be expected to increase as reduction proceeds. For instance, there is a strong linear correlation between the Average Kuhn reduction index and the length of retouch on each complete specimen (r = 0.83, d.f.=154, p<0.001). In this regression analysis no constant is employed, thereby forcing the regression line through origin. Because the two variables compared must both start at 0 for a flake without retouch this is the appropriate regression model. A regression with constant gives a reduced coefficient but is still significant (p<0.001). This relationship holds for all dorsally retouched flakes in our sample. Hiscock and Attenbrow (2003) have established

equally strong correlations between the proportion of the flake perimeter that was retouched and the Average Kuhn reduction index. These relationships exist because the values of all these variables (i.e. Average Kuhn reduction index, length of retouch, and proportion of flake perimeter) are higher on more heavily retouched specimens.

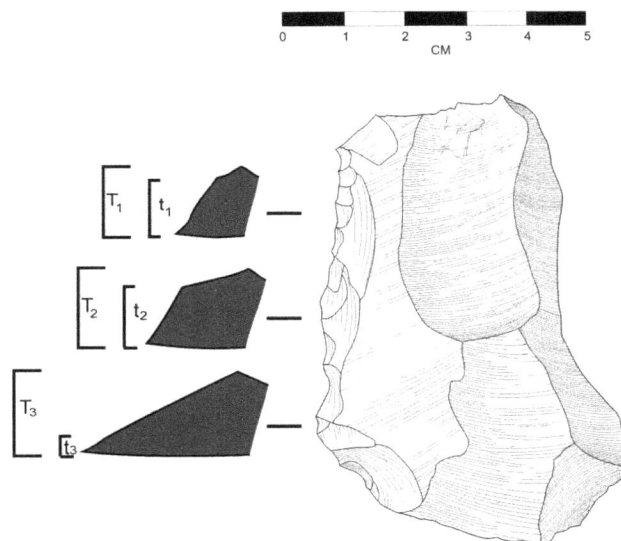

Figure 2. Illustration of a retouched flake from Capertee 3 (ESP1024, Square 9 Level G), showing the measurement of retouch intensity. The Average Kuhn reduction index is calculated as $(t_3/T_3 + t_2/T_2 + t_1/T_1)/3$.

If the length of margin that was retouched increased as reduction proceeded then at least the aspects of McCarthy's classification that are based on the number of retouched edges are likely to vary with the extent of reduction. To evaluate this proposition we also measured the amount of retouch by recording the number of locations on which retouch occurs on the sample of complete retouched flakes. We recorded the presence or absence of retouch in eight notional sections (proximal end, distal end, and for each margin the proximal, medial, and distal thirds). Each implement could have between one and eight of these sections retouched. The number of retouched sections shows a strong linear relationship with the Average Kuhn reduction index (r = 0.86, d.f. = 151, p<0.001), such that the extent of reduction expressed by the Kuhn index explains more than 74% of variation in the number of retouched sections. This pattern is congruent with the hypothesis that as reduction proceeds additional sections of the flake margin are retouched. Hiscock and Attenbrow (2003) have also shown that in the Capertee assemblage the expansion of retouch around the perimeter of a flake proceeded in a regular way: often starting with blows to the distal portion of the left lateral margin and/or distal end, and spread to other sections of the flake as reduction progressed. This explains why the specimens that McCarthy described variously as side scrapers or end scrapers have low Average Kuhn reduction indices.

Increased retouching that lengthens the retouched edge and involves retouching a second or third margin is likely to also change the curvature of the retouched edge. This prediction can be evaluated with a simple quantitative measure of retouched edge shape obtained by the calculation of an 'Index of retouch curvature'[1]. This index is created by using the equation (R6 / R3), which expresses the depth of concavity or convexity of the retouched edge in millimeters (a value labeled R6) relative to a notional 'baseline' represented by a straight line between the ends of the retouch, the length of which was measured in millimeters (a value labeled R3). These dimensions were measured in the plane of ventral surface, as illustrated in Figure 3, with a retouched edge protruding beyond the R3 line being given a positive R6 value while a retouched edge retreating from the R3 line being given a negative R6 value. Measured in this way the 'Index of retouch curvature' is 0 for a straight edge, negative for concave edges, and positive for convex edges. The larger the positive value the more convex is the edge. For the Capertee assemblage this index ranged from a slightly concave value of -0.19 through to highly convex value of 13.42, with most specimens being slightly or moderately convex ($\bar{x}$ = 0.34, s.d. = 1.15, N = 154). The positive relationship between this index of flake shape and the extent of reduction can be evaluated in several ways.

Two illustrations of this connection between retouch curvature and reduction are provided by the box plots drawn in Figure 4. Median values, upper quartiles and most lower quartiles of the retouch curvature index consistently increase with higher categories of the Kuhn index (Figure 4A). A strong linear correlation exists between the retouch curvature index and the Average Kuhn reduction index (r = 0.77, d.f. = 150, p<0.001). This measurement indicates the extent of reduction explains more than 60% of variation in shape of the retouched edge as we have measured it. A similar pattern is revealed in the progressive increase in median and upper quartile values of the retouch curvature index as the number of retouched sections increased (Figure 4B).

Correlation statistics of the number of retouched sections and the curvature of the retouched edge also indicate a significant positive relationship, as calculated using Spearman's rho (r_s = 0.523, d.f. = 151, p<0.001,) and Pearson's r (r = 0.544, d.f. = 151, p<0.001).

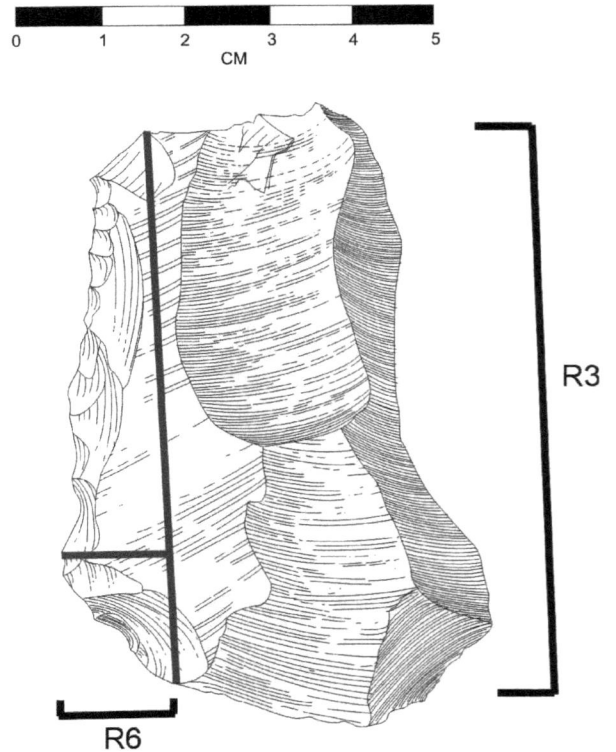

Figure 3. Illustration of a retouched flake from Capertee 3 (ESP1024, Square 9 Level G), showing the calculation of the Index of retouch curvature (R6/R3).

All of this evidence is consistent with the reduction model described above, demonstrating that not only are there morphological continuums within this assemblage but also that this pattern displayed by the assemblage is best explained in terms of the extent of knapping each specimen has undergone. For the Capertee 3 assemblage we can offer the following normative depiction of the reduction process that resulted in the dorsally retouched flakes. Retouch, beginning in a restricted area of one margin, typically produced a slightly concave or convex edge, but as reduction proceeded and retouching was carried out on adjacent margins of the flake the retouched edge became progressively more convex until semi-discoidal specimens retouched on three or four margins were produced. This progression of retouching is illustrated in Figure 5, which uses values predicted in the regression analyses discussed here to give an inferred interpretation of the typical morphological changes that would have taken place as reduction proceeded.

We therefore conclude that variation in the location of retouch and the shape of retouched edges is largely

---

[1] In two previous publications (Hiscock and Attenbrow 2002, 2003) we have employed the Index of retouch curvature exactly as described here but inadvertently and incorrectly gave the calculation as (R3 / R6). The equation and description of procedure provided here is the correct one.

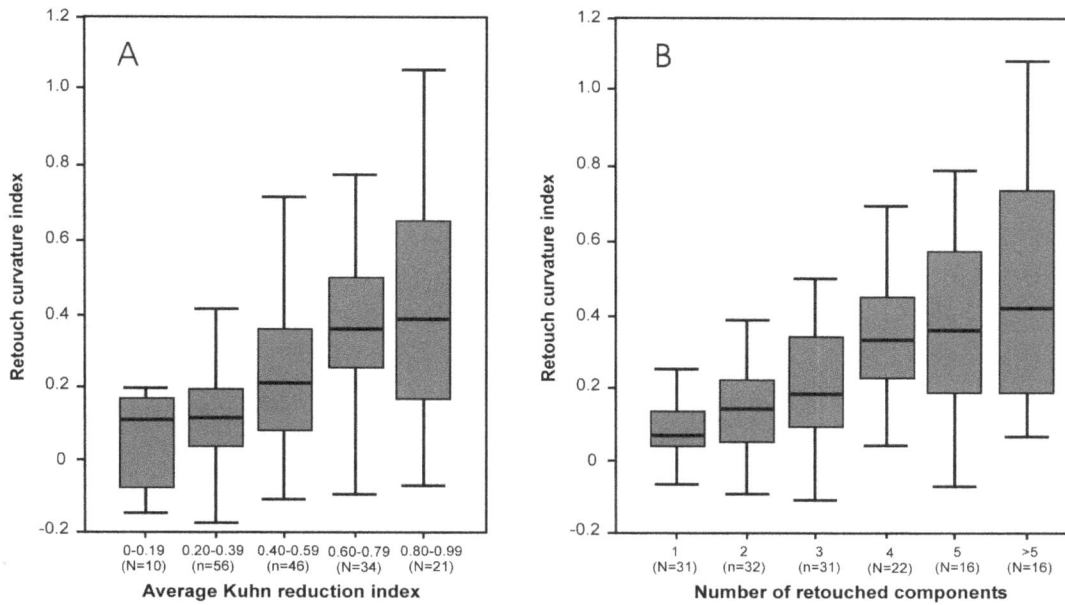

Figure 4. Box plots illustrating the positive relationship of the retouch curvature index to two measures of the extent of reduction: A = Average Kuhn reduction index, and B = Number of retouched sections.

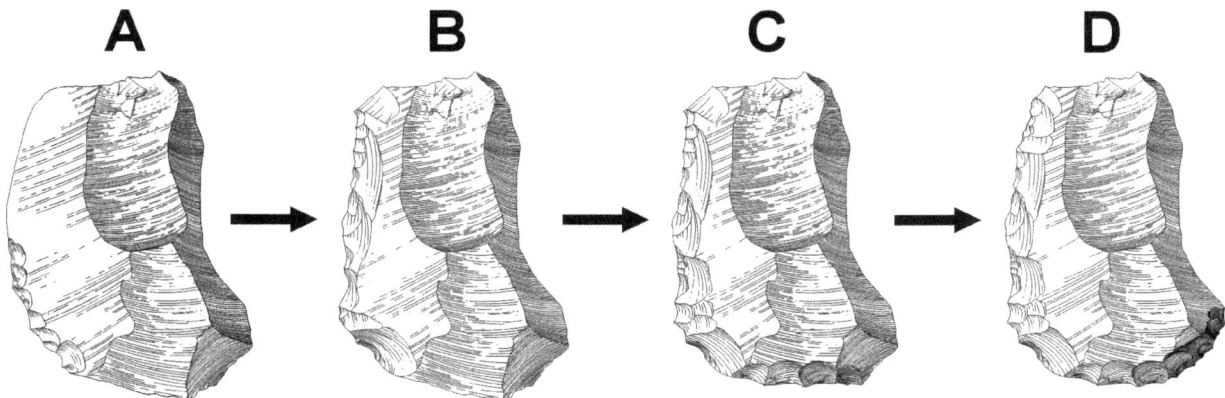

Figure 5. Illustration of typical reduction continuum inferred at Capertee 3. (A) has Curvature Index of 0.15 and Reduction Index of 0.38, (B) has Curvature Index of 0.27 and Reduction Index of 0.65, (C) has Curvature Index of 0.38 and Reduction Index of 0.74, and (D) has Curvature Index of 0.57 and Reduction Index of 0.92.

explicable in terms of the extent of reduction undertaken on specimens. Since shape and extent of retouch is the basis McCarthy used in classifying implements into different types this inference reveals that the difference between many of the McCarthian types merely reflects different amounts of reduction. The implication of this conclusion for functional interpretations of scraper morphology is potentially dramatic, and is worth exploring further.

Changes to the Retouched Edge Associated With Reduction

In addition to the inference that can be drawn from the above, that the continuous morphological variation in these dorsally retouched flakes from Capertee 3 is largely a reflection of the different amounts of reduction to which

specimens have been subjected, there are also many specific characteristics of the retouched edge that are clearly related to the extent of retouching. Reduction-related changes for a number of these edge characteristics on complete dorsally retouched chert flakes are summarised in Figure 6, using a common graphical system. In these diagrams the vertical bars denote the 95% confidence interval for mean in each 0.2 increment of the reduction index, the node on each bar marks the arithmetic mean, the stippled envelope encloses the 95% confidence interval for categories of reduction index, and the broken line illustrates the median trend line. Expressed graphically in these ways the differences in typical values between the five 0.2 categories of the reduction index trace obvious trends in edge characteristics as reduction proceeds. The key trends identified can be summarised as follows.

Lateral expansion of retouched edge

As we have already discussed, the retouched edge expanded laterally around the margins of the flake as retouching continued. This expansion can be measured by counting the number of sections retouched around the circumference of each specimen. As retouch expands around the margin the count of retouched sections is increased. Consequently the measurement of the average or median number of retouched sections per 0.2 category expresses the lateral extent of retouching for each phase of reduction, and as revealed in Figure 6a there is a consistent increase in the relative length of retouch as reduction continues. As retouch expands the retouched edge becomes increasingly convex in plan shape, as discussed earlier. This trend is illustrated in Figure 6b.

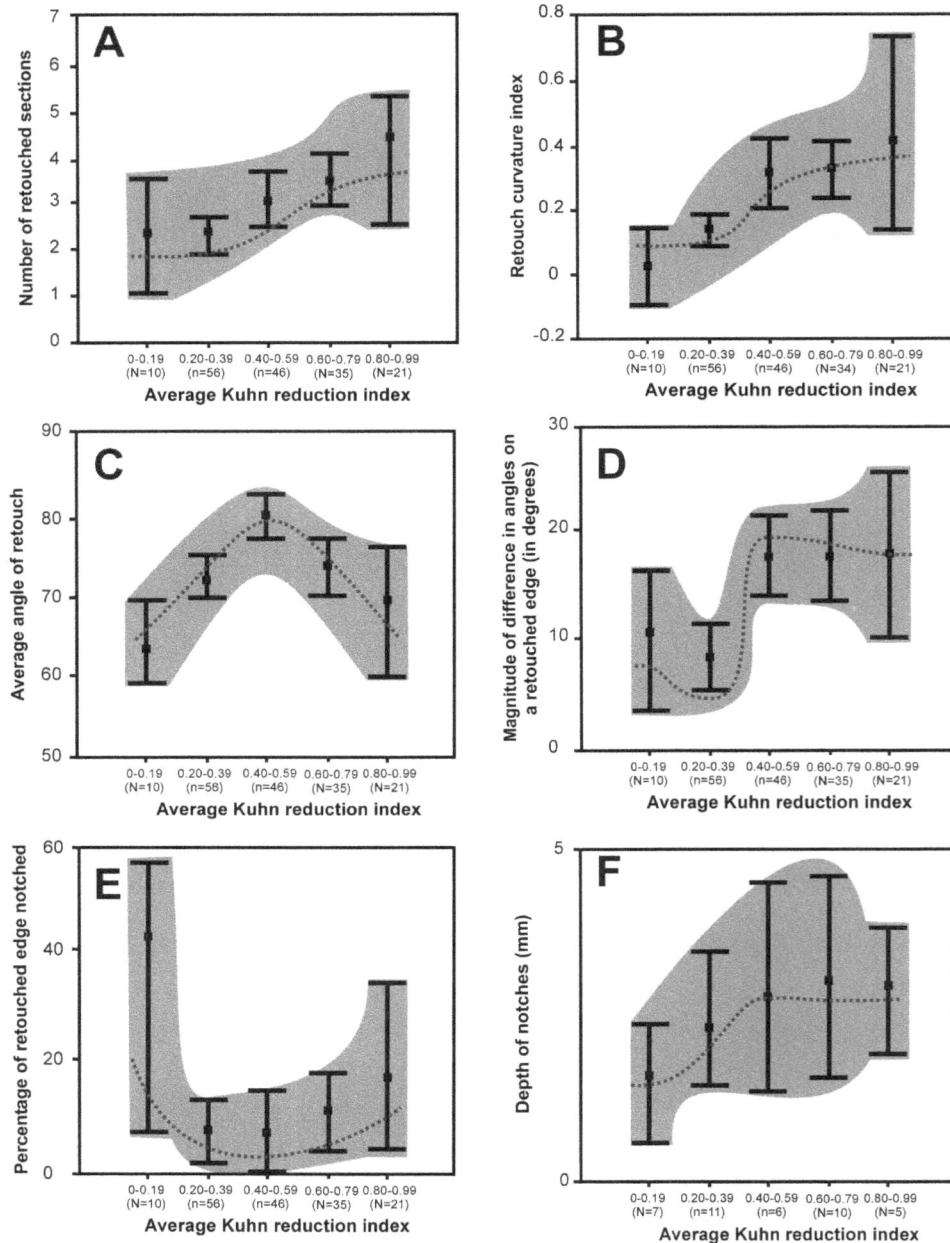

Figure 6. Illustration of the relationship between selected morphological characteristics and the Average Kuhn reduction index for complete chert dorsally retouched flakes (scrapers). The characteristics are A) Number of retouched sections per specimen, B) Retouch curvature index, C) Average retouch angle, D) Range of average retouch angles, E) Percentage of the retouched edge that was notched, and F) Average depth of notches. Vertical bars denote the 95% confidence interval for mean in each category of the reduction index. The node on each bar marks the arithmetic mean and the envelope encloses the 95% confidence interval for categories of reduction index. The broken line illustrates the median trend line.

These changes during reduction, from short and straight or concave retouched edges after a small amount of retouching to long and convex edges after extensive retouching, create the pattern that has already been depicted in Figure 5.

Alteration of Edge Angle

Average edge angle increases during the early and middle phases of reduction, as expressed in the Kuhn index, until retouched edges are typically quite steep, often being close to or exceeding $80°$ (Figure 6c). Increased edge angles were commonly associated with greater frequencies of abruptly terminated flake scars on the retouched edge. Average edge angles then decline during later phases of retouching, eventually reaching values nearly as low as those at the beginning of the retouching process. This reversal of the trend in edge angles can largely be explained as the result of changed knapping practices later in the retouching sequence, effectively rejuvenating the edge and enabling reduction to continue with a lower probability of creating abrupt terminations or breaking the specimen. Rejuvenation was accomplished by striking thicker, wider flakes from the retouched edge. As reduction continued the range of angles exhibited by retouched edges becomes larger, as some edges and sections of edges are rejuvenated while others are not (Figure 6d).

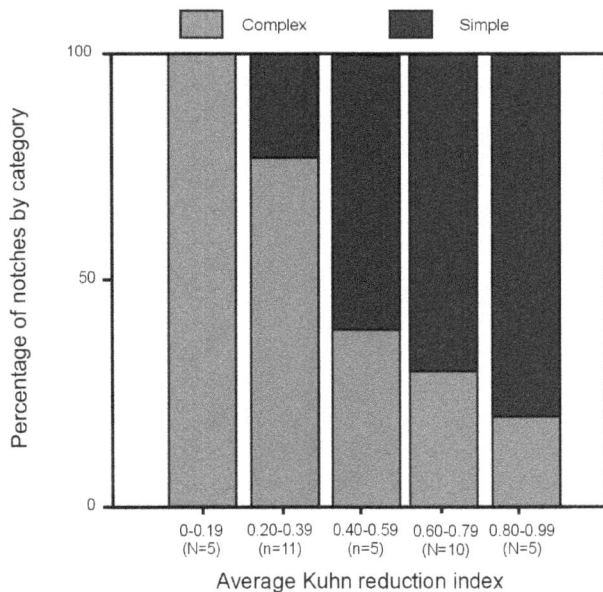

Figure 7. Changes in the frequency of simple and complex notches during reduction.

Edge Shape

One consequence of the shift to removing larger flakes later in the retouching sequence is the change in the shape of the retouched edge. Several trends in the plan shape of retouched edges are apparent as reduction proceeds. One pattern already discussed is the increasing curvature of the edge that usually accompanied expansion of retouching around the flake perimeter. Although the extension of

retouching around the flake circumference means that more extensively retouched specimens have convex edges, there may be straight or even concave sections along the length of the generally convex edge. One way to express such differences in the edge shape is by measuring the characteristics of 'notches', concave retouched areas arbitrarily defined as concavities in the retouched edge wider than 10mm. Figure 6e illustrates that as a percentage of retouched edge notching is relatively common at the start of the retouching process, becomes comparatively rare as reduction proceeds, but again becomes more common in extensively retouched specimens. The increase in notching later in the retouching sequence is partly a result of the creation of more notches but also a result of the creation of different kinds of notches. Late in the reduction process notches are both wider and deeper (Figure 6f) than those produced when retouching is initiated on a flake. These large notches are typically created by the removal of a single large flake. This is revealed in Figure 7 which shows that simple notches (ie. concavities produced by single flakes) are the dominant kind of concavity in heavily retouched specimens, whereas complex notches (ie. concavities produced by multiple flakes) were the only ones created when retouching commenced. The production of simple notches occurred when blows were placed relatively far from the edge and removed longer, slightly more invasive, and wider flakes – flakes that were effective in removing step terminations and lowering edge angles.

Reduction Coontinuums and Tool Use: Alternative Models

Evidence we have presented in this paper indicates that the reduction model outlined earlier, in which there is a positive relationship between morphological characteristics such as the curvature of retouched edges and the amount of retouching, can be extended to explicate many of the edge features that have frequently been taken to indicate artefact function, such as angle of retouch, shape of retouched edge and nature and abundance of notching. As discussed above morphological differences between specimens in characteristics of edge length, shape and angle have often been interpreted as reflections of functional differences. However, it has been shown that for the Capertee assemblage the length and shape of retouched edges, the angle of retouch scars on those edges, and the nature and frequency of notches are all changed as retouching proceeded. These characteristics are not independent of, but are intertwined with, the amount of reduction. (Intriguingly this conclusion echoes earlier observations of the relationship between reduction and edge angle in Australian assemblages – see Hiscock 1982a, 1982b, 1983).

In light of this inference we note the more obvious models that might describe the relationship between changing artefact morphology and artefact use. Each of these models can be appraised as follows:

- *Model 1: Artefact use changes as morphology changes.* This model is based on the principle that form and function are strongly connected, and consequently the expectation would be that as morphology changed during reduction the artisan chose to employ the artefact for different uses. The difficulty that arises in this model is that many specimens in an assemblage often display similar reduction-related morphological changes. This is the case for Capertee 3 where there are dramatic alterations in artefact form strongly correlated with the level of reduction, as demonstrated earlier, and also for the Ingaladdi assemblage reported on by Clarkson (this volume). European assemblages of the Middle Palaeolithic have also been demonstrated to display similar reduction-related changes to form (eg. Dibble 1995; Holdaway et al. 1996). The consequence of such a pattern is that most or all of the artefacts within any assemblage or technological system would need to progress through a regular sequence of functions if a strict relationship between form and function is to be maintained. This might have been an advantage to prehistoric foragers, who might have used the predictability of morphological shifts to assist in their planning of tool kit composition so that the necessary functions could be carried out with the appropriate tools.

However, regularity in reduction related morphological change between specimens would probably create complications for stone users in a number of ways if they insisted on performing tasks with specifically suited edges. For example, in order to have tools available for a large range of tasks foragers might need to transport a collection of specimens representing different levels of reduction or else risk wasting edges of a specimen by retouching it until the morphology suited the task at hand. The strategy that might be effective would at least partly depend on the rate at which particular categories of edge morphology occurred during the reduction sequence. In the case of the Capertee 3 pattern presented here, in which edge angles typically oscillated from medium to steep and back to medium during reduction, it would have been easier to obtain medium angled tools (say 55-70°) than ones with higher angles (say >75°). If these patterns of edge characteristics and specimen size and morphology are directly related to the technology of reduction, as we have argued them to be, and prehistoric foragers insisted on a specific form for each kind of task, then we would be in the curious position of being obliged to argue that the nature and/or timing of activities of a foraging group (at least those involving stone tools) were constrained or determined by the stoneworking technology. The idea that reduction strategies shaped functional options available to prehistoric groups is unlikely to be a popular conclusion amongst archaeologists, but at least in those assemblages in which morphological variation is explicable as a technological byproduct of reduction the question researchers must pose is: "what explanatory power can concepts of tool design and tool efficiency provide"?

In this model use-wear and residues studies of discarded artefacts may not be capable of providing a reliable indication of the tasks for which those artefacts were used. This difficulty reflects two processes connected to flake retouching. Firstly, the retouching of used edges removes much evidence of use. Secondly, the change in function as reduction progressively creates different morphologies means that the use evidence on the discarded specimen is not indicative of uses of the specimen earlier in its history; a principle clearly enunciated by Frison (1968). Consequently use analyses that examine a small number of discarded retouched flakes should be interpreted with care, and inferences about site functions based on those analyses should be regarded with considerable skepticism. Use wear and residue studies must not only seek to employ large samples, irrespective of the large labour costs incurred, but must also measure the nature of functional change associated with reduction. The latter goal could be accomplished through methods such as use studies of flakes conjoined onto implements and/or by studies of samples with small, medium and large values of Kuhn's reduction index.

- *Model 2: Artefact use remains unchanged during reduction.* This hypothesis avoids the complications inherent in Model 1 by predicting that despite morphological changes during reduction the knapper is able to continue using the specimen for the same activities. Such a model would at first sight appear to make sense of artefact resharpening: implying that continued retouching served merely to extend a specimens' duration of use, without requiring that the nature of the use must change. However, the unchanged use of specimens despite substantial alterations to edge angle, edge length and edge shape must signal the unimportance, perhaps even irrelevance, of morphology for function.

This principle might operate in a number of ways. For instance, it might be that edge characteristics are not a fundamental determinant of the uses to which a specimen can be put, because on specimens with edges containing a variety of shapes the artisan can sufficiently manipulate the orientation of the tool, angle of contact with worked material, and motion of tool so that a wide range of tasks can be accomplished. This hypothesis, that almost any edge may be used for any purpose, is not consistent with the traditional conclusion of many functional studies, and while it is testable is unlikely to be generally applicable.

An alternative possibility is that edge characteristics are important for the efficiency of any particular use, with specific edge angles and edge shapes being more effective and efficient for some tasks than others, but that efficient tool use was not critical for the performance of a task. This principle would mean that there is indeed a theoretical association between use and the edge characteristics best suited to the task, but that sadly covariation between implement forms and kinds of uses would often be very poor, simply because the user of the implement continued to use the specimen in the same way even when its morphological characteristics had changed to a less suitable state. The implication of unchanging patterns of use through a reduction sequence even though the edge characteristics at any particular point in the sequence were efficient for one use and not others would logically be that prehistoric tool users were prepared to employ inefficient tools.

The level of inefficiency represented by tool use in any assemblage might usefully be evaluated experimentally, and may also be a noteworthy feature in the construction of models explaining the selective context in which any foraging group was operating. For instance, this kind of functional inefficiency may be a cost worth paying by foragers who cannot predict the nature and timing of activities, and for whom multi-functionality confers substantial benefits (see Hiscock in press b). Additionally, in locations far from replacement raw material the cost of employing inefficient, even barely functional, tools may be outweighed by the benefits gained from conserving the stone material at hand. This notion of tool inefficiency being a strategy for raw material conservation raises the possibility that within any region the inefficiency of tool use may vary spatially, becoming more pronounced as distance to source and other economic factors make tool replacement more expensive.

Yet another example of how the identification of this kind of form-function relationship might be informative is in debates about the selective advantage of one group over another. For instance when comparing chronological change between technological systems emphasizing extended tool resharpening and potential (see Shott 1996) and one with short-lived specific tools, a comparison often suggested for the Middle- to Upper-Palaeolithic transition, this issue of tool inefficiency might be critical in developing explanations of group success.

- *Model 3: Artefact use is minimal.* This third model posits minimal use of retouched specimens, perhaps with use taking place only towards the end of the reduction process. In this model the variety of morphological states within the reduction sequence would be explained by a purpose other than resharpening of a blunt working edge. The implication of such a pattern is that use occurred at only one phase in the history of a specimen, perhaps when the object

was already shaped to a specific form, and that extended use requiring resharpening did not take place. This, of course, was the proposition underlying the conventional notion of implement types as being designed as functionally proficient tools, and this model is incompatible with the arguments advanced by Dibble and others that resharpening is a primary role for retouching. Alternatives to this traditional idea of implement types exist, such as the proposition that flake retouching was frequently unsuccessful in creating functionally suitable edges, and consequently specimens were not used during much of the mass removal achieved by retouching. Irrespective of which mechanism was in place the question raised by any variant of this model is why it was cost-effective to expend so much stone material for a minimally used tool. In some senses this model is one of wasteful tool production, representing a strategy which would be effective when raw material conservation was a minimal concern and other factors more powerful stimulants.

These three models describe the inability of stoneworkers to conserve stone by extending the use of a tool through retouching while also using each tool for a specific function and having that tool operate in an efficient way throughout its entire use-life. For the reasons provided here it may not be possible for a knapper to create tools that satisfy all of these qualities, and knapper's may have to choose between the models discussed here.

In constructing these models it is not our intention that they be perceived as competing universal explanations. We can see no reason that each model might not be applicable in some situations but not others, and might therefore represent alternative strategies. We suggest that these models therefore represent structural differences in the articulation of tools and production systems, and it is therefore conceivable that one model might describe the typical form-function relationship in one region but not in another. Furthermore, all three models may be represented in a single behavioural system, although the relative emphasis on any one approach may indicate the strategies being emphasized by any foraging group in response to local economic circumstances. If that is a reasonable summary of the status of these models it becomes imperative to test the relationship between use and artefact morphology in each assemblage, rather than presume universal relationships exist. This would require that use evidence be studied in the context of a technological analysis of the reduction process.

Conclusion

Our hope is that this paper will stimulate more extensive discussions of the articulation of artefact production and use, and provoke more sophisticated conceptualization of tool use and toolkits. We have advocated the need to move beyond the naïve presumption that conventionally recognized implement types have a simple association with particular uses and that by implication those types must have been designed to be optimal in the particular use to which they were constructed. The fundamental issue we have raised is the contradiction that exists between two central principles in modern interpretations of lithic assemblages. On the one hand researchers investigating implement function have frequently had an expectation of a distinct form-function relationship, usually expressed as a distinct relationship between the angle, shape and edge of retouch. On the other hand researchers investigating the technology of implement production have increasingly theorized, and sometimes demonstrated, the progressive alteration of implement form. Tension between these two seemingly incompatible propositions creates an interpretative paradox: *"how can implements be designed for, and be efficient in, a specific use if their morphology is continuously changing?"* Future studies should actively pursue issues that may help answer this question, such as experimental and archaeological investigations into the differential efficiency of tool forms, quantification of the nature of morphological change during artefact reduction, and the evaluation of the relationship between use evidence and the reduction process. We have formulated and discussed three models of this relationship, and the testing of these models in specific archaeological assemblages will represent an initial step in understanding the interaction between past reduction continuums and tool use.

Acknowledgments

We thank Chris Clarkson and Lara Lamb for the invitation to include our paper in this significant volume. The Capertee collection is housed at the Australian Museum in Sydney, and we thank the Trustees of the Australian Museum for access to the material. Artefact recording was carried out during September 2000, October 2001, February 2002, July 2002, October 2002 and November 2002 at the Australian Museum, which provided laboratory space and facilities. We acknowledge the assistance of Leanne Brass in organising access to the collection. Chris Clarkson, Lara Lamb and Oliver McGregor provided valuable comments on drafts of this paper. Finally, we thank Chris Clarkson for drawing Figure 5.

References

Beyries, S. 1988 Functional variability of lithic sets in the Middle Palaeolithic. In A. Montet-White and H. Dibble (eds) *Upper Pleistocene Prehistory in Western Eurasia.* Pp.213-224. Philadelpia: University of Pennsylvania Museum.

Birford, L.R. 1973 Interassemblage variability - the Mousterian and the 'functional' argument. In C. Renfrew (ed.) *The Explanation of Culture Change.* Pp.227-254. Surrey: Duckworth.

Birford, L.R. and S.R.Binford 1966 A preliminary analysis of functional variability in the Mousterian of Levallois Facies. *American Anthropologist* 68:238-295.

Bisson, M.S. 2001 Interview with a Neanderthal: an experimental approach for reconstructing scraper production rules, and their implications for imposed form in Middle Palaeolithic tools. *Cambridge Archaeological Journal* 11:165-184.

Bordes, F., 1961. Mousterian cultures in France. *Science* 134:803-810.

Bordes, F., 1972. *A Tale of Two Caves.* New York: Harper and Row.

Bordes, F., 1973. On the chronology and contemporaneity of different palaeolithic cultures in France. In C. Renfrew (ed.) *The Exploration of Culture Change.* Pp.217-226. Surrey: Duckworth.

Bordes, F. and de Sonneville-Bordes, D., 1970. The significance of variability in Paleolithic assemblages. *World Archaeology* 2:61-73.

Dibble, H. L. 1984 Interpreting typological variation of Middle Paleolithic scrapers: Function, style, or sequence of reduction? *Journal of Field Archaeology* 11:431-436.

Dibble, H. L. 1987 The interpretation of Middle Paleolithic scraper morphology. *American Antiquity* 52:109-117.

Dibble, H. L. 1995 Middle Paleolithic scraper reduction: Background, clarification, and review of evidence to date. *Journal of Archaeological Method and Theory* 2:299-368.

Ferguson, W.C. 1980 Edge-angle classification of the Quininup Brook implements: testing the ethnographic analogy. *Archaeology and Physical Anthropology in Oceania* 15:56-72.

Frison, G.C. 1968 A functional analysis of certain chipped stone tools. *American Antiquity* 33:149-155.

Gordon, D. 1993 Mousterian tool selection, reduction, and discard at Ghar, Israel. *Journal of Field Archaeology* 20:205-218.

Hiscock, P. 1982a The real meaning of edge angles? *Australian Archaeology* 14:79-85.

Hiscock, P. 1982b More about edge angles. Reply to 'A different angle', W.C. Ferguson. *Australian Archaeology* 15:116-119.

Hiscock, P. 1983 From simple suggestion to complex debate: a reply to Hallam. *Australian Archaeology* 16:171-174.

Hiscock, P. 1996 Transformations of Upper Palaeolithic implements in the Dabba industry from Haua Fteah (Libya). *Antiquity* 70:657-664.

Hiscock, P. in press a Looking the other way. A materialist/technological approach to classifying tools and implements, cores and retouched flakes. In S. McPherron and J. Lindley (eds), *Tools or Cores? The Identification and Study of Alternative Core Technology in Lithic Assemblages.* Philadelphia: University of Pennsylvania Museum.

Hiscock, P. in press b Blunt and to the Point: Changing technological strategies in Holocene Australia. In I. Lilley (ed.) *Archaeology in Oceania: Australia and the Pacific Islands.* New York: Blackwell.

Hiscock, P. and V. Attenbrow 2002 Reduction continuums in Eastern Australia: measurement and implications at Capertee 3. In Sean Ulm (ed.) *Barriers, Borders, Boundaries.* Tempus Volume 7.

Brisbane: The University of Queensland.

Hiscock, P. and V.Attenbrow 2003 Early Australian implement variation: a reduction model. *Journal of Archaeological Science* 30: 239-249.

Holdaway, S, S. McPherron and B. Roth 1996 Notched tool reuse and raw material availability in French Middle Paleolithic sites. *American Antiquity* 61:377-387.

Holmes, W.H. 1890 A quarry workshop of the flaked stone implement makers in the District of Columbia. *American Anthropologists* 3:1-26.

Holmes, W.H. 1891 Manufacture of stone arrow points. *American Anthropologist* 4:49-58.

Holmes, W.H. 1892 Modern quarry refuse and the Paleolithic theory. *Science* 20:295-297.

Holmes, W.H. 1893 Distribution of stone implements in the Tide-Water Country. *American Anthropology* 6:1-14.

Jelinek, A.J. 1976 Form, function and style in lithic analysis. *In* C.B.Cleland (ed.) *Cultural change and continuity: essays in honor of J.G. Griffin*. Pp.19-33. New York: Academic Press.

Kuhn, S. 1990 A geometric index of reduction for unifacial stone tools. *Journal of Archaeological Science* 17:585-593.

Kuhn, S. 1992 Blank form and reduction as determinants of Mousterian scraper morphology. *American Antiquity* 57:115-128.

Kuhn, S. 1995 *Mousterian Lithic Technology*. Princeton, New Jersey: Princeton University Press.

Kuhn, S. and M. Stiner 1998 Middle Paeolithic 'creativity': reflections on an oxymoron? In S. Mithen (ed.) *Creativity in Human Evolution and Prehistory*. Pp.143-164. Routledge.

McCarthy, F.D. 1964 The archaeology of the Capertee Valley, N.S.W. *Records of the Australian Museum* 26:197-246.

McPherron, S. P. 2000 Handaxes as a measure of the mental capabilities of early hominids. *Journal of Archaeological Science* 27: 655-663.

Mulvaney, D.J. and J. Kamminga 1999 *Prehistory of Australia*. Sydney: Allen and Unwin.

Neeley, M. P. and C. M. Barton 1994 A new approach to interpreting late Pleistocene microlith industries in southwest Asia. *Antiquity* 68:275-288.

Rolland, N. and H. L. Dibble 1990 A new synthesis of Middle Paleolithic assemblage variability. *American Antiquity* 55:480-499.

Shott, M.J. 1996 An exegesis of the curation concept. *Journal of Anthropological Research*. 52:259-280.

Whallon, R. and J.A. Brown (eds). 1982 *Essays on Archaeological Typology*. Evanston: Center for American Archaeology Press.

Wilmsen, E.N. 1968 Functional analysis of flaked stone artefacts. *American Antiquity* 33:156-161.

6 | Abrupt Terminations and Stone Artefact Reduction Potential

Oliver J. Macgregor

Abstract

This paper considers ways in which flaked stone artefact technologies could be organised to incorporate strategies which economise the useage of raw materials through maximising artefact reduction potential. The morphological characteristic of abruptly terminated flake scars is identified as a factor inhibiting the reduction process and thus affecting reduction potential. The results of a controlled experimental program of flake production are presented, which indicate that the occurrence of abruptly terminated flake scars presents a problem for further reduction of an artefact. Furthermore, the experimental results show that problems of reduction are more pronounced according to artefact edge angle, and according to the size of the abruptly terminated scar. The ways in which these data can be used to better understand the strategies being employed in prehistoric assemblages to increase artefact reduction potential are discussed.

Introduction

The maintenance of a flaked stone technological system requires the progressive reduction of artefacts in order to supply functional tools. Functional tools are created through reduction by the production of useable flakes, and by the reshaping and resharpening of artefacts. This reduction is costly in terms of raw material useage and the associated provisioning cost. In circumstances where the cost of supplying replacement stone is high, it would be advantageous for human groups to employ reduction strategies which conserve raw material. As a consequence, the organisation of flaked stone artefact technologies will vary according to the pressures operating on the human groups which produce them (Andrefsky 1994; Jochim 1989; Kelly 1988; Kelly & Todd 1988; Myers 1989). An increase in the cost of supplying replacement stone could be the result of a number of factors, including distance to raw material sources, group mobility, familiarity with the landscape, and the nature of foraging activities (Bamforth & Bleed 1997; Bleed 1986; Hiscock in press; Jeske 1989; Kelly 1988; Lurie 1989). One way in which a technological system can adapt to conditions of higher procurement cost is through the production of artefacts with a higher "reduction potential" (Hiscock in press).

The issue of reduction potential is the focus of this paper. This term is related to the concept of artefact use-life (Shott 1989), in that it refers to the potential amount of reduction which can be carried out on an artefact. In terms of stone artefacts, the concept of maintainability (Bleed 1986) is equivalent to reduction potential, which is the term which will be used in this paper. When raw material procurement costs are high (see Bleed 1986; Hiscock in press; Myers 1989), technological strategies developed to heighten artefact reduction potential would have been advantageous, since these strategies would have the effect of increasing the number of times an artefact could be modified through reduction, either to provide functional edges or to reshape the artefact to perform a different

function (Hiscock in press). In other words, increasing reduction potential will increase the length of time over which a unit of raw material can be used, and may also increase the multifunctionality of the technological system. It is important, therefore, to be able to develop measures of reduction potential, if we are to test the proposition that observable changes in artefact technology are brought about by strategies employed in response to ecological stress varying costs and benefits in procurement and use.

Central to the objective of measuring artefact reduction potential is understanding the situations under which reduction can become problematic. During the reduction process, a number of situations can arise which make further reduction difficult. One such situation is the occurrence of flakes which terminate abruptly, either in a step termination or a hinge termination. The occurrence of abrupt terminations has been cited by knappers as presenting a problem to the subsequent removal of flakes from an artefact (Cotterell & Kamminga 1987:700; Cundy 1990; Hiscock in press; Whittaker 1994). If we are to gain an understanding of artefact reduction potential, therefore, it is vitally important to understand the ways in which the occurrence of abrupt terminations affects the reduction process, and to quantify how problematic abrupt terminations are.

This paper presents the results of experiments carried out to answer these questions. These experiments confirm that the existence of an abruptly terminated flake scar on the free surface of an artefact creates a problem for the successful removal of flakes from the artefact. Furthermore, the results suggest that the degree of difficulty posed to the reduction process by abruptly terminated flake scars is variable, and is most noticeably affected by the platform angle of the artefact. The experimental results make it possible to discuss strategies which can be employed to reduce the risks of abrupt terminations occurring in the reduction process, and strategies which can be used to increase the probability of successfully overcoming the problems which an abrupt termination creates.

The Experimental Method: Controlled Flake Production

A controlled experimental approach was used to investigate the effects of abrupt terminations on the flaking process. The advantage of a controlled experimental design is that it eliminates the effects of extraneous variables, which might otherwise have had a confounding effect on the results. For this reason, variables such as the force and angle with which percussive force was applied to the cores were held constant throughout the different experimental series. Core morphology was also held constant within each experimental series. This standardisation of the experimental replicates enabled a reliable observation of the differences in flake morphology within and between the different experimental series.

Flakes were struck from glass cores by dropping a ball bearing onto the platform surface. To ensure that the force with which the ball bearing struck the platform was constant for all experiments, the ball bearing was dropped from an electromagnet held at a constant height above the core. Cores were held immobile in a vice throughout the procedure.

The point at which the ball bearing struck the platform was accurately pre-determined. The electromagnet which held the ball bearing prior to dropping it had a 2mm hole drilled through its centre. A plumb-line was suspended through this hole, and the position of the core could then be adjusted to ensure that the desired point of impact was located directly below the electromagnet (Figure 1).

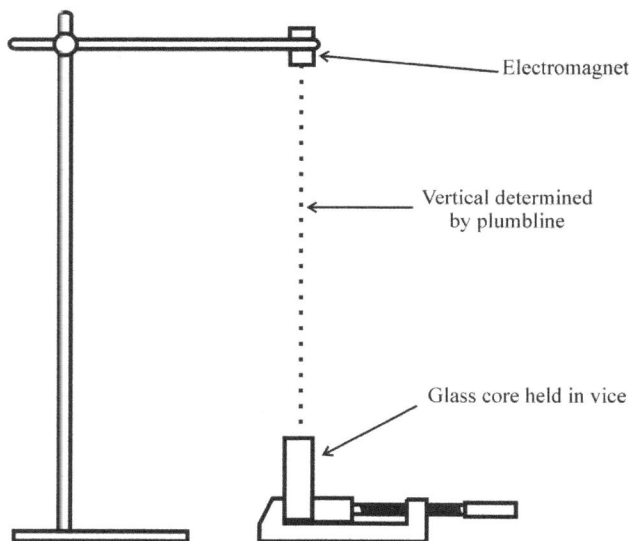

Electromagnet

Vertical determined by plumbline

Glass core held in vice

Figure 1. The apparatus used to strike flakes from glass cores.

The controlled fracture experiments are divided into eight experimental series, according to the morphology of the cores from which flakes were struck in each series (Table 1). Four of the experimental series used cores with exterior platform angles (EPA's) of 70 degrees, while four used cores with EPA's of 45 degrees. For each EPA, cores without flake-scars cut into their free surfaces were used as the control group. In addition to these, three core types with abruptly terminated flake scars cut into their free surfaces were experimented on. The abruptly terminated scars were cut into these cores using a diamond saw. The basic scar used in the experimental cores was 5mm in depth, and 20mm in length. For the sake of brevity, these abruptly terminated flake scars will be referred to as 5 x 20 mm scars. The second scar type was twice as deep, being 10 x 20 mm. The third scar type was twice as long as the 5 x 20 mm scar, being 5 x 40 mm.

For all the experimental series, the conditions of force application were held constant. The ball bearings used to strike the flakes were 20 mm in diameter, and weighed 32.2 grams. The height from which the ball bearings were dropped was 900 mm. The force of impact was therefore the same throughout all the experimental series. The angle at which the ball bearings impacted the platform surface of the core was held at a constant 20 degrees from a line perpendicular to the platform surface (Figure 2).

Table 1. The different core types from which flakes were struck in the controlled fracture experiments, and the number of experimental replicates for each core morphology.

	Exterior Platform Angle	Flake Scar Depth	Flake Scar Length	Number of Replicates
Series 1	70 degrees	No flake scar		19
Series 2	70 degrees	5 mm	20 mm	19
Series 3	70 degrees	10 mm	20 mm	14
Series 4	70 degrees	5 mm	40 mm	18
Series 5	45 degrees	No flake scar		14
Series 6	45 degrees	5 mm	20 mm	19
Series 7	45 degrees	10 mm	20 mm	19
Series 8	45 degrees	5 mm	40 mm	17
Total				139

Experimental Results

In each experimental series, a number of cores were machined and had flakes struck from them (Table 1). From each core morphology, flakes were struck from a range of platform thicknesses. Platform thickness was measured along the platform, from the dorsal face of the core to the point of fracture initiation. Since this was a continuous variable in each experimental group, and since it transpired that platform thickness has a significant effect on the fracture path, the most informative way in which to communicate the results of the fracture experiments is to describe the fracture patterns which occurred at different values of platform thickness.

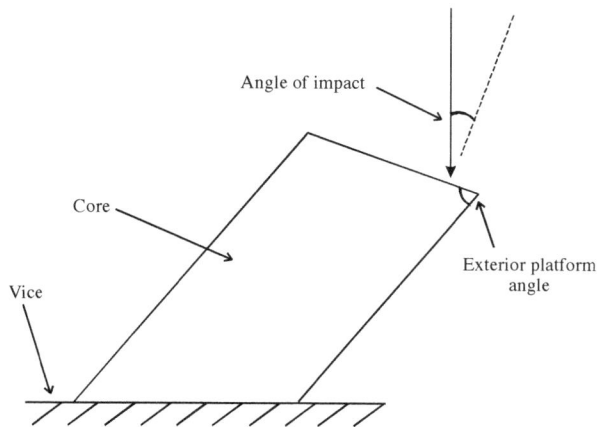

Figure 2. The angle of impact in the controlled fracture experiments was held constant at 20 degrees. The angle is measured between the vertical path of the falling ball bearing (arrow in diagram), and a line perpendicular to the platform surface of the core (dotted line).

In the unscarred cores, the size of flakes struck increased in proportion to the platform thickness (Figure 3). These results agree well with the results of previous researchers (Dibble & Pelcin 1995; Dibble & Whittaker 1981; Faulkner 1972; Pelcin 1996; Pelcin 1997a; Pelcin 1997b; Pelcin 1997c; Speth 1974; Speth 1975; Speth 1981). When the platform thickness reached a certain point, however, the force provided by the impact of the ball

bearing was insufficient to detach a flake, leaving only an incipient Hertzian cone on the surface of the core. This value of platform thickness, above which the force supplied is insufficient to detach a flake, is termed the "detachment threshold" for the purposes of this paper.

The scarred cores displayed more complex fracture patterns. I will discuss the patterns which emerged in general terms first, before describing the differences between the individual core morphologies in more detail. At low values of platform thickness, the length of flakes corresponds roughly to the length of the scar (Figure 4): these flakes propagated through the core until they reached the distal end of the scar, and then stepped, hinged or inflexed (see Cotterell & Kamminga 1987) to reach the corner of the scar. Once the platform thickness was sufficiently high, however, the fractures were able to propagate past the scar, terminating further down the free surface and removing the scar from the core. The value of platform thickness above which the fracture was able to propagate past the scar is termed the "scar threshold" for the purposes of this paper, since it is the threshold value below which the fracture path is affected by the scar. Plotting flake length against platform thickness illustrates how sudden the change in flake length is, once this critical platform thickness has been exceeded.

Even above this critical platform thickness, the flakes struck often snapped transversely as they were being removed from the core, the snap fracture running from the ventral surface to the corner of the scar. Furthermore, these snapped flakes often exhibited a complex and unpredictable fracture path below the snap, often with pronounced undulations. If the platform thickness was increased still further, this transverse snapping of the flakes ceased, and complete flakes were removed which

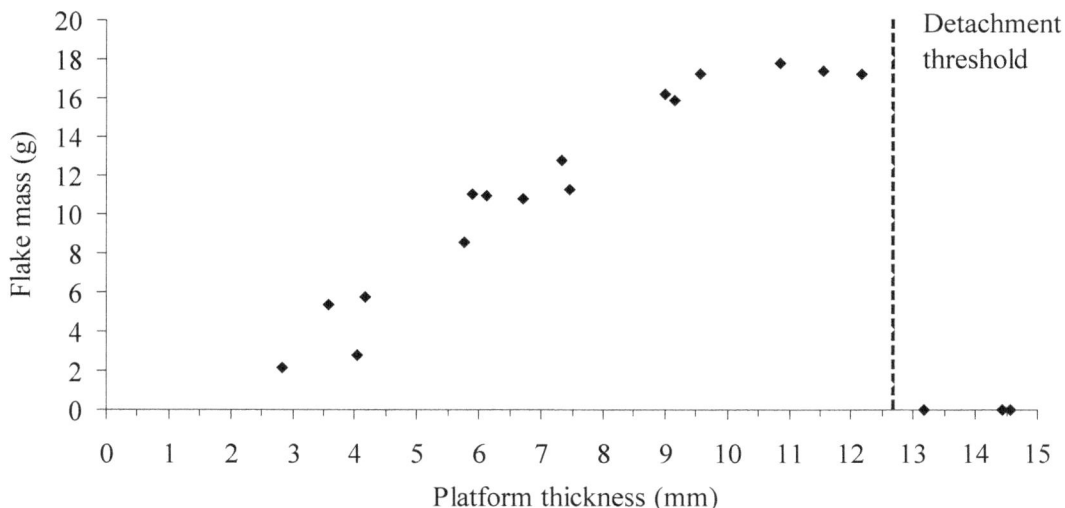

Figure 3. Flake mass plotted against platform thickness, for flakes struck from unscarred cores, with exterior platform angles of 70 degrees. The incipient Hertzian cones are represented as points with mass equal to zero. The detachment threshold is shown with a dotted line.

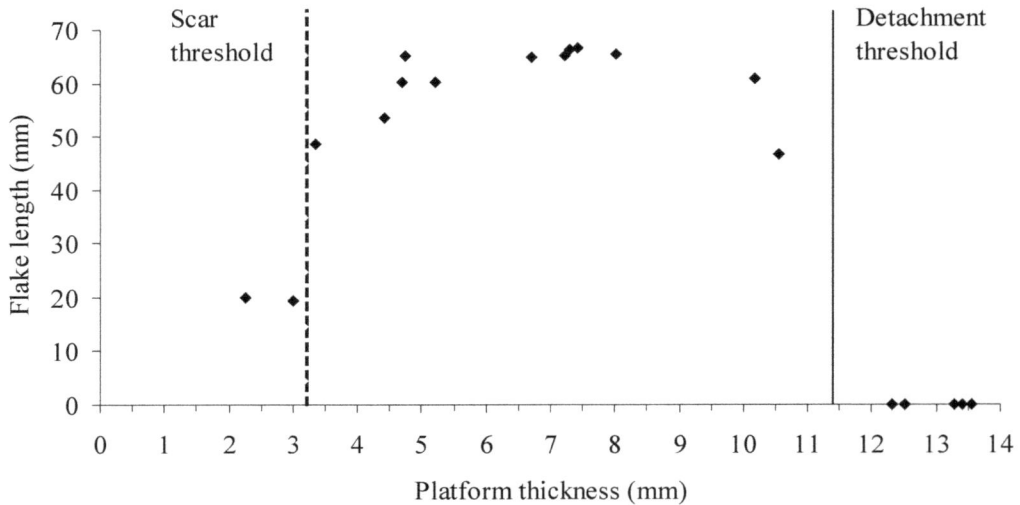

Figure 4. Flake length plotted against platform thickness for flakes struck from 70 degree EPA cores with 5x20mm scars. At low values of platform thickness the fractures hinge or step terminate to meet the distal corner of the scar: this is the reason why, in this case, all the flakes with platform thickness less than approximately 3mm have the same length. The scar threshold is shown by the dotted line, and the detachment threshold is shown by the solid line.

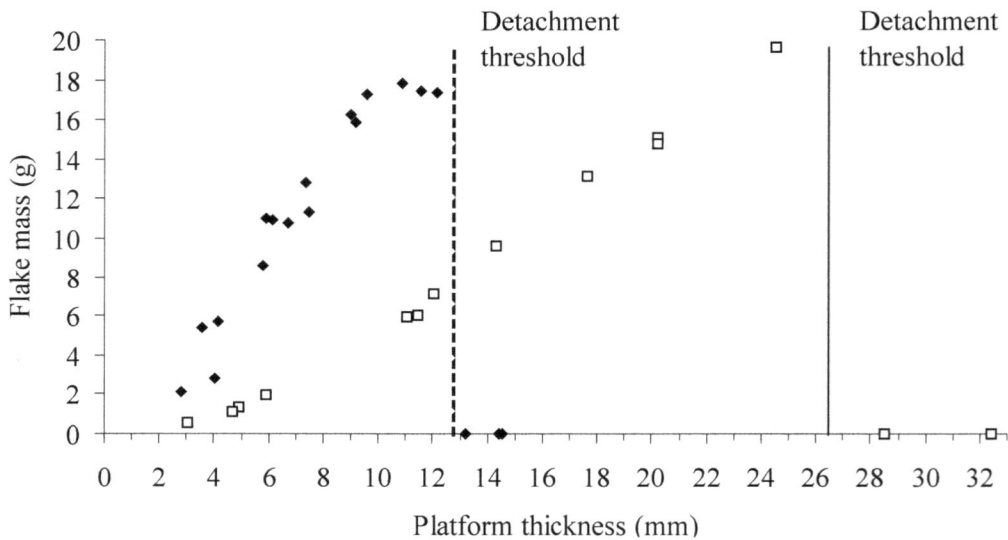

Figure 5. Flake mass plotted against platform thickness for unscarred cores, with exterior platform angles of 70 degrees (diamonds) and 45 degrees (squares).

propagated past the scar, terminating further down the core. This pattern of flake continued as platform thickness increased, until the detachment threshold was reached, at which point flakes could not be detached, and the impact of the ball bearing left only an incipient cone in the platform surface.

The fracture patterns which occurred were markedly different between cores with 45 degree EPA and 70 degree EPA. Most importantly, flakes could be struck over a much wider range of platform thicknesses from cores with exterior platform angles of 45 degrees. In other words, the detachment threshold, above which there was insufficient energy to successfully strike a flake,

occurred at a much higher platform thickness in cores with exterior platform angles of 45 degrees than it did in cores with 70 degree exterior platform angles (Figure 5).

The exterior platform angle also had a significant effect on the critical value of platform thickness below which flakes hinged to meet an abruptly terminated scar on the free surface. For the cores with the lower platform angle, this threshold was consistently higher than in for the cores with a 70 degree platform angle. This is clear when comparing graphs of cores with different platform angles but the same sized scar. For example, for cores with 10 x 20 mm scars, the threshold of platform thickness which must be exceeded to successfully remove the scar is

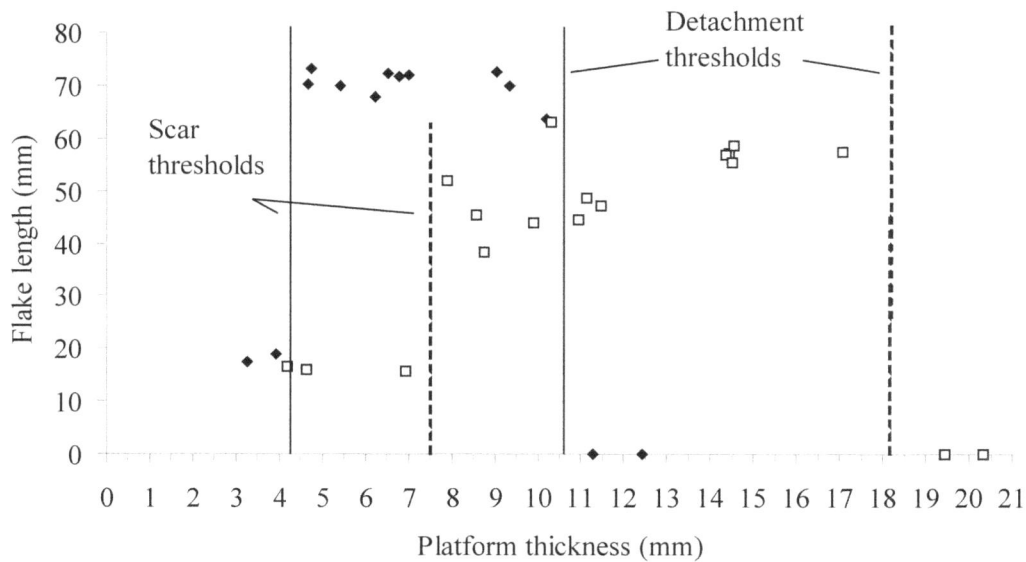

Figure 6. Flake length plotted against platform thickness for cores with 10x20mm scars, with exterior platform angles of 70 degrees (diamonds) and 45 degrees (squares). The scar thresholds and detachment thresholds are shown by solid lines for the 70 degree cores, and dotted lines for the 45 degree cores.

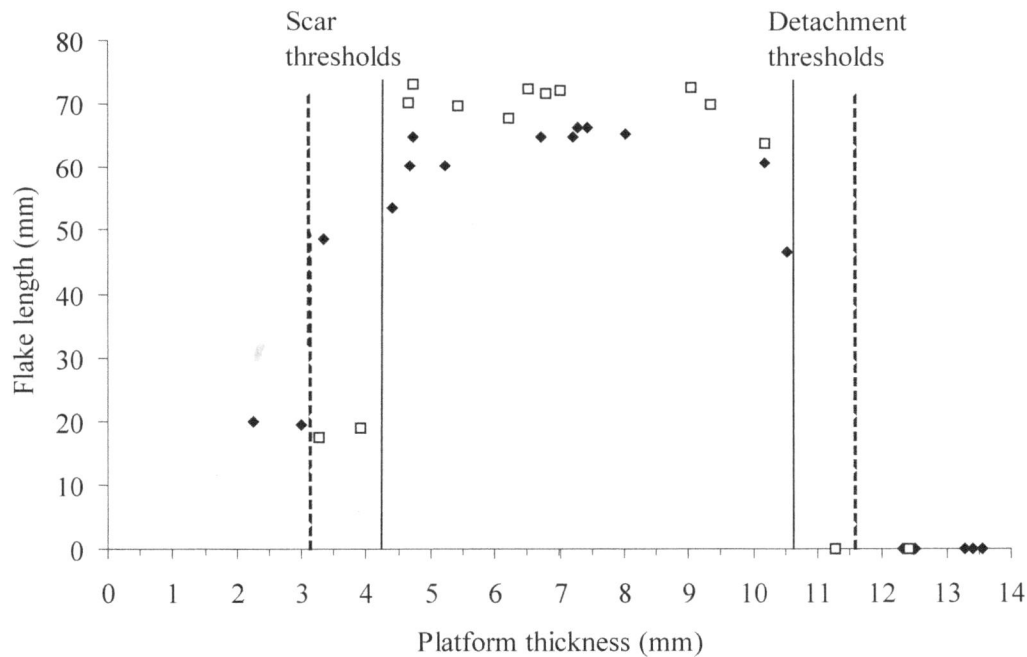

Figure 7. Flake length plotted against platform thickness for scarred cores with exterior platform angles of 70 degrees. One set of flakes were struck from cores with 5x20mm scars (diamonds: scar and detachment threshold shown with dotted lines), and the other set of flakes were struck from cores with 10x20mm scars (squares: scar and detachment threshold shown with solid lines).

around 7.5 mm in 45 degree EPA cores, but only around 4 mm in 70 degree EPA cores (Figure 6). This difference in scar threshold values can be explained by the different angles which the fracture path takes through the differently shaped cores. In cores with a low EPA, the fracture path typically heads toward the free surface more rapidly than it does in a core with a higher EPA. Since the fracture path in the 45 degree EPA cores approaches the free surface at a steeper angle than fractures in 70 degree

EPA cores, these fractures fall under the influence of the scar, even when they have been initiated at a point relatively far from the free surface.

Although a flake must be initiated at a higher platform thickness in a core with a low EPA in order to successfully remove the flake, it should be noted that this disadvantage of the low EPA cores is offset by the fact that the upper limit of platform thickness is consistently higher, as discussed above. Therefore, the range of platform thicknesses between the two thresholds is consistently greater for the 45 degree EPA cores than it is for the 70 degree EPA cores (Figure 6). Since this inter-threshold range represents the range of platform thicknesses from which flakes successfully remove the scar from the core, it can be concluded that it is on the whole easier to successfully strike a flake which removes the scar from a core with a low EPA, since to do this requires less precision in positioning the point of impact.

For cores of the same EPA, the scar threshold varies according to the size of the scar. As the depth of the scar is increased, the threshold is slightly higher (Figure 7). This difference is slight, though it should be remembered that the measurement of platform thickness used here does not include the depth of the scar itself. In other words, the difference in the scar threshold is much greater if the measurement of platform thickness includes the length of the platform removed by the scar.

The scar threshold is altered dramatically when the length of the scar is increased. In cores with a 70 degree exterior platform angle, this threshold is increased from 3 mm to 8.5 mm when the length of the scar is doubled (Figure 8). In addition, increasing the length of the scar on the cores with 70 degree EPA dramatically decreases the region between the scar threshold and the detachment threshold.

Increasing the length of the scar had a similar effect on the scar threshold in the case of cores with exterior platform angles of 45 degrees (Figure 9). Doubling the length of the scar raised the value of the scar threshold from 7 mm (in cores with 5x20 mm scars) to around 12 mm (in cores with 5x40 mm scars). Interestingly, however, the region between the scar threshold and the

detachment threshold was not decreased by this increase in scar length. In other words, increasing the length of the scar on the cores with lower EPA does not restrict the range of platform thicknesses from which a flake can be detached to successfully remove the scar. Comparing this with the situation in Figure 8 indicates that an increase in scar length creates a greater problem for reduction on a core with a higher EPA, since more precision is required in applying the force to the platform.

Summary of Results
The experiments confirmed that the presence of an abruptly terminated scar on the free surface of a core can have a dramatic effect on the paths of fractures travelling through the core. The experiments also made it apparent that the effect of the scar depended upon the distance into the core at which the fracture was initiated. On all the scarred cores, there existed a threshold of platform thickness, below which fractures hinged or stepped to meet the distal corner of the scar, and above which they travelled past the scar, terminating further down the core. In other words, a pre-existing scar on the free surface of a core can only be removed by applying the force at a point above this "scar threshold".

As platform thickness increases, another threshold was encountered, beyond which the impact force proved insufficient to detach a flake at all. Confirming the results of previous experiments, this study found that the exterior platform angle had a major effect on the detachment threshold (Dibble & Pelcin 1995; Dibble & Whittaker 1981; Pelcin 1997c; Speth 1981). Cores with a platform angle of 45 degrees could have flakes struck from much higher platform thicknesses than cores with a 70 degree platform angle. Previous experimenters have agreed that the detachment threshold can be increased if a greater

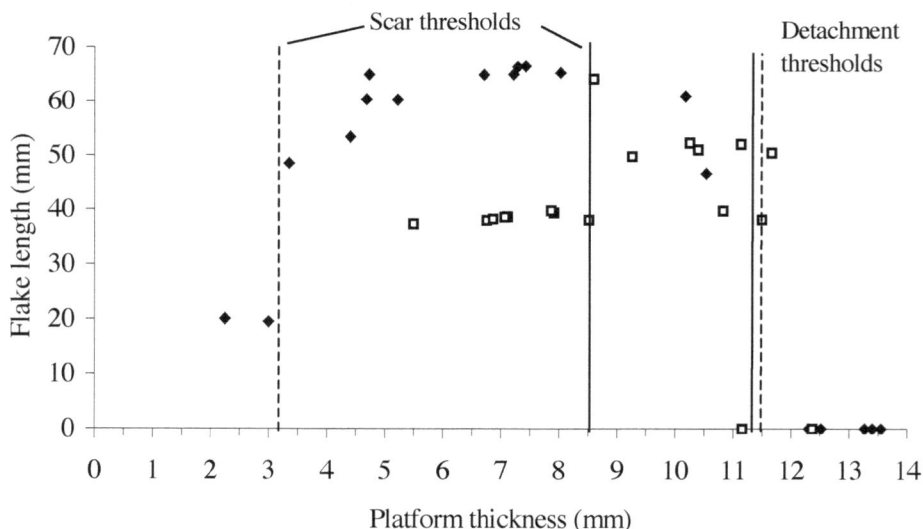

Figure 8. Flake length plotted against platform thickness for flakes struck from cores with exterior platform angles of 70 degrees. One set of flakes was struck from cores with 5x20mm scars (diamonds: scar and detachment thresholds shown with dotted lines), while the other set of flakes was struck from cores with 5x40mm scars (squares: scar and detachment thresholds shown with solid lines).

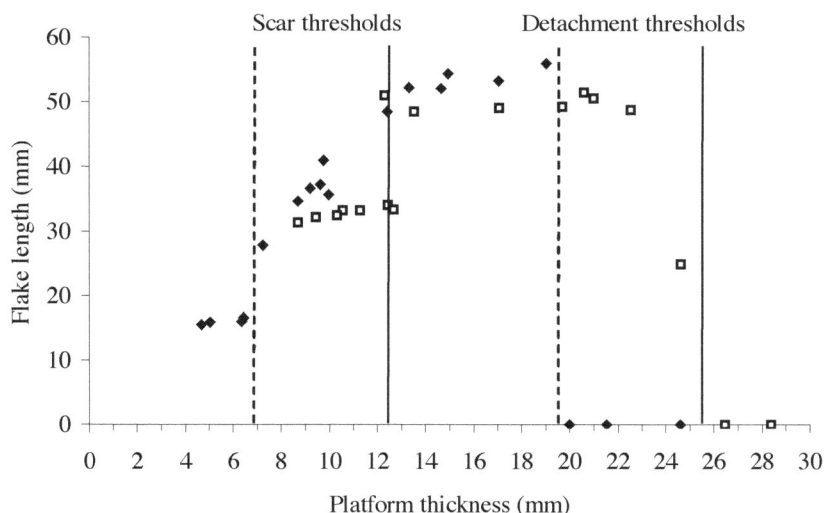

Figure 9. Flake length plotted against platform thickness for flakes struck from cores with exterior platform angles of 45 degrees. One set of flakes was struck from cores with 5x20mm scars (diamonds: scar and detachment thresholds shown with dotted lines), while the other set of flakes was struck from cores with 5x40mm scars (squares: scar and detachment thresholds shown with solid lines).

force is applied to the core (Dibble & Pelcin 1995; Speth 1974). In other words, a larger force is required to strike a flake with a thicker platform. Since there is a limit to how much force any particular knapping technique can apply to a core, it is reasonable to assume that knappers encounter detachment thresholds, just as controlled experiments do.

Given the existence of the detachment threshold as a factor limiting the knapper's ability to detach a flake, it is perhaps most important to examine the distance between the two thresholds. It is the area between the two thresholds which represents the range of platform thicknesses from which a flake can be struck to successfully remove the abruptly terminated scar from the free surface. Therefore, as the distance between the two thresholds decreases, detaching a flake which successfully removes the scar becomes more difficult. The experiments showed that the distance between the two thresholds was smaller for the cores with the higher EPA. In addition, the cores with higher EPA experienced a decrease in this inter-threshold distance if the length of the scar was increased. By contrast, the inter-threshold range did not decrease when the length of the scar was increased in the case of cores with lower EPA. These results clearly show that the occurrence of abruptly terminated flake scars is more problematic on artefacts with high platform angles.

Discussion
The experimental results demonstrate that abrupt terminations have the potential to cause problems for the reduction process, in that they increase the probability that subsequent flakes struck from the same platform will also terminate abruptly. To reduce the problems

occurring as a result of abrupt terminations, knappers could employ strategies of reduction which decrease the chances of abrupt terminations occurring, or which increase the chances of successfully overcoming the problems posed when abrupt terminations occur.

There are several possible strategies which could be employed to reduce the likelihood of abrupt terminations occurring. Many of these strategies involve the way in which force is applied to the core: Crabtree, for example, found that pressure flaking of blades was less likely to cause hinging or stepping than percussion flaking (Crabtree 1968:457), and that decreasing the outward or tangential force as the flake was detached will also decrease the occurrence of abrupt terminations (Crabtree 1968:466). Unfortunately, strategies like these which vary the force application are invisible to the archaeologist.

Aspects of artefact morphology will also affect the probability of abrupt terminations occurring. Since these morphological variables may be visible archaeologically, they offer a chance of identifying when strategies have been employed to increase artefact reduction potential. Previous experimental studies have demonstrated that abrupt terminations are more likely to occur when the edge angle of the artefact is high (Pelcin 1997c). Therefore, the knapper can reduce the chances of abrupt terminations occurring by maintaining a low edge angle on the artefact throughout reduction. Analysis of artefact morphology throughout a reduction sequence has shown that knappers were capable of rejuvenating the edge of an artefact by reducing the edge angle (Hiscock & Attenbrow this volume; see also Clarkson this volume; White 1969). Hiscock and Attenbrow argue that this reduction of the edge angle was specifically to reduce the probability of abrupt terminations occurring in the reduction sequence.

When abrupt terminations do occur, two broad strategies may be employed to overcome the problem and continue reduction of the artefact. First, flaking may be carried out on a different area of platform. This flaking may serve to remove the abruptly terminated flake scar, and so allow reduction to continue on the original platform. Second, as the results presented here show, an abruptly terminated flake scar can be removed from the artefact, if a sufficiently large flake is struck from the same platform.

The costs involved in carrying out these problem solving strategies will vary according to the type of artefact being reduced. The first strategy, of carrying out reduction from a different platform, may be quite costly for some artefact types. For example, single platform artefacts such as unifacial cores and scrapers may be disrupted by the necessity of removing flakes from a second platform. If a pattern of ridges has been set up on the free surface adjacent to the first platform, removing flakes from a second platform may wholly or partially destroy these ridge patterns. This in turn will create problems if flaking is moved back to the original platform.

Other artefact types will not be as badly affected by the necessity to continue reduction on a different platform. In particular, bifacial artefacts will experience little or no problem in incorporating this strategy: if an abruptly terminated flake scar occurs on one face, then reduction can be carried out on the other face. This reduction will have the effect of reducing the length of the abruptly terminated flake scar, making it easier for a flake struck from the original face to remove the scar altogether (Whittaker 1994).

Bifacial reduction has the additional advantage of maintaining low edge angles around the margin of the artefact being reduced. As has already been discussed, this reduces the probability of flakes terminating abruptly. It also increases the probability, if abrupt terminations do occur, that subsequent reduction will successfully remove the abruptly terminated flake scar, allowing reduction to continue unhindered. Maintaining low edge angles on an artefact being reduced, therefore, has a double advantage in terms of reducing the risks and problems associated with abrupt termination occurrence. The data presented here are in agreement with other studies which have identified bifacial artefacts as having a high reduction potential (Ahler & Geib 2000; Jeske 1989; Kelly & Todd 1988).

Our knowledge of the mechanics of abrupt terminations allows us to predict the types of technological behaviour we would expect to see in situations where knappers were preoccupied with reducing the risks of abrupt terminations occurring in the reduction sequence. Such assemblages will have a relatively low proportion of

single-platform artefacts, will show evidence of core rotation, or of reduction from multiple platforms (e.g. Hiscock 1996), and will be comprised of artefacts with relatively low edge angles throughout the reduction sequence. Analysis of reduction sequences according to reduction intensity indices (Clarkson 2002; Kuhn 1990), are expected to be of considerable value in identifying these characteristics (e.g. Clarkson this volume; Hiscock & Attenbrow this volume).

Identifying assemblages in which artefact reduction strategies have been used which lessen the risks associated with the occurrence of abrupt terminations will be informative of the raw material procurement costs faced by the human group which produced the artefacts. In situations where procurement costs are high, for example when raw material sources or foraging opportunities are scarce and unpredictable, strategies which lessen the risks of abrupt terminations will be more pronounced, in order to increase artefact reduction potential and create a more maintainable technology.

The example of abrupt terminations demonstrates the advantages to archaeology in understanding the mechanics of the problems which can occur during artefact reduction. Such an understanding is expected to be of value to theories attempting to explain observable transitions in the archaeological record in terms of the changing pressures experienced by past human groups. In order to test such theories, it is vital to have a body of data detailing the mechanical factors of flake production, and the observable characters of artefact morphology, which function to increase or decrease artefact reduction potential.

Acknowledgements
I would like to thank Chris Clarkson, Peter Hiscock, Barry Cundy and Sophie Collins for the encouragement, advice and criticism they provided during the writing and revision of this paper. The experimental program benefited greatly from the advice of Zbigniew Stachurski.

References
Ahler, S.A. & P.R. Geib. 2000 Why flute? Folsom point design and adaptation. *Journal of Archaeological Science* 27:799-820.

Andrefsky, W. 1994 Raw-material availability and the organization of technology. *American Antiquity* 59:21-34.

Bamforth, D.B. & P. Bleed. 1997 Technology, flaked stone technology, and risk (trans.) M.E. Whalen. In C.M. Barton & G.A. Clarke (eds) *Rediscovering Darwin: Evolutionary Theory and Archaeological Explanation*. Archaeological Papers of the American Anthropological Association. Arlington, Virginia: American Anthropological Association.

Bleed, P. 1986 The optimal design of hunting weapons: maintainability or reliability. *American Antiquity* 51:737-747.

Clarkson, C. 2002 An index of invasiveness for the measurement of unifacial and bifacial retouch: a theoretical, experimental and archaeological verification. *Journal of Archaeological Science* 29:65-76.

Clarkson, C. this volume. Tenuous types: 'scraper' reduction and typological continuums in Wardaman Country, Northern Australia.

Cotterell, B. & J. Kamminga. 1987. The formation of flakes. *American Antiquity* 52:675-708.

Crabtree, D.E. 1968 Mesoamerican polyhedral cores and prismatic blades. *American Antiquity* 33:446-478.

Cundy, B.J. 1990. An Analysis of the Ingaladdi Assemblage: A Critique of the Understanding of Lithic Technology. Unpublished PhD Thesis, Australian National University.

Dibble, H.L. & A.W. Pelcin. 1995 The effect of hammer mass and velocity on flake mass. *Journal of Archaeological Science* 22:429-439.

Dibble, H.L. & J.C. Whittaker. 1981 New experimental evidence on the relation between percussion flaking and flake variation. *Journal of Archaeological Science* 8:283-296.

Faulkner, A. 1972 Mechanical Principles of Flintworking. PhD, Washington State University.

Hiscock, P. 1996. Transformations of Upper Palaeolithic implements in the Dabba industry from Haua Fteah (Libya). *Antiquity* 70:657-664.

Hiscock, P. in press. Blunt and to the point: changing technological strategies in Holocene Australia. In I. Lilley (ed.) *Archaeology in Oceania: Australia and the Pacific Islands*. New York: Blackwell.

Hiscock, P. and V. Attenbrow this volume Reduction continuums and tool use.

Jeske, R. 1989 Economies in raw material use by prehistoric hunter-gatherers. In R. Torrence (ed.) *Time, Energy and Stone Tools* Cambridge, Cambridge University Press.

Jochim, M.A. 1989 Optimization and stone tool studies: problems and potential. In R. Torrence (ed.) *Time, Energy and Stone Tools*. Cambridge: Cambridge University Press.

Kelly, R.L. 1988 Three sides of a biface. *American Antiquity* 53:717-734.

Kelly, R.L. & L.C. Todd 1988 Coming into the country: early Palaeoindian hunting and mobility. *American Antiquity* 53:231-244.

Kuhn, S.L. 1990 A geometric index of reduction for unifacial stone tools. *Journal of Archaeological Science* 17:583-593.

Lurie, R. 1989 Lithic technology and mobility strategies: the Koster site Middle Archaic. In R. Torrence (ed.) *Time, Energy and Stone Tools*. Cambridge: Cambridge University Press.

Myers, A. 1989 Reliable and maintainable technological strategies in the Mesolithic of mainland Britain. In R. Torrence (ed.) *Time, Energy and Stone Tools*. Cambridge: Cambridge University Press.

Pelcin, A.W. 1996 Controlled Experiments in the Production of Flake Attributes. Unpublished PhD Thesis: University of Pennsylvania.

Pelcin, A.W. 1997a The effect of core surface morphology on flake attributes: evidence from a controlled experiment. *Journal of Archaeological Science* 24:749-756.

Pelcin, A.W. 1997b The effect of indenter type on flake attributes: evidence from a controlled experiment. *Journal of Archaeological Science* 24:613-621.

Pelcin, A.W. 1997c The formation of flakes: the role of platform thickness and exterior platform angle in the production of flake initiations and terminations. *Journal of Archaeological Science* 24:1107-1113.

Shott, M.J. 1989 On tool-class use lives and the formation of archaeological assemblages. *American Antiquity* 54:9-30.

Speth, J.D. 1974 Experimental investigations of hard-hammer percussion flaking. *Tebiwa* 17:7-36.

Speth, J.D. 1975 Miscellaneous studies in hard-hammer percussion flaking: the effects of oblique impact. *American Antiquity* 40:203-207.

Speth, J.D.1981 The role of platform angle and core size in hard-hammer percussion flaking. *Lithic Technology* 10:16-21.

White, J.P. 1969 Typologies for some prehistoric flaked stone artefacts of the Australian New Guinea Highlands. *Archaeology and Physical Anthropology in Oceania* 4:18-46.

Whittaker, J.C. 1994 *Flintknapping: Making and Using Stone Tools*. Austin: University of Texas Press.

7

Stone Artefact Assemblage Variability in Late Holocene Contexts in Western New South Wales: Burkes Cave, Stud Creek and Fowlers Gap

Justin Shiner, Simon Holdaway, Harry Allen and Patricia Fanning

Abstract

Harry Allen excavated Burkes Cave in the Scopes Ranges, western New South Wales (NSW), Australia in 1970, revealing a deeply stratified deposit dated by a single radiocarbon determination to 2,000 BP. Despite its name, the excavation actually occurred on a terrace outside the front of the rockshelter.. The site rapidly became identified as one of the artefactually richest open sites in the arid zone, featuring in a number of early settlement and subsistence models for arid Australia with regular mentions in textbooks on Australian prehistory. In this paper we report on a new study based on a reanalysis of the Burkes Cave stone artefact assemblage now housed in the Australian Museum, Sydney. We compare the results of this with two assemblages recorded during Western New South Wales Archaeological Program (WNSWAP) fieldwork at Stud Creek and Fowlers Gap. All three locations are in the arid rangelands and so feature a broadly similar range of resources important to their prehistoric inhabitants. Fieldwork also clarified the range and accessibility of lithic raw materials at each location, and each assemblage can be shown, through an extensive dating program, to have accumulated over the last 1000 to 2000 years of Aboriginal occupation. Thus, having controlled for geographic setting, raw material accessibility and chronology, we seek to determine the degree to which stone artefact assemblage variability can be used to detect regional differences in place use history among three quasi contemporaneously occupied locations. In so doing, we are able to reaffirm the significance of Burkes Cave, some 30 years after its excavation.

Introduction

Stone artefact assemblages have played an important role in the formation of Australian arid zone settlement and subsistence models (e.g. Allen 1972, Cane 1984, Veth 1993). Comparisons are often made between assemblages derived from a range of environments to investigate variation in lithic reduction and discard across space. From such studies have come models that contrast locations where people spent longer periods of time versus places that were used more ephemerally. Reasons put forward to explain differences in the duration of place use have varied from seasonal variation in resource availability through to the importance of ceremonies that bring together relatively large numbers of people at one location (e.g. Ross 1981, Smith 1989, 1996, Thorley 1998, Veth 1989, 1993). However, of central concern in all studies is the ability to differentiate place use history as a function of the intensity of stone reduction.

While there are no simple ways to measure this relationship in absolute terms, there are some relative measures with which we can begin. Much can be inferred from stone artefact assemblage composition by applying some generalisations that predict the outcomes from using raw materials of variable quality spaced at different distances from the occupation location (e.g. Hiscock 1986, 1996). As distance from the source increases, evidence for raw material conservation is expected, producing a pattern that is recognised word wide (Odell 1996). To this may be added the concept of artefact use

life. Clearly, some artefacts were used for longer than others, often being reworked as the edge became unusable. When combined, these factors allow a series of predictions that relate assemblage composition to occupation duration.

A number of authors have commented that short duration occupations by groups will lead to the deposition of a few flakes and tools manufactured from materials carried by the group (e.g. Kuhn 1995). In these situations, local material, particularly if it is of inferior quality for tool edge manufacture, will be under-represented. In contrast, less mobile groups will make greater use of local materials since the opportunity to visit more distant sources of material is restricted simply because mobility is reduced (Elston 1990). Torrence (1989) uses a similar set of principles to differentiate more sedentary from more mobile groups, but bases the distinction on the degree of tool design. Less mobile groups will also tend to abandon artefacts with long-use lives since occupation duration will approach, or at times exceed, the use-life of a particular artefact (Shott 1997, 2003). For short duration occupations the probability of abandoning a long-use-life artefact will be lower since many will be taken elsewhere before they reach the point of abandonment. Thus, based on the degree that mobility equates with occupation duration, the latter can be determined by analysing assemblage composition as a reflection of the intensity with which material was worked (Bird 1985).

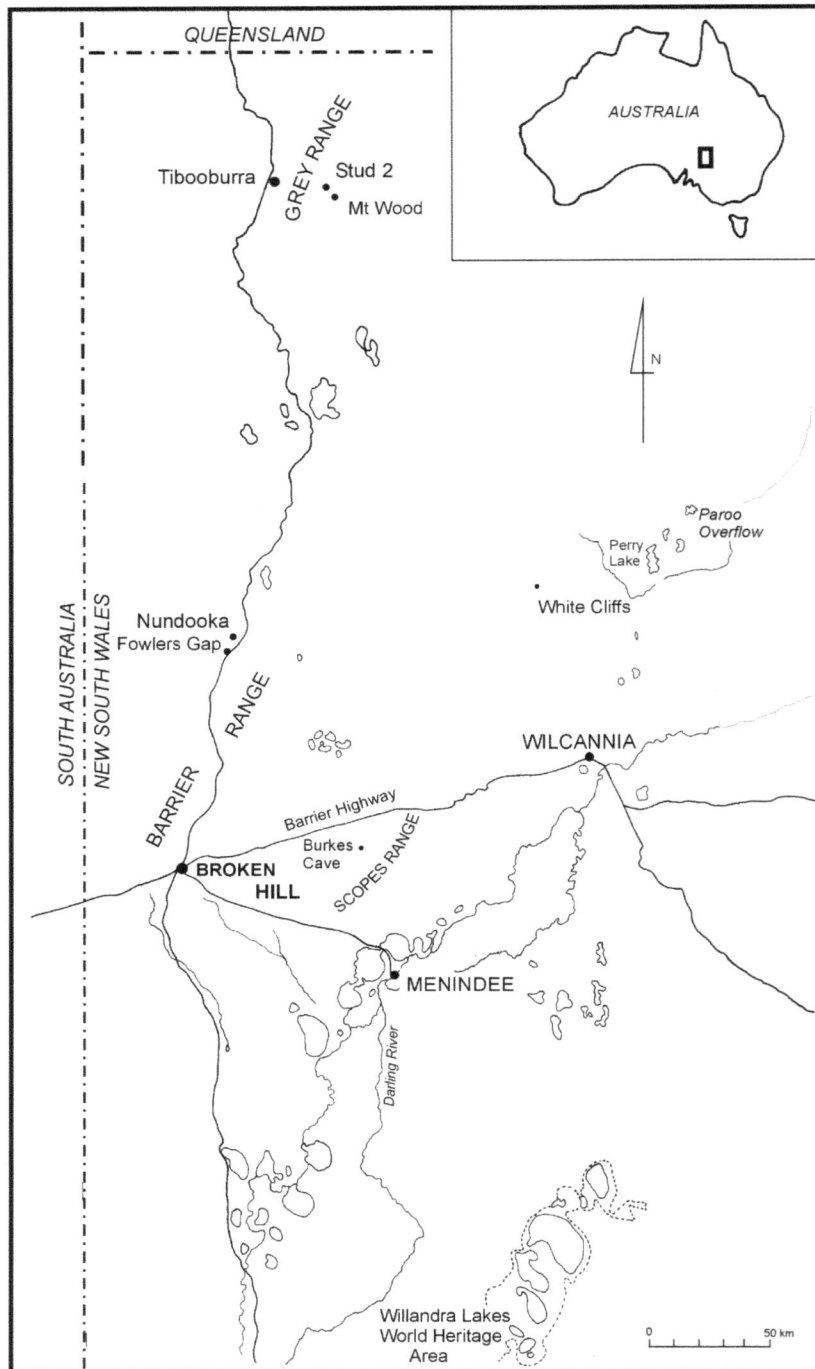

Figure 1. Location of the assemblages.

Occupation duration is frequently discussed in the singular, but the vagaries of determining an archaeological chronology mean that most assemblages represent a mixture of material derived from several distinct occupations; or, a point accepted implicitly by most archaeologists. This is particularly true for assemblages derived from surface scatters as with two of the examples discussed here. Developing chronologies for surface scatters presents further difficulties. Recent approaches rely on correlations with occupational chronologies derived from stratified rockshelters (e.g.

Veth 1993), or the use of typology as a means of linking rockshelter and surface assemblages together (e.g. Thorley 1998). Such approaches provide general temporal sequences but are often not particularly sensitive to variation in occupation duration at one location.

In this paper we address similar questions to those investigated by many authors interested in the Australian arid zone (e.g. Veth 1993, Thorley 1998, Barton 2001): we attempt to derive measures of relative occupation duration where precise chronologies are difficult to generate using methods based on an analysis of assemblage composition, raw material distance to source as well as absolute dating techniques. We illustrate these methods using three assemblages from western NSW: one from Burkes Cave and two others derived from surface contexts: Stud 2 from Sturt National Park and Nundooka on Fowlers Gap Arid Zone Research Station (Figure 1).

The Temporal Context
Chronologies at Stud Creek and Nundooka result from combining age estimates of the surfaces on which the artefacts rest with radiocarbon determinations of a series of heat retainer hearths. It is clear at both locations that geomorphological changes are a key component of the age of archaeological materials.

At Stud Creek, a detailed sedimentary sequence, much longer than the archaeological chronology, provides a picture of a changing sedimentary environment (Fanning and Holdaway 2001). The record is discontinuous, reflecting a limited sediment supply, and it is dominated by erosion. Unstable or nonequilibrium conditions over the valley floor predominate throughout a dated sequence that spans the late Pleistocene through to the mid-to-late Holocene, meaning that it is unlikely that evidence of Aboriginal occupation before the last 2000 years has survived.

A radiocarbon chronology for the last 2000 years at Stud Creek, obtained from a number of heat retainer hearths, indicates two phases of hearth construction separated by a clear gap of about 200 years (Holdaway *et al.* 2002). During each phase, hearths were constructed every few decades. However, from 1100 to 900 BP, hearth construction appears to have ceased altogether, since there are no hearths dating to this time period. It was this finding that first alerted us to the problem of treating palimpsest deposits as accumulations of material derived from a series of similar occupations. The apparent cessation of heat-retainer hearth construction suggests that the nature of occupation may have changed at Stud Creek. Since they were lagged onto a common surface, the artefacts from each geographic location at Stud had to be treated as one assemblage. However, some variability in assemblage composition, that reflects change in the nature of occupation, is expected.

In fact, as will be discussed below, it is the assemblage from Nundooka, rather than that from Stud 2, that produced the evidence of variable occupation history. Jansen's (2001) geomorphological work provides an estimate of the age of the Nundooka assemblage at Fowlers Gap. The gorge in which Nundooka is located retains stratigraphic evidence of occasional catastrophic floods that scour sediments from the floor of the gorge. The most recent superflood of this type is bracketed by radiocarbon determinations to between 3390 and 1710 BP (Jansen 2001:238). Fine-grained slackwater deposits

draping high terraces along the margins of the gorge began accumulating at least 800 years ago (Jansen 2001:239). These data correlate well with dates of 709±128 BP and about 930 cal. BP (Jansen 2001) obtained from radiocarbon determinations on charcoal from heat retainer hearths excavated on two of these high terrace surfaces at Nundooka. Thus, as at Stud 2, the age of the surface stone artefact deposits can be estimated by combining the results of geomorphological studies of surface age together with dates obtained from heat retainer hearths. Both analyses indicate the Nundooka assemblage accumulated over a period no longer than 1000 years.

Chronology at Burkes Cave was obtained more conventionally, with one of us (HA) excavating a square into the location searching for a stratified deposit. A single radiocarbon determination of 1850±240 BP (ANU-704) uncorrected was obtained at a depth of 610mm out of a total depth of c.1000mm in Square 2. This date provides a maximum age for the artefacts analysed here as more than 95% of all artefacts recovered at the site came from this level or above. Although the deposit was stratified, no other determinations were obtained from higher in the sequence. Thus, radiocarbon dating tells us nothing about the chronology of occupation during the last 2000 years. In this sense, despite the site having been excavated, the assemblage differs little from the assemblages derived from lagged deposits at Stud Creek and Nundooka, in that only the maximum age of the deposit is known. Therefore, in the analyses detailed below, the Burkes Cave assemblage is treated in the same way as those from the other two locations.

Thus, in terms of absolute chronology, we know the maximum age of the assemblages at all three of the locations considered here. The Stud 2 and Burkes Cave assemblages accumulated over a period of 2000 years, while that from Nundooka represents less total time, the assemblage accumulating over no longer than 1000 years.

Raw Material Reduction and Assemblage Composition
While our chronologies permit a general indication of the maximum length of occupation at the three locations we are no more able to determine how many occupations are represented nor the duration of any particular occupation than authors who have come before us. It is very unlikely that either of these questions will be answered by conventional dating techniques, at least none that would work with the materials with which we are dealing, therefore we turn our attention to the analysis of assemblage composition as a means to obtain a relative measure of occupation frequency and/or duration. As discussed above, a combination of measures of the intensity with which materials from different sources were reduced as well as the production of tools may be used to indicate whether assemblages represent long or short duration occupations (Shott 1997). We begin our consideration of the three assemblages with raw material.

Raw Material Composition

The three locations considered here are situated within rich lithic landscapes, with a wide range of potential raw material sources suitable for the production of stone artefacts. The same types of raw material occur in broadly similar forms within each area. Quartz occurs as nodules within gibber pavements within the immediate context of Burkes Cave and Nundooka, although it is less common around Stud 2. Quartzite is also widely available within the gibber pavements. Silcrete occurs as both outcrops and within gibber pavements as pebbles. The grain composition of silcrete varies from clast silcrete (large to small quartz clasts with medium to high densities) to non-clast silcrete (either no quartz clasts or minor percentages of small quartz clasts) within individual outcrops. Doelman *et al.* (2001) note that in the area surrounding Stud 2, non-clast silcrete more readily occurs in outcrop form while gibber is mostly composed of clast silcrete (although these categories are not mutually exclusive). Clast silcrete is more readily available than the non-clast variety around Burkes Cave and Nundooka. Silcrete outcrops on the eastern flank of the Scopes Range at a minimum distance of five kilometres from Burkes Cave and outcrops also occur on several hilltops within a minimum of 1.5 kilometres of Nundooka. A few silcrete gibbers are also found in the immediate vicinity of Nundooka

Several different methods exist for determining the relative proportions of artefacts manufactured from different raw materials within an assemblage. Although all methods are related, each provides a slightly different picture of relative raw material abundance. The first method uses the number of individual artefacts. More artefacts manufactured from one raw material will lead to greater relative abundance, however for raw materials that produce large amounts of shatter during reduction, simply counting pieces irrespective of their technological attributes may over-estimate the importance of some materials in the raw material economy (Holdaway and Stern in press). The second method, summing the volume (maximum length x maximum width x maximum thickness, an alternative to weight when taking this measurement is not practical) of artefacts manufactured from each raw material overcomes this problem to some extent. However, as is the case with basic counts, volume does not consider the technological composition of assemblages. The third alternative, the Minimum Number Flakes (MNF) calculation is a measure of raw material proportion that considers the relative abundance of flakes by counting each individual piece with a platform or point of force application (longitudinal splits were divided by two) (Hiscock 2002, Shott 2000).

The proportion of raw materials per assemblage calculated by the three different methods (Figure 2) indicates significant differences among the assemblages. Stud 2 is consistently dominated by silcrete, with slightly more clast than non-clast material. Quartz at this location, which is included in the 'other' category, accounts for less than five percent. Silcrete is also abundant at Burkes

Cave, but not to the same extent as at Stud 2. Clast silcrete consistently accounts for approximately 40% of raw materials at Burkes Cave followed by non-clast silcrete varying between 15% based on volume measures and 30% based on MNF. Quartz at Burkes Cave accounts for 30% by number and volume, but decreases to approximately 20% by MNF. Other materials account for less than 10%. Nundooka has the least amount of silcrete, overall accounting for approximately 45% of raw materials. Clast silcrete varies between 25% and 30% depending on the abundance measure and non-clast silcrete is 20% by MNF but as low as 10% by volume. Quartz consistently accounts for approximately 50% of raw materials and other materials less than 10%.

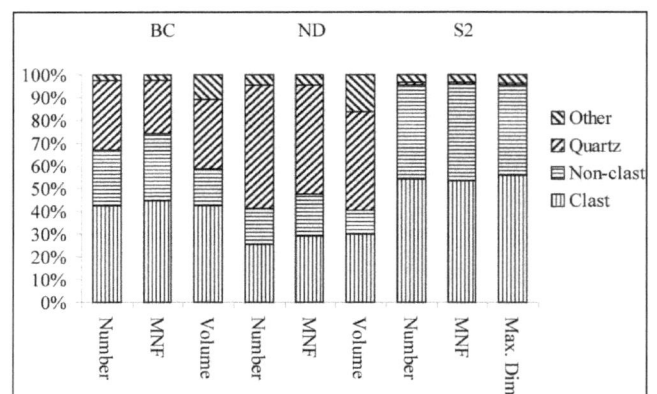

Figure 2. Raw material proportions.

Difference in raw material access is likely to account for some of the variability in relative raw material proportions between the three assemblages. Stud 2 and Nundooka are both located relatively close to abundant raw material sources and they both contain a large proportion of these raw materials (clast silcrete and quartz respectively). Imported raw materials (defined here simply as stone not present at the site location), non-clast silcrete at Stud 2 and both silcrete types at Nundooka, account for relatively smaller proportions of artefacts. The pattern is different at Burkes Cave, where non-local raw materials, in this case silcrete, predominate. Significantly, silcrete sources are located furthest from Burkes Cave compared to the other two assemblages.

Raw Material Reduction and Utilisation

Access to raw material is clearly an important determinant of assemblage variability in the three assemblages considered. In the rangelands of western NSW exposure of raw material is unlikely to have been a limiting factor since landscapes are mostly erosion dominated, and outcrop and gibber sources are abundant (e.g. Doleman et al. 2001). Instead, access to raw material sources is likely to have varied as a function of variables like group mobility and occupation duration. The significance of these variables can be assessed by using a series of technological measures related to the intensity of the stone artefact reduction process.

70

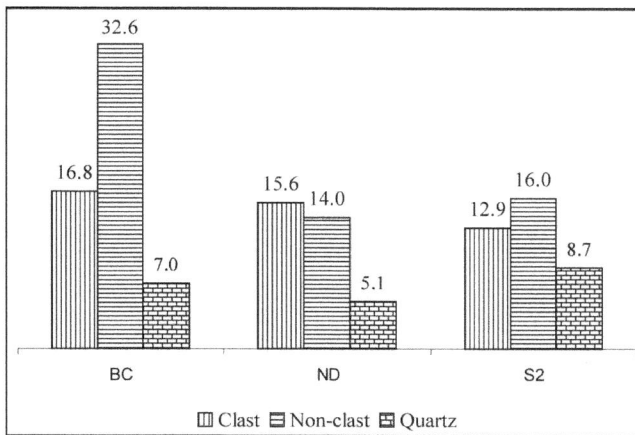

Figure 3. Flake to core ratio.

Flake to core ratio: One of the keys to inferring occupation duration is to determine how completely cores were reduced. The ratio of flakes to cores is one such measure. Longer duration occupations by less mobile groups will lead to the more complete reduction of cores producing more flakes from each core so the flake to core ratio will rise (Dibble 1995).

Plotting this ratio for each raw material type (Figure 3) indicates both similarities and differences among the assemblages. In both the Burkes Cave and Stud 2 assemblages, non-clast silcrete has the highest flake to core ratio followed by clast silcrete and quartz, suggesting that non-clast cores were more intensively reduced than those of either clast silcrete or quartz. However, this is not true for the Nundooka assemblage, where clast silcrete has the highest ratio followed by non-clast silcrete and quartz. Comparison by location indicates that the Burkes Cave assemblage has the highest flake to core ratio for both types of silcrete. This suggests that greatest reduction occurred at Burkes Cave, and by implication that Burkes Cave saw the longest occupations of the three locations. However, the flake to core ratio is only one measure of core reduction intensity.

Non-cortical Core to Cortical Core Ratio: As the intensity of reduction increases more flakes will be produced per core and the proportion of cortical surfaces on cores will decrease (Dibble 1995). Therefore, the non-cortical core to cortical core ratio provides another measure of core reduction intensity. Values for this ratio by location and raw material are provided in Figure 4. Burkes Cave has the highest ratio for both types of silcrete, and these ratio are higher than those from both Nundooka and Stud 2, confirming the inference concerning the relative reduction intensity among the locations discussed above. Among the raw materials, the ratio is highest for non-clast silcrete consistent with the results of the flake to core ratio, although the small number of quartz artefacts (n=15) at Stud 2 also indicate intense reduction. At Nundooka, the situation is more complex with the non-cortical to cortical core ratio suggesting non-clast silcrete is worked most intensively

but the flake to core ratio indicating that it is clast silcrete that is being more reduced.

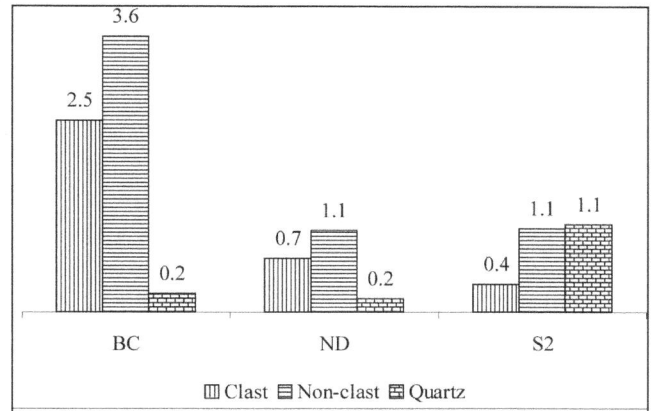

Figure 4. Non-cortical core to cortical core ratio.

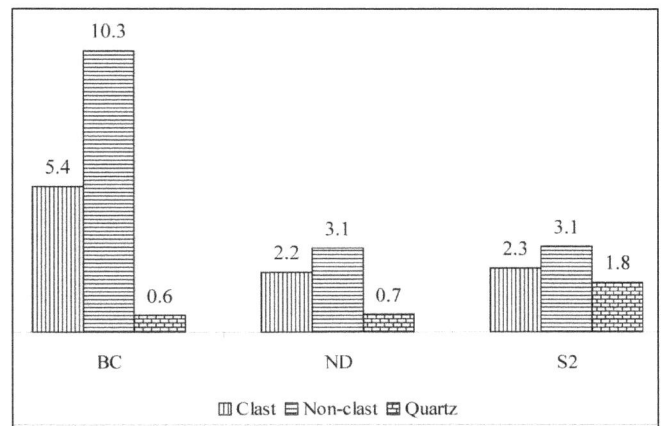

Figure 5. Non-cortical complete flake to cortical complete flake ratio.

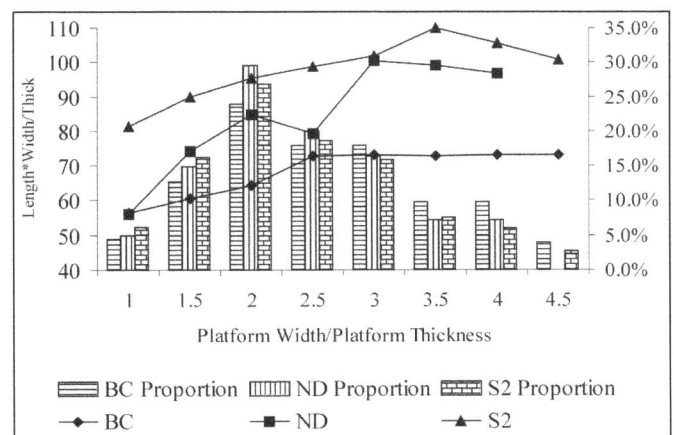

Figure 6. Clast silcrete flake shape plot.

Table 1. Length (mean and standard deviation in millimetres) and frequency of clast cortical complete flakes (F = 63.4, d.f. = 2. 2593, p = <.001).

Assemblage	Number	Mean	Std. Deviation
Burkes Cave	177	22.60	7.88
Nundooka	148	28.64	10.84
Stud 2	2271	32.64	12.26

Table 2. Length (mean and standard deviation in millimetres) and frequency of non-clast cortical complete flakes (F = 20.1, d.f. = 2, 1206, p = <.001).

Assemblage	Number	Mean	Std. Deviation
Burkes Cave	65	21.88	6.72
Nundooka	67	26.70	10.16
Stud 2	1077	30.27	11.32

Table 3. Length (mean and standard deviation in millimetres) and frequency of quartz cortical complete flakes (F = 26.4, d.f. = 2, 929, p = <.001).

Assemblage	Number	Mean	Std. Deviation
Burkes Cave	403	21.38	5.67
Nundooka	495	23.88	6.98
Stud 2	34	22.95	8.22

Non-cortical Complete Flake to Cortical Complete Flake Ratio: An equivalent to the non-cortical to cortical core ratio can be calculated for flakes and provides a third measure of reduction intensity. Increased core reduction will produce relatively larger numbers of non-cortical to cortical complete flakes hence increasing the value of this ratio (Dibble *et al.* 1995, Roth and Dibble 1998). Results, provided in Figure 5, indicate that the highest values occur for Burkes Cave in comparison to Nundooka and Stud 2. In each assemblage, non-clast silcrete is the most heavily reduced raw material followed by clast silcrete and quartz. Thus, the results from this measure closely follow those obtained from the non-cortical core to cortical core ratio.

Nodule Size and Form: Nodule size is an important factor influencing the degree and format of core reduction (Kuhn 1995). Only a limited number of flakes above a certain size cut-off can be produced from small nodules, therefore interpretations of core reduction intensity based on the flake to core ratio should include a consideration of the effect of nodule size.

However, estimating original nodule size can be difficult, especially when the entire core reduction sequence is not represented in an assemblage. The average length of complete flakes that retain dorsal cortex offers one opportunity for investigating the effects of nodule size on core reduction. Cortical flakes are usually, but not always, removed during the early stages of reduction (Baulmer 1988), therefore their dimensions provide a relative indication of nodule size.

The length of complete cortical flakes (Tables 1-3) indicates that the largest silcrete nodules of both types were flaked at Stud 2 with the smaller mean cortical flake lengths at Nundooka and then Burkes Cave. Thus, based on this measure, there is a clear order in nodule size among the assemblages but one that runs in the opposite direction to the intensity of core reduction. Nodules are smallest at Burkes Cave, yet this assemblage shows the highest values for the flake to core ratio, suggesting the most intensive core reduction. The simplest interpretation for these findings is that the inhabitants of Burkes Cave were maximising the potential of non-local raw material that had to be brought in over the relatively greatest distance.

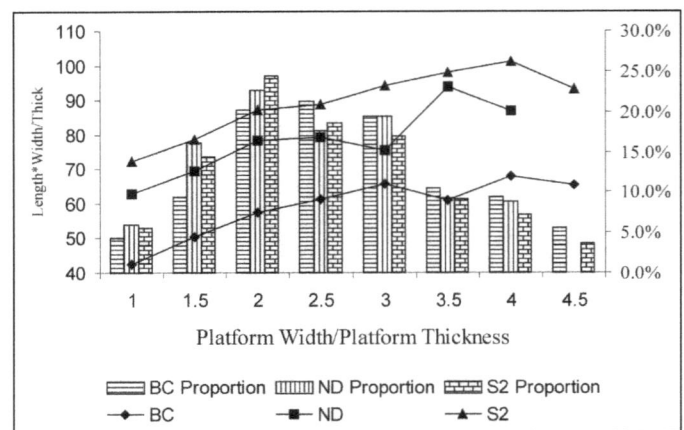

Figure 7. Non-clast silcrete flake shape plot.

Flake Shape: A final measure of raw material reduction and utilization is based on a plot of relative flake shape. For a given exterior platform angle, increasing the thickness of the platform will produce a heavier flake. However, increasing the platform width relative to the thickness will change the distribution of this weight, producing flakes that have larger surface areas (length x width) relative to their thickness (Dibble 1997). Thus, flake shape measures the influence of raw material access on reduction, because flake surface area is often maximised when raw material conservation is important (Pelcin 1997:749).

Figures 6-8 present shape plots for clast silcrete, non-clast silcrete and quartz complete flakes respectively with histograms of the proportions of flakes that fall into platform ratio size classes. Due to the small number of complete quartz flakes at Stud 2, flake shape for quartz could not be examined at this location. For each of the raw material classes, flakes in the Burkes Cave assemblage (diamonds in the Figure 6 and 7) on average have a smaller surface area to thickness ratio than flakes from the Nundooka and Stud 2 assemblages. This supports the interpretation that core reduction was more intensive at Burkes Cave because flakes that are thick relative to their surface area are more likely to be produced towards the end of the reduction process than at its beginning.

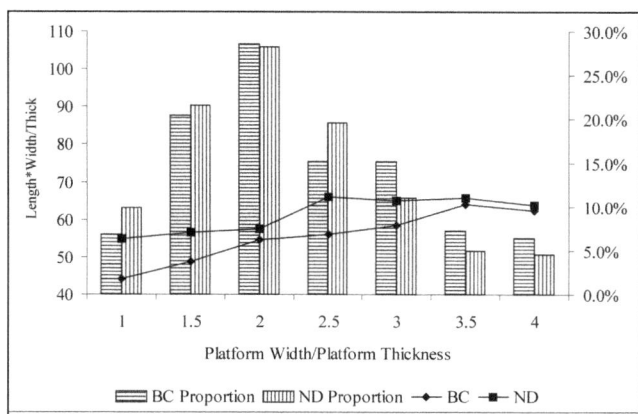

Figure 8. Quartz flake shape plot.

However, the relationship between flake shape, core reduction and raw material access is not always this clear-cut. Clast and non-clast silcrete flakes at Stud 2 (triangles in the Figures 6 and 7) have the largest surface area relative to thickness, suggesting that core reduction was least intensive, a result not always reflected in the earlier measures of core reduction according to which the Nundooka assemblage was the least intensively reduced for some raw materials. This anomaly may be explained to some extent by the larger nodule size at Stud 2 compared to Nundooka (Tables 1-3) since increased nodule size permits a greater proportion of flakes with a high surface area to thickness ratios to be produced.

Summary: When combined, the measures of raw material reduction indicate the most intensive reduction of clast and non-clast silcrete occurred at Burkes Cave. Quartz appears to be most intensively reduced at Stud 2, however, the total number of quartz pieces is low at this location. Comparison within raw material types between assemblages suggests that non-clast silcrete is generally the most intensively reduced material. However, this pattern is not as clear at Nundooka, where the flake to core ratio is highest for clast instead of non-clast silcrete. At face value, these results might suggest that occupation duration was longest at Burkes Cave since core reduction was most intensive at this location. This location is also the most distant from any raw material outcrop, so the results might equally reflect raw material conservation or some combination of the two. Distance to raw material source does not preclude mobility as an explanation of assemblage composition; neither does the reverse. However, analytically it is necessary to control for one so that the other may be investigated. It is not sufficient to simply assume that either raw material distance to source or mobility is dominant as has sometimes been suggested.

Tool Production and Discard
Tools represent flakes (and sometimes cores) where one or more of the edges have been modified either through retouch or use. Tool form and proportions of different types within assemblages vary as a result of several factors, including the mobility of the people who

manufactured them and the duration the location was occupied (Shott 2003). However, the rate of tool production and discard is somewhat independent of flake production (Dibble 1995). For example, increased core reduction does not always correlate with increased tool production, especially in situations where abundant high quality local raw materials are available and there is little incentive for conservation (Elston 1990). The opposite may be true of situations where access to raw material sources is constrained either through reduced mobility arising from increased occupation span or natural scarcity of stone. In such cases a greater emphasis on maximising the potential of available lithic stocks can be expected, including increased core reduction and increased tool production, maintenance and resharpening.

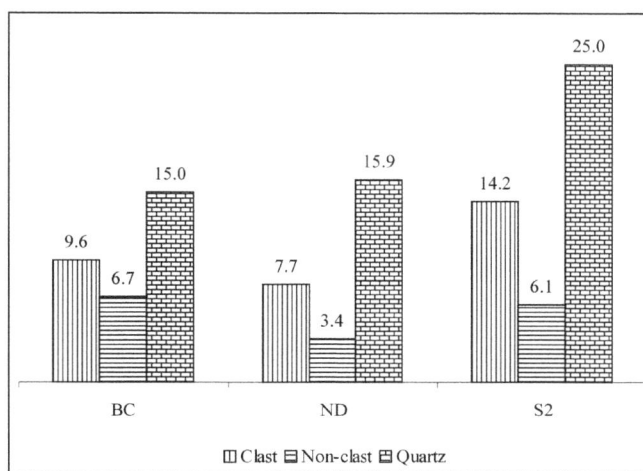

Figure 9. Flake to tool ratio.

Burkes Cave saw increased levels of core reduction, and so is a good candidate for increased levels of tool production. A low proportion of flakes relative to tools would suggest that flake and tool production were related and that occupations at Burkes Cave were of a longer duration than that for the other two locations. On the other hand, Elston (1990) predicts that low flake to tool ratios reflect short duration occupations. In instances of high residential mobility, the amount of raw material that can be accumulated and transported is limited; therefore there is a greater emphasis on "gearing-up" with tools (Elston 1990:158). In this instance, high tool proportions at one of the locations might indicate shorter occupation durations.

Flake to Tool Ratio: The flake to tool ratio is the simplest measure of tool production. Low values of this ratio imply that proportionally, more flakes have been modified into tools. Figure 9 indicates that Nundooka has the lowest flake to tool ratio followed by Burkes Cave and Stud 2. According to this measure, while flake production at Burkes Cave was more intensive than at the other locations, this did not involve the conversion of large numbers of flakes to tools.

Complete Tool Surface Area to Complete Flake Surface Area Ratio: More intensive tool production sometimes correlates with more intensive tool resharpening (Dibble 1995). Therefore the most intensive tool resharpening might be expected in the Nundooka assemblage given the results of the flake to tool ratio from this location. There are many methods of quantifying tool resharpening; reduction indices, for instance, are one method that has received recent attention in Australia (e.g., Clarkson 2002). A method that has received less attention, however, involves the calculation of the mean complete tool surface area to mean complete flake surface area ratio. This measures the change in flake surface area produced by tool formation in relation to the size of the unmodified flakes. The surface area of both tools and flakes is over-estimated by assuming that the artefacts are rectangular in shape, however an advantage of this method is that tool resharpening is investigated in relation to the population of flakes from which blanks were selected for retouch, thereby providing a measure of the relative intensity of tool formation in comparison to flake production.

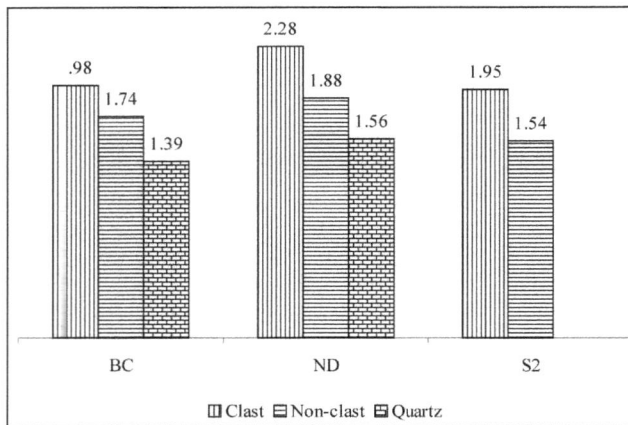

Figure 10. Complete Tool Surface Area to Complete Flake Surface Area Ratio.

Figure 10 presents the results of this calculation for scrapers and complete flakes from the three assemblages. There are three things to note. First, scraper resharpening in all of the assemblages is not very intensive; the mean surface area of scrapers exceeds that of complete flakes in all of the assemblages. Values in excess of one for this ratio indicate that tools are made on relatively large blanks compared to the unmodified flakes and that retouch has removed relatively little of the tool blank surface area. Second, quartz tools have the lowest ratio value at both Burkes Cave and Nundooka, suggesting that they were the most intensively retouched of the three raw material types, a result that is surprising given the results of the flake to tool ratio measure which indicated non-clast silcrete flakes were most frequently converted into tools. Third, comparing the values among the locations, both clast and non-clast silcrete scrapers are more intensively retouched at Stud 2 followed by Burkes Cave and Nundooka. Although a greater proportion of flakes

were retouched into tools at Nundooka compared to the other two locations (Figure 9), these tools were not intensively retouched. Clearly, tool production, retouch intensity and core reduction are largely independent of each other in the three assemblages considered.

Mean Number of Retouched Quadrants: The intensity of tool resharpening can also be investigated through an examination of the mean number of retouched edges. Following Dibble's (1984, 1987) reduction model, more intensive resharpening will result in an increase in the number of edges retouched.

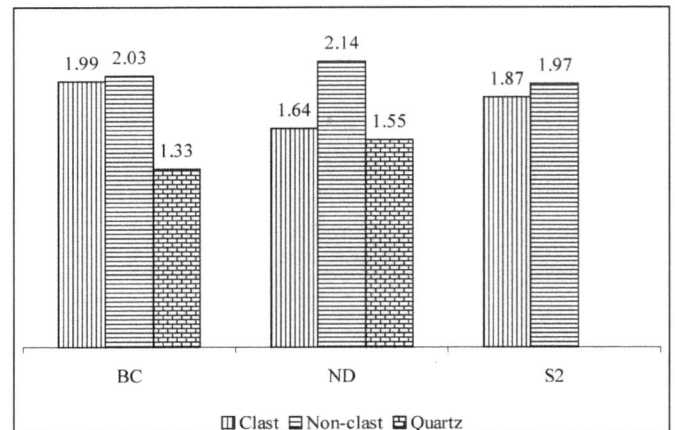

Figure 11. Mean number of retouched quadrants on complete scrapers

The location of retouch in all three assemblages was recorded using a quadrant system described elsewhere (Holdaway and Stern in press). Figure 11 and Tables 4 -5 indicate that when divided by material, non-clast silcrete scrapers have the highest mean number of retouched quadrants in all three assemblages and quartz the lowest. However, only the differences in means for clast silcrete approach significance. Amongst the three locations, Nundooka shows the most variability. This location records the highest mean number of tool edges for non-clast silcrete amongst the assemblages, however the mean for clast silcrete at Nundooka is lower than the values for both Burkes Cave and Stud 2. At Burkes Cave the mean number of retouched edges is similar for both types of silcrete. The value for quartz scrapers at Nundooka is higher than that for Burkes Cave. Differences among the locations are small and only sometimes approach significance suggesting that at least according to this measure, resharpening of scrapers is a minor influence on assemblage composition. Nevertheless, when compared with the measures of intensity of tool production discussed above, these results strengthen the previous suggestion that tool production, resharpening and core reduction are not closely correlated.

Tool Proportions: Tools occur in a variety of different forms, reflecting a number of processes. Function, resharpening and style have frequently been discussed in the literature however a rather different approach to tool proportions involves thinking about tools as indicators of the duration of occupation (Bird 1985, Holdaway et al. 2000). Many tools were manufactured and used at locations away from places where they were discarded. Tools with long use lives will be disposed of at locations where occupation duration is longer, since they will wear out and be replaced more often at places where people spend more time. Thus, concentrations of certain forms with long use lives, in contrast to forms that imply shorter use lives, will allow inferences to be made concerning the temporality of occupation.

Table 4. Mean number of retouched quadrants for complete clast scrapers
(F = 2.49, d.f. = 2, 264, p = .085).

Assemblage	Number	Mean	Std. Deviation
Burkes Cave	88	1.99	.80
Nundooka	39	1.64	.78
Stud 2	140	1.87	.83

Table 5. Mean number of retouched quadrants for complete non-clast scrapers
(F = .6, d.f. = 2, 321, p = .552).

Assemblage	Number	Mean	Std. Deviation
Burkes Cave	59	2.03	.91
Nundooka	29	2.14	.74
Stud 2	236	1.97	.82

Among the three assemblages considered here, obvious differences exist in the proportions of tool forms manufactured from different raw materials (Tables 6-8). Much of the contrast seems to be between tool forms that imply long use lives (scrapers, thumbnail scrapers and tula slugs) versus those that were used and discarded more rapidly (utilised artefacts and notches). For instance, Burkes Cave has the greatest proportion of scrapers (48%) and the lowest proportion of utilised and notched tools on both types of silcrete and quartz among the three assemblages. The proportion of non-clast

silcrete scrapers at Nundooka and Stud 2 is broadly similar (33% and 34%), however there are proportionally more utilised tools at Stud 2 (33%) than at either Burkes Cave or Nundooka. The proportion of clast silcrete scrapers at Nundooka (53%) is much larger than that at Stud 2 (36%). Nundooka has the greatest proportion of non-clast silcrete tula slugs (24%), while the proportion of these is identical at Burkes Cave and Stud 2 (13%). The proportion of clast silcrete tula slugs is low in all assemblages, but is highest at Burkes Cave (3%). Tula are not represented in quartz and quartz tool proportions could not be assessed at Stud 2 because of the small number of quartz tools found (N=5). If all potentially long-life tools (at least compared to flakes) are combined (scrapers, thumbnail scrapers and tula slugs), Burkes Cave has the largest proportion of these artefacts (non-clast silcrete 67%, clast silcrete 72%, quartz 60%) followed by Nundooka (non-clast silcrete 61%, clast silcrete 57%, quartz 48%) and Stud 2 (non-clast silcrete 47%, clast silcrete 37%).

Some of the variability no doubt continues to reflect raw material access. The large proportion of scrapers at Burkes Cave for instance, compared to the other assemblages, may be indicative of maximising the potential of raw material stocks in the face of a greater distance to source. It is also significant that the greatest proportion of lightly retouched tools (Utilised) occurs at Stud 2 where raw material sources are most abundant. However, the overall similarity in the proportion of long use-life tools at Burkes and Nundooka is surprising, particularly given the large proportion of tula slugs at Nundooka compared to Burkes Cave and Stud 2. Silcrete raw material sources are relatively close at Nundooka yet the location shows the highest proportions of the tool form that is likely to have the longest use life. It might be expected that tula slugs would be more common at Burkes Cave, where there is a greater emphasis on raw material conservation since accessible raw material is at some distance. As noted above, what is of interest is the interplay between mobility and raw material distance.

Table 6. Clast silcrete tool type frequency and proportion (in brackets).

Tool Type	Burkes Cave	Nundooka	Stud 2
Backed Blade	9 (6.8)	5 (6.5)	27 (5.3)
Denticulate	9 (6.8)	6 (7.8)	66 (13)
Notch	4 (3)	4 (5.2)	74 (14.6)
Pirri		1 (1.3)	1 (0.2)
Scraper	88 (66.7)	40 (51.9)	183 (36)*
Thumbnail	3 (2.3)	2 (2.6)	
Tula Slug	4 (3)	1 (1.3)	5 (1)
Utilised	15 (11.4)	18 (23.4)	151 (29.8)
Total	132 (100)	77 (100)	507

*Thumbnail scrapers were not recorded as a separate type at Stud 2

Table 7. Non-clast silcrete tool type frequency and proportion (in brackets).

Tool Type	Burkes Cave	Nundooka	Stud 2
Backed Blade		1 (1.1)	29 (3.3)
Burin	1 (0.8)		
Burren Slug	2 (1.7)	1 (1.1)	5 (0.6)
Denticulate	2 (1.7)	6 (6.7)	60 (6.9)
Notch	7 (5.8)	7 (7.8)	84 (9.6)
Pirri		2 (2.2)	2 (0.2)
Scraper	59 (49.2)	30 (33.3)	295 (33.8)*
Thumbnail	7 (5.8)	4 (4.4)	
Tula Slug	15 (12.5)	21 (23.3)	114 (13.1)
Utilised	27 (19.2)	18 (20)	283 (32.5)
Total	120 (100)	90 (100)	872 (100)

*Thumbnail scrapers were not recorded as a separate type at Stud 2

Table 8. Quartz tool type frequency and proportion (in brackets).

Tool Type	Burkes Cave	Nundooka	Stud 2
Backed Blade	5 (10.6)	2 (3.3)	1 (20)
Denticulate	2 (4.3)	7 (11.5)	
Notch	3 (6.4)	3 (4.9)	1 (20)
Scraper	27 (57.4)	29 (47.5)	1 (20)
Thumbnail	1 (2.1)		
Utilised	9 (19.1)	20 (32.8)	2 (40)
Total	47 (100)	61 (100)	5 (100)

Discussion

In this paper we have focused on analysing the variability between three different assemblages that have similar arid rangeland settings, chronological contexts and conditions of access to raw material sources. Broadly, these assemblages might be expected to represent the deposits created by groups with similar mobility patterns. If this were so, similarities in assemblage composition should outweigh differences. However, despite some similarities there is also significant variation illustrated by a variety of assemblage composition measures perhaps suggesting that these three localities record regional variation in occupation duration and by inference, levels of mobility. Technological measures, the flake to core, non-cortical to cortical complete flake and non-cortical core to cortical cores ratio as well as the analysis of flake shape indicate that clast and non-clast silcrete core reduction is most intensive at Burkes Cave. In addition, analysis of scraper retouch indicates that although Burkes Cave scrapers are not consistently the most intensively retouched, they are relatively intensively retouched compared to all other scrapers except those manufactured from non-clast silcrete in the Nundooka assemblage. At least a portion of this variability can be accounted for by distance to raw material source. Of the three locations, Burkes Cave is located furthest from potential silcrete sources and the increased core reduction and production of scrapers may indicate an emphasis on maximising the potential of a non-local lithic resource.

Having said this, it must be admitted that the distances involved, at the most a few kilometres, pale into insignificance compared to ethnohistoric accounts of movement by Aboriginal people in the recent past (e.g. Myers 1986). Studies of the distribution of axes (e.g. McBryde 1984) indicate that some artefact types were moved over very long distances, however these are probably movements of artefacts through exchange rather than movements by individual people. By far the majority of stone artefacts in western NSW do not reflect very long distance movement by people at all. Thus despite the ethnographic accounts of movement, the archaeological record is made up of 'imported' and 'locally' available stone materials all of which are available in the immediate region. The influence of distance to source is still apparent, but as a product of relatively short lineal distances. Close (2000) makes the point that based on refit studies (which she argues do reflect the movement of people), the archaeological record from many locations primarily reflects movements measured in hundreds of meters rather than hundreds of kilometres. While some people probably did move very large distances across NSW and beyond in the past, the archaeological record they left behind primarily reflects movement over very much shorter distances.

Distance to source is clearly important but it forms only part of the story. There are other aspects of the Burkes Cave assemblage that fit rather less well with a simple distance to source model. Local raw materials are not

76

dominant at Burkes Cave, as might be expected if restricted access to distant high quality raw material sources forced a greater reliance on local sources. Imported silcretes, especially non-clast silcrete, are intensively worked, however locally available quartz and quartzite only account for approximately one third of the assemblage at Burkes Cave and quartz was not intensively reduced. Following suggestions by Elston (1990), who equates greater levels of local material reduction with longer duration occupations, these results may indicate that occupation lengths at Burkes Cave were always relatively short, not of sufficient duration to result in the intensive reduction of local raw materials.

At first glance, the intensity of core reduction at Burkes Cave appears to suggest that the location was occupied more often and for longer periods of time than either Nundooka or Stud 2. For instance, Burkes Cave consistently shows higher levels of core reduction than seen at the two other locations. However, consideration of core reduction within the context of the lithic resource base around Burkes Cave suggests that much of this difference may simply reflect distance to source. As discussed above, this result is not surprising. Similar models of raw material exploitation are well known from other parts of the arid zone (e.g., Hiscock 1986, O'Connell 1977) and as noted by Odell (1996), raw material conservation should be expected in many circumstances. Among the assemblages discussed here, the significance of the distance to source only becomes apparent when comparisons are made to the two other assemblages.

The Stud 2 assemblage is not as intensively worked as the assemblage from Burkes Cave, largely, we suggest, because Stud 2 exhibits different conditions of raw material access compared to Burkes Cave. Abundant high quality raw materials are situated within several hundred metres of Stud 2 and as a consequence, Stud 2 has the highest proportion of utilised artefacts and proportionally fewer flakes retouched into tools than either Burkes Cave or Nundooka. Clearly, in contrast to Burkes Cave, there was little need to maximise raw material reduction potential at Stud 2.

However, if the variability introduced by distance to raw material at Burkes Cave and Stud 2 is treated as a constant, and assemblage composition compared in ways that inform on the duration of occupation, the two assemblages appear much closer to each other in composition. The proportion of non-clast silcrete tula slugs, for instance, is identical in both assemblages and the difference in tool proportions reduces to the proportion of lightly retouched non-clast silcrete tool forms at Stud 2 (33%) that find their equivalent in the high proportion of the rarely resharpened scrapers at Burkes Cave (48%). A similar change is apparent for clast silcrete tools. The proportion of clast silcrete scrapers at Burkes Cave (67%) is close to the proportion of clast silcrete scrapers and Utilised pieces combined at

Stud 2 (66%). If tula slugs reflect long use-life histories, and therefore they have a low probability of discard because their use-life will often exceed occupation duration, Burkes Cave and Stud 2 may reflect similar occupation durations.

For large numbers of tula slugs to be discarded requires that either occupation span exceeds use-life or that occupation occurs often enough for the probability of discard to increase. Alternatively it is possible that the proportion of tula and other tool forms are not closely correlated. In the Boulia District of western Queensland, Hiscock (1988) identified a cache of tula adzes and blanks interpreted to represent a manufacturing sequence. He argued that only blanks with certain types of attributes were selected for manufacture into tula adzes and these blanks might be expected to have quite restricted sources. Based on this interpretation, it is possible that the tula discarded at the three locations considered here did not derive from flake populations manufactured locally, but were produced at other locations and on raw materials whose source is quite distant. In this situation, tula slugs would not necessarily vary in the same way as scrapers manufactured from raw materials closer to hand.

No matter what the explanation, Nundooka appears to have a more variable occupational history compared to either Burkes Cave or Stud 2. While differences in access to raw material sources can explain much of the variability in the intensity of core reduction between Burkes Cave and Stud 2, this is not true of Nundooka. At this location, raw materials are relatively abundant, however measures of the intensity of core reduction, and the production and resharpening of tools, do not indicate a simple pattern of increased reduction with distance to source. At Nundooka core reduction is the least intensive of the three assemblages yet the tools would imply relatively long duration occupations.

In addition, the chronology at Nundooka is significant since it may reflect a reduced occupation span relative to the other two locations (although as pointed out by a reviewer, we have no way at present to demonstrate this). Nundooka represents no more than 1000 years of occupation, while at both Burkes Cave and Stud 2 accumulation spans a maximum of 2000 years. While clearly these spans do not reflect the actual duration of individual occupations at these locations, it is not unreasonable to suggest that both the Stud 2 and Burkes Cave assemblages reflect individual occupations that sum to a greater total occupation duration than do the total of individual occupations at Nundooka. It is therefore possible that repeated, relatively short-term occupations at Burkes Cave and Stud 2 are combining to reduce the variability in these assemblages by effectively swamping the evidence for occasional occupations of longer duration. At Nundooka it may be that the larger proportion of long use-life tools represents longer duration occupations, but these longer duration occupations are not apparent in the level of core reduction. In effect, not enough occupation time has elapsed at Nundooka for all technological indices to revert to a pattern of increased flake, core and tool reduction with increasing distance from raw material source. Nundooka reflects more clearly the nature of variability introduced by other factors such as flexible levels of group size, mobility, and the span of time over which multiple visits are occurring.

Conclusion

The Burkes Cave, Nundooka and Stud 2 localities are clearly not part of a single settlement system. However, the broadly similar geographic setting of the three locations suggests that they can be expected to reflect a broadly similar range of resources. Controlling for chronology, access to potential raw material sources and landscape context provides the best opportunity to identify similarities and differences between the assemblages. Analysis indicates that while there are significant similarities in approaches to raw material reduction, there are just as many differences in the overall composition of the assemblages.

The major similarity between the assemblages is the consistent hierarchy of raw material reduction. Non-clast silcrete is the most intensively worked raw material followed by clast silcrete and quartz. This pattern is confirmed by several different measures of raw material utilisation intensity. However, variability in the degree of raw material reduction among the assemblages coupled with differences in the proportion of tools discarded suggests that the history of occupation at each of the locations was different.

The Burkes Cave assemblage is clearly the most intensively worked and we would argue that this reflects restricted access to silcrete sources rather than occupations whose duration was longer than those evidenced at either Stud 2 or Nundooka. Two factors support this interpretation. First, locally available quartz and quartzite is not intensively worked at Burkes Cave and neither raw material is dominant in the raw material proportions. Clearly occupation duration at Burkes Cave did not exceed the reduction potential of the silcrete imported to the site since the inhabitants did not make intensive use of local material. Second, tula slugs account for an identical proportion of complete tool types at both Burkes Cave and Stud 2. Therefore it is distance to raw material source, rather than differences in occupation duration that account for much of the distinction between Burkes Cave and Stud 2.

Nundooka has a different assemblage composition. Core reduction is least intensive at this location, yet there are proportionally more tools relative to flakes compared to the two other assemblages. Accepting that the total occupation span is different at Nundooka compared to Burkes Cave and Stud 2, Nundooka appears to retain a more historically variable record than the other two locations. Because less time has elapsed at Nundooka, the effect of distance to raw material source is less pronounced hence the technological measures discussed here paint a less uniform picture of assemblage variability.

If our results can be reproduced at other locations there are clear implications for the way settlement pattern analyses should be undertaken. Not only must contemporaneity be established but assemblages must also be subjected to a range of technical assessments in order to determine the occupational variability they record.

A number of years ago Gould (1980:225) suggested that Burkes Cave was one of the richest sites in the Australian arid zone. Re-analysis and comparison of Burkes Cave with other assemblages calls into question its status as a semi-permanent base camp and suggests that it shares many similarities with surface scatters located in comparable environmental situations. The formation processes responsible for the Burkes Cave artefact assemblage include the intensive use of preferred raw materials and artefact variability that reflects frequent but short duration visits. The reanalysis indicates that Burkes Cave, some 30 years after it was excavated, continues to have a part to play in changing the configuration of Australian arid zone archaeology.

Acknowledgements

Research at Stud Creek was funded by a Collaborative Australian Research Council (ARC) grant to SH and the NSW National Parks and Wildlife Service, a Small ARC Grant to SH and a Macquarie University Research Grant to PF. Research at Fowlers Gap was funded by an Australian Research Council (ARC) grant to SH and PF. A University of Auckland Graduate Research Fund Grant to JS funded the re-recording of the Burkes Cave assemblage. Permission to conduct the study at Stud Creek from the Wangkumara Cultural Heritage Management Committee (traditional owners), the Tibooburra Local Aboriginal Land Council and the NSW National Parks and Wildlife Service is gratefully acknowledged. Permission to conduct the study at Fowlers Gap from the Broken Hill Local Aboriginal Council, the University of New South Wales and the NSW National Parks and Wildlife Service is gratefully acknowledged. Thanks also to students from La Trobe, Macquarie and Auckland Universities for their valuable input of labour and to Leane Brass at the Australian Museum for facilitating access to the Burkes Cave assemblage. Finally thanks Joan Lawrence and Tim Mackrell for preparing Figure 1 and to the Edward's family of Broughton Vale Station for allowing us to revisit the Burkes Cave locality.

References

Allen, H. 1972 Where the Crow Flies Backwards: Man and Land in the Darling Basin. Unpublished PhD Thesis, The Australian National University, Canberra.

Barton, H. J. Mobilising Lithic Studies: An Application

of Evolutionary Ecology to Understand Prehistoric Patterns of Human Behaviour in the Simpson Desert, far western Queensland. Unpublished PhD thesis, Department of Archaeology, The University of Sydney.

Baulmer, M.F. 1988 Core reduction, flake production and the Middle Paleolithic industry of Zobište (Yugoslavia). In H.L. Dibble and A. Monet-White (eds) *Upper Pleistocene Prehistory of Western Eurasia*. Pp.255-274. University of Pennsylvania Museum, Philadelphia.

Bird, C.F..M., 1985 Prehistoric Lithic Resource Utilisation: A case study from the Southwest of Western Australia. Unpublished PhD thesis, Centre for Prehistory, The University of Western Australia.

Cane, S. 1984 Desert Camps. Unpublished PhD Thesis, The Australian National University, Canberra.

Clarkson, C. 2002 An index of invasiveness for the measurement of unifacial and bifacial retouch: a theoretical, experimental and archaeological verification. *Journal of Archaeological Science* 29: 65-75.

Close, A. 2000 Reconstructing movement in prehistory. *Journal of Archaeological Method and Theory* 7(1):49-77.

Dibble, H.L. 1984 Interpreting typological variation of Middle Paleolithic scrapers: function, style or sequence of reduction? *Journal of Field Archaeology* 11:431-436.

Dibble, H.L. 1987 The interpretation of Middle Palaeolithic scraper morphology. *American Antiquity* 52(1):109-117.

Dibble, H.L. 1995. Raw material availability, intensity of utilization, and Middle Paleolithic assemblage variability. In H. Dibble and M. Lenoir (eds) *The Middle Paleolithic Site of Combe-Capelle Bas (France)*. Pp.289-315. University of Pennsylvania Museum, Philadelphia.

Dibble, H.L. 1997 Platform variability and flake morphology: a comparison of experimental and archaeological data and implications for interpreting prehistoric lithic technological strategies. *Lithic Technology* 22: 150-170.

Dibble, H.L, Roth, B.J. and Lenoir, M. 1995 The use of raw materials at Combe-Capelle Bas. In H. Dibble and M. Lenoir (eds) *The Middle Palaeolithic Site of Combe Capelle Bas (France)*. Pp.259-287. University of Pennsylvania Museum, Philadelphia.

Doelman, T., Wedd. J And Domanksi. M. 2001 Source to discard: patterns of lithic raw material procurement and use in Sturt National Park, northwestern New South Wales. *Archaeology in Oceania* 36(1):15-33.

Elston, R.G. 1990 A cost-benefit model of lithic assemblage variability. In R. G. Elston and E. E. Budy (eds) *The Archaeology of James Creek Shelter*. Pp. 153-164. University of Utah Anthropological Papers 115, Salt Lake City.

Fanning, P.C. and Holdaway, S.J. 2001 Temporal limits to the archaeological record in arid Western NSW, Australia: lessons from OSL and radiocarbon dating

of hearths and sediments. In M. Jones and P. Sheppard (eds) *Australasian Connections and New Directions Proceedings of the 7th Archaeometry Conference.* Pp. 85-104. Department of Anthropology, The University of Auckland, Auckland.

Gould, R.A. 1980 *Living Archaeology*. Cambridge University Press, Cambridge.

Hiscock, P. 1986 Raw material rationing as an explanation of assemblage differences: a case study of Lawn Hill, northwest Queensland. In G.K. Ward (ed.) *Archaeology at ANZAAS, Canberra: a collection of papers presented to Section 25A of the 54th Congress of the Australian and New Zealand Association for the Advancement of Science in May 1984*. Pp.178-190. Canberra Archaeological Society, Canberra.

Hiscock, P. 1988 A cache of tulas from the Boulia district, western Queensland. *Archaeology in Oceania* 23:60-70.

Hiscock, P. 1996 Mobility and technology in the Kakadu coastal wetlands. *Indo-Pacific Prehistory Association Bulletin* 15:151-57.

Hiscock, P. 2002 Quantifying the size of artefact assemblages. *Journal of Archaeological Science* 29:251-58.

Holdaway, S.J., Fanning, P.C. and Witter, D.C. 2000 Prehistoric Aboriginal occupation of the rangelands: interpreting the surface archaeological record of far western New South Wales, Australia. *Rangelands Journal* 22(1):44-57.

Holdaway, S.J., Fanning, P.C., Jones, M., Shiner, J., Witter, D.C. and JONES, M. 2002 Variability in the chronology of late Holocene Aboriginal occupation on the arid margin of southeastern Australia. *Journal of Archaeological Science* 29:351-363.

Holdaway, S. and Stern. N. In Press. *Written in Stone: Decoding the Australian Flaked Stone Record.* Canberra: Australian Institute of Aboriginal and Torres Studies.

Jansen, J.D. 2001 Bedrock Channel Morphodynamics and Landscape Evolution in an Arid Zone Gorge: Sandy Creek Gorge, northern Barrier Range, south-eastern Central Australia. Unpublished PhD Thesis, Macquarie University, Sydney.

Kuhn, S. 1995 *Mousterian Lithic Technology: An Ecological Perspective*. Princeton University Press, Princeton.

McBryde, I., 1984 Kulin greenstone quarries: the social contexts of production and distribution for the Mt William site. *World Archaeology* 16(2):267-85.

Myers, F. R., 1986. *Pintupi Country: Pintupi Self: Sentiment, Place and Politics among Western Desert Aborigines*. Canberra: Australian Institute of Aboriginal Studies.

O'Connell, J.F. 1977 Aspects of variation in central Australian lithic assemblages. In R.V.S. Wright (ed) *Stone Tools As Cultural Markers: Change, Evolution and Complexity*. Pp.269-281. Australian Institute of Aboriginal Studies, Canberra.

Odell, G.H. 1996 Economizing behavior and the concept

of 'curation'. In G.H. Odell (ed) *Stone Tools: Theoretical Insights into Human Prehistory*. Pp.51-80. Plenum Press, New York.

Pelcin, A. 1997 The effect of core surface morphology on flake attributes: evidence from a controlled experiment. *Journal of Archaeological Science* 24:749-756.

Ross, A. 1981 Holocene environments and prehistoric site patterning in the Victorian Mallee. *Archaeology in Oceania* 16:145-154.

Roth, B.J. and Dibble, H.L. 1998 Production and transport of blanks and tools at the French Middle Paleolithic site of Combe-Capelle Bas. *American Antiquity* 63:47-62.

Shott, M. J. 1997 Activity and formation as sources of variation in Great Lakes Paleoindian assemblages. *Midcontinental Journal of Archaeology* 22(2):197-236.

Shott, M. J. 2000 The quantification problem in stone-tool assemblages. *American Antiquity* 64(4):725-38,

Shott, M.J. 2003 Size as a Factor in Old World Middle Palaeolithic Assemblage Variation: A North American Perspective. In N. Moloney and M. Shott (eds) *Lithic Analysis at the Millennium*. Pp 137-149. Archtype, London.

Smith, M.A. 1989 The case for a resident human population in the Central Australian Ranges during full glacial aridity. *Archaeology in Oceania* 24(3):93-105.

Smith, M.A. 1996 Prehistory and human ecology in central Australia: an archaeological perspective. In S. R. Morton and D. J. Mulvaney (eds) *Exploring Central Australia: Society, the Environment and the 1894 Horn Expedition*. Pp. 61-73. Surrey Beatty and Sons, Chipping Norton.

Thorley, P. 1998 Shifting location, shifting scale: a regional landscape approach to the prehistoric archaeology of the Palmer River catchment, central Australia. Unpublished PhD Thesis, Anthropology, School of Southeast Asian and Australian Studies, Northern Territory University.

Torrence, R. 1989 Retooling: towards a behavioural theory of stone tools. In R. Torrence (ed.) *Time, Energy and Stone Tools*. Pp.57-66. Cambridge: Cambridge University Press.

Veth, P. 1989 Islands in the interior: a model for the colonisation of the arid zone of Australia. *Archaeology in Oceania* 24(3):81-92.

Veth, P. 1993 *Islands in the Interior: The Dynamics of Prehistoric Adaptations within the Arid Zone of Australia*. International Monographs in Prehistory, Archaeological Series 3, Ann Arbor.

Stone Artefact Reduction, Mobility and Arid Zone Settlement Models: A Case Study from Puritjarra Rockshelter, Central Australia

8

W. Boone Law

Abstract
This paper presents the results of two techniques used to measure the amount of reduction incurred on a population of retouched flakes from Puritjarra rockshelter. The data indicates a change in the reduction of retouched flakes that begins during the mid-Holocene and continues throughout the late Holocene. This increase is most pronounced for retouched flakes manufactured from non-local raw materials. It has been suggested by some archaeologists that the intensity of stone artefact reduction is a key indicator of residential mobility (Bamforth 1986, 1991, Bamforth and Bleed 1997, Binford 1979, 1980, Bleed 1986, Kelly 1992, Kuhn 1995, Shott 1986, Torrence 1983, 1989). In central Australia, there is still much debate centring on the level of mobility exhibited by mid-late Holocene resident populations. Past and present models of Holocene residential mobility are reviewed and the implications of the observed Puritjarra reduction patterns are discussed.

Introduction

The archaeological study of Australia's arid regions has been important in building an understanding of Australian prehistory. The Australian arid zone encompasses nearly 70% of the continent and is considered by many to include some of the most inhospitable environments on earth. Humans entered this region some 32,000 years ago and over a long period have been able to reorganise their settlement patterns to adapt to fluctuations in climatic conditions (eg.; Hiscock 1994, Smith 1988, 1996, Thorley 1998a, 1998b, 2001, Veth 1989, 1993). Investigating how, when and where these adjustments took place is a crucial step in understanding the long term settlement of the Australian arid zone.

Residential mobility has been a key feature of most models put forward to explain chronological and spatial variations in arid region settlement. Information from stone artefact assemblages has largely been used to support these models, including conventional artefact typology, artefact densities (#/vol. or #/kg.), and artefact discard rates (#/kya). While this sort of information is useful for investigating broad archaeological patterns in the arid zone, it has been pointed out by Hiscock (1986) that these measures do not clearly assess greater or lesser residential mobility. For example, chronological increases of artefact densities or artefact discard rates may be measuring changing patterns of artefact reduction rather than population increases or increased sedentism (Hiscock 1986). Resolving this problem requires that we develop both theory and techniques that allow us to measure residential mobility using a combination of variables. In this paper, two techniques will be used to measure the intensity of retouched flake reduction at Puritjarra, a large rockshelter in the centre of Australia (Figure 1). The results of this analysis suggest that exploring retouch intensity provides a useful way of detecting chronological changes in residential mobility.

Models of Arid Zone Settlement and Subsistence During the Holocene

Over the last few decades, arid zone researchers have proposed several settlement and subsistence models based on archaeological and ethnographic evidence to explain Holocene archaeological patterns. Mobility—or the range, frequency and nature of residential moves—has featured prominently in all of these models. Gould (1978:93), for example, argued that desert Aborigines demonstrate "perhaps the greatest amount of nomadism reported for any known hunting-and-gathering society in the world (Gould 1977:170)." Coupled with his archaeological investigations, Gould's extensive ethnographic work in central Australia also led him to the conclusion that Australia's contemporary desert populations are likely representative of an unchanging desert culture that has survived for the past 10,000 years. The only technological change he acknowledges during this sequence is the emergence of a suite of composite stone tools including unifacial points, backed artefacts, and tulas (Figure 2). Gould (1969, 1977, 1978) conceded that the "sudden appearance" of these stone tool types in the mid-Holocene marks the introduction of a new "small tool tradition" beginning around 4000BP. Although Gould (1969, 1977, 1978) effectively demonstrated this technological change at several arid zone sites, he argued that the change was associated only with the use of new maintenance tools "which cannot be linked directly to the food quest or other aspects of prehistoric procurement" (Gould 1977:170).

Gould's (1977, 1978) model of an unchanging Australian desert culture is hard to assimilate with the long, dynamic record of climate change in the region (c.32,000 B.P.). For instance, recent climatic research by Lambeck and Chappell (2001) suggests that the hyperarid conditions that peaked during the last glacial maximum (LGM) 16,000-20,000 years ago may have initially begun to impact the arid region by 30,000 B.P. Starting around 13,000-14,000 years ago, the climatic record suggests conditions warmed and became moister than present day

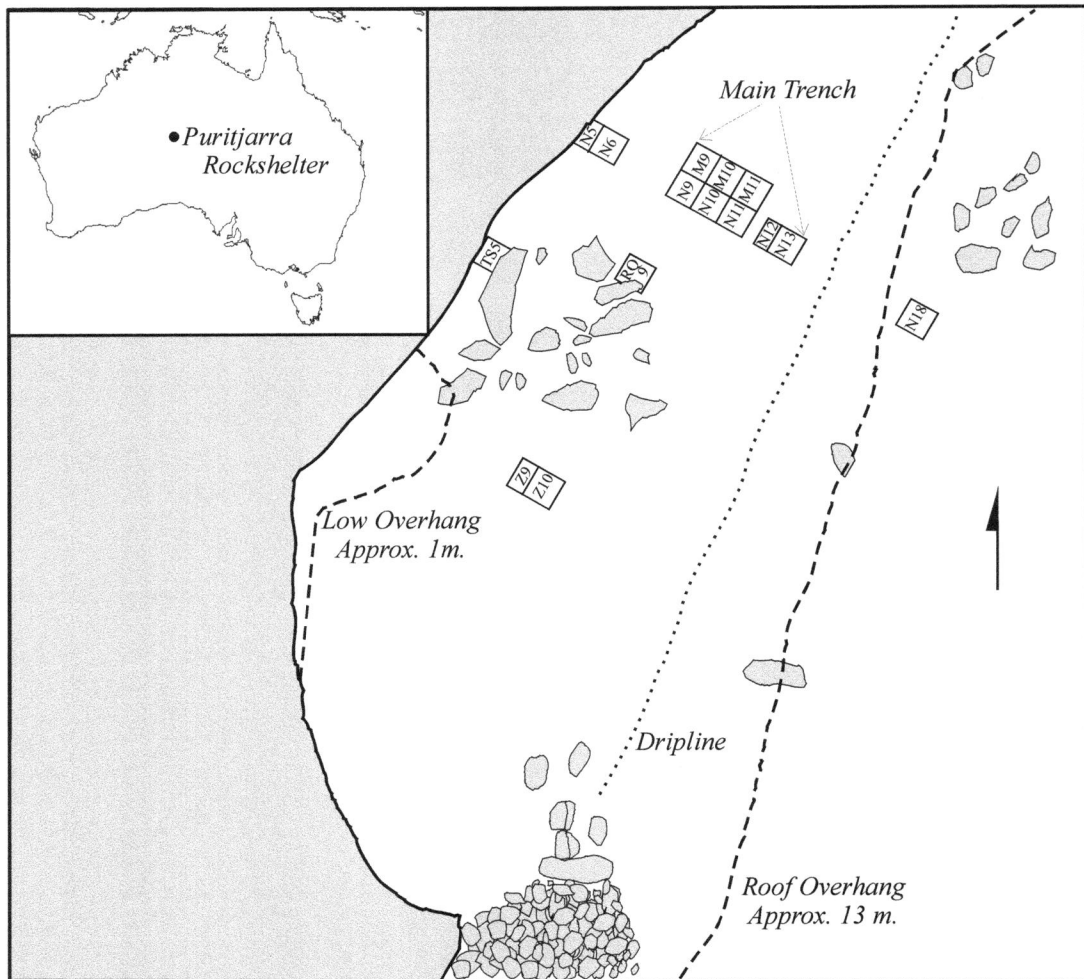

Figure 1. Location and site plan of Puritjarra rockshelter.
Adapted from Smith (1988, Smith et al. 1997) and Bowdery (1998).

and this trend is believed to have continued throughout the early Holocene until at least 7,000 B.P. (Kershaw 1995, McCarthy and Head 2002, Wyrwoll and Miller 2001). The mid-Holocene (7,000-3,500 B.P.), on the other hand, shows a climatic pattern that is characterised by an extensive period of decreased and unpredictable rainfall patterns beginning sometime between 6-4kya (Cupper 2002, Cupper *et.al.* 2000, Dimitriadis and Cranston 2001, Hiscock and Kershaw 1992, McCarthy and Head 2002). Many palaeoclimatic models indicate that this dry period persisted in parts of the arid zone (Cupper 2002, Cupper *et.al.* 2000, McCarthy and Head 2002) until 2-1kya when climatic conditions begin to ameliorate. The final 1,500 years of the late Holocene is believed to have experienced a significant improvement in rainfall patterns (Cupper 2002, McCarthy and Head 2002) and is most similar to that of the present-day arid region climate.

Contrary to Gould's model, Veth (1989, 1993, 2000) argues that there are changes in the residential mobility of Holocene desert populations and that these are largely timed around climatic changes. For instance, Veth (1993) contends that a mid-Holocene territorial expansion into the arid zone takes place shortly after c.5,000 B.P. He proposes that the advent of developed social networks and some key arid zone adapted artefact technologies (ie. seed grinding implements, backed artefacts, and tulas) allowed mid-Holocene populations to expand into previously unoccupied regions. Veth (1993:95) also suggests that residential mobility of prehistoric populations was governed by the availability of permanent water sources, so that archaeological sites with the greatest artefact densities and frequencies of retouched flakes should be located near permanent waters.

Thorley (1998b, 2001) presents a model of late Holocene desert resource use for the Palmer River catchment, a region located east of Puritjarra rockshelter in the central Australian ranges. Thorley's (2001) research demonstrates that late Holocene stone artefact assemblages located at sites near ephemeral water sources have much greater artefact densities than those closer to

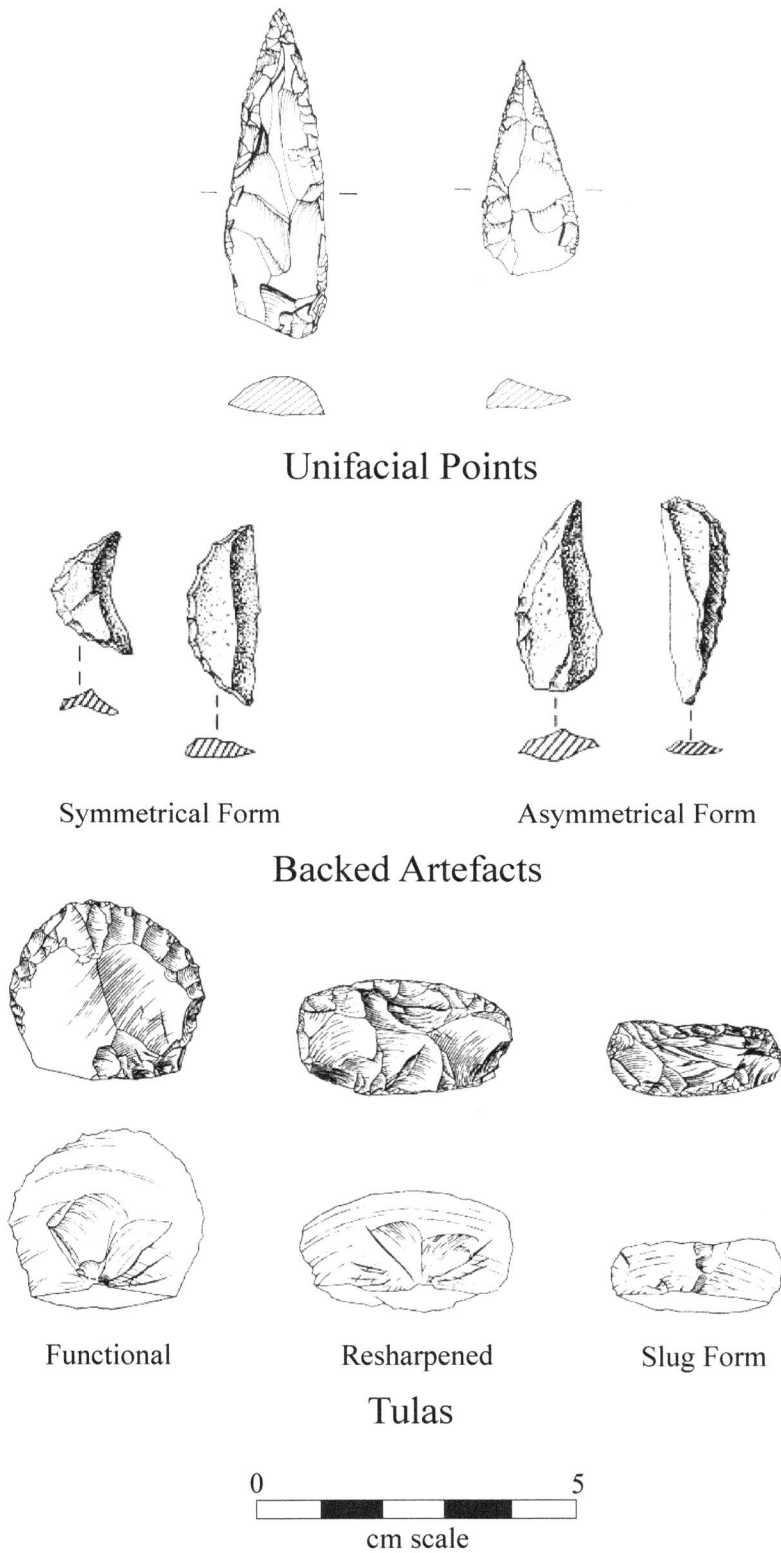

Figure 2. Conventional types of the "small tool tradition" from Australia's arid zone. Unifacial points (after White and O'Connell 1982: Fig.5.6), backed artefacts (after Gould 1977: Figs.59-60), and tulas (after Mulvaney 1969: Fig.23).

permanent waters. Instead of resident populations concentrating their food gathering activities around permanent waterholes, Thorley (2001) suggests that late Holocene populations exercised a "risk minimisation" settlement system. Instead of relying on the resources surrounding permanent waters, desert groups took full advantage of the temporary sites and resources located near ephemeral waters. In doing so, populations conserved the more permanent water related resources for the more stressful, drier climatic periods. This settlement system effectively reduced the risk of exhausting resources near permanent waters and enhanced the probability of group survival. Since improved rainfall patterns widened the available foraging area, group mobility potentially increased. If Thorley's model is correct, we can expect there to be a large number of late Holocene archaeological sites around both ephemeral and permanent waters.

Hiscock (1994) offers another interpretation of arid zone prehistoric subsistence activities in terms of a "risk reduction" model that places special emphasis on the role of stone technologies. Hiscock (1994) argues that mid-Holocene populations experienced climatic stresses that would have caused many resource restrictions. Consequently, new problem solving strategies would be required to overcome these stresses. Hiscock (1994) proposes that the specialised, curated technologies that emerge during the mid-Holocene (e.g. backed artefacts, points, and tulas) were part of a portable, multifunctional, and maintainable mobile tool kit. He adds that the greatest advantage of these artefact forms came from their performance as reliable composite tools that effectively reduced the risk of foraging failure during a climatically stressful period.

Smith (1988, 1996) acknowledges a mid-Holocene archaeological sequence similar to Gould (1977, 1978), Veth (1993), and Hiscock (1994), but argues that the most striking change that occurs in the arid zone archaeological record happens in the late Holocene around the time climatic conditions begin to improve. Across the arid zone, Smith (1988, 1996) reports that after 1,500B.P there is an increased intensity of site use as reflected in the "greatly increased artefact densities of chipped stone artefacts, grindstones, charcoal, bone, and other types of occupation debris after this date". Smith (1996) argues that these patterns mark a "late Holocene intensification" of human occupation in the arid region. Smith (1988, 1996) uses a number of temporal trends in stone artefact production to support his late-Holocene intensification model. For instance, Smith (1988:131) documents a steady increase in artefact densities, discard rates, and core reduction throughout the Holocene sequence. All of these trends are argued to have changed and peaked during the last 1,000 years, which Smith (1996 68) believes to demonstrate "the residue of a substantial and probably more sedentary population."

Presently, there are several settlement and subsistence

models proposed for the Holocene archaeological record of the arid zone where residential mobility has been attributed to the formation of stone artefact assemblages. For the most part, however, the composition of stone artefact assemblages have tended to be under-utilised in testing these models, and when changes in assemblage variation are invoked, inferences tend to be overly simplistic. Archaeologists working in the arid zone must therefore develop a more sophisticated theoretical basis from which to interpret patterning in stone artefact assemblages. Only then can robust reconstructions of residential mobility be established.

Residential Mobility and Provisioning Strategies

Residential mobility refers to the frequent or infrequent rate that hunter-gatherers relocated their resident base camps (Binford 1980). Residential mobility ranges from low to high, and is often argued to affect the composition of stone artefact assemblages as well as the intensity of reduction incurred upon individual artefacts in predictable ways. Kuhn's (1995) recent provisioning model provides one of the most coherent formulations of the effect that residential mobility may have on assemblage composition, toolkit design, and reduction intensity. His model cross-cuts the concepts of curated and expedient technologies and integrates many previous studies of technological organisation (e.g.; Bamforth 1986, 1991, Binford 1979, 1980, Bleed 1986, Kelly 1992, Kelly 1995, Nelson 1991, Shott 1986, Torrence 1983,1989).

According to Kuhn (1995:22), provisioning refers to the "depth of planning in artefact production, transport, maintenance, and the strategies by which potential needs are met." Kuhn contends it is most unlikely that any prehistoric group relied solely upon unplanned artefact technologies because resources are rarely ubiquitous across a landscape and all human technologies incorporate a planned component to insure that stone tools or raw materials are available for future needs. Even on-the-spot expedient stone tool manufacture is intertwined with some level of future planning. For instance, the choice to conserve a limited, non-local raw material or a specialised stone tool may in some instances underlie the seemingly "expedient" use of a locally derived material of low-quality. Thus, the use of expedient tools may be part of a larger plan to conserve limited resources or items for future needs.

Kuhn (1995) describes two strategies that may be employed in the design of stone artefact technologies; They are the *provisioning of individuals* and the *provisioning of places*. Kuhn terms the strategy of transporting materials in anticipation of potential future need as the *provisioning of individuals* (Kuhn 1995:22). In this strategy it is assumed that there are limits tp the number and size of tools, spare artefacts, and raw materials mobile individuals can effectively carry. Consequently, mobile individuals will carry a portable tool kit that includes stone tools that can be maintained and reworked to increase their multifunctionality (Bleed

1986; Shott 1986). The components of a portable tool kit are expected to have extensive "use-lives" and should exhibit evidence of successive reduction (Dibble 1995; Hiscock and Attenbrow 2003). Greater mobility is also often correlated with greater uncertainty over opportunities to reprovision with raw materials. Hence mobile foragers may also tend to make use of higher quality raw materials that will increase the performance and reliability of their toolkits (Goodyear 1989; Bleed 1986). Also, since mobility sets limits on what people can carry, individuals likely employed strategies to conserve their "mobile gear" by utilizing the immediate resources encountered on their journeys (Kelly 1988; Kuhn 1989, 1995). These resources may include local raw materials suitable for manufacture of expedient tools or the scavenging and rejuvenation of previously discarded artefacts made from higher quality raw materials.

The *provisioning of places* is a strategy that copes with the anticipated requirements of stone tools by stocking those places where stone tools are likely to be needed with the appropriate raw materials, artefacts, or implements (Kuhn 1995:22). Assemblages formed by this planning strategy are characterised by their toolmaking potential (Kuhn 1995). Large cores, large flakes, and unmodified non-local raw materials are examples of goods that may be stock-piled with excellent toolmaking potential. Smaller, previously shaped artefacts and artefacts made of lower quality raw materials are potentially less versatile and lack the reduction potential of large cores and flakes of high quality raw material. Also, smaller artefacts or heavily reduced raw materials are less able to accommodate or satisfy technological needs. Kuhn (1995:24) states:

> Tactics for extending the utility of tools—resharpening and situational reworking—would be less important in a situation where many functionally redundant implements or large quantities of raw material can be kept at hand. Comparatively frequent discard and replacement of worn or broken tools, and relatively little reuse or resharpening, can thus be expected to characterize the strategy of provisioning places.

Since stone artefact assemblages are formed from the discard of planned stone artefact technologies, assemblages will manifest different characteristics of provisioning strategies. Determining which provisioning strategy had greater influence on the formation of a stone artefact assemblage can help archaeologists reconstruct patterns of residential mobility. Kuhn (1995:25) argues that the more frequently people move their residential locus, the more they must depend on strategies of provisioning individuals. Conversely, more sedentary populations will need to employ a strategy of provisioning places where suitable quantities of raw materials can be stock-piled to meet their potential technological needs. The daunting task of the archaeologist is to determine which of these strategies best characterises a stone artefact assemblage and how they may be unambiguously separated.

Measuring Intensity of Retouched Flake Reduction

One way that it may be possible to distinguish the different provisioning strategies that formed a stone artefact assemblage is by measuring the intensity of retouched flake reduction. The tactic of flake retouching extends the use-life of stone tools and allows for a greater reliance on transported items. Increases in non-local retouched flake reduction may indicate an increasing dependence on transported artefacts which, in turn, suggests an increased focus on the strategy of provisioning individuals.

A retouched flake is created by a single or combination of successive reduction processes which may be staged or continuous in nature (Bleed 2002). For example, a retouched flake may be reduced by continuous utilisation and maintenance activities or it may be specifically reduced in a single step to meet an intended functional purpose. Whatever the case, the reduction incurred by a retouched flake is visible by the negative scars along the retouched flake margins. The resulting size, number or nature of these flake scars can be used to effectively measure the intensity of reduction incurred on the artefact specimen before discard (Barton 1988, Clarkson 2002, Hiscock and Attenbrow 2003, Kuhn 1995).

This paper employs two techniques to accurately measure retouched flake reduction at Puritjarra rockshelter. These methods have successfully been applied to the majority of the retouched flake assemblage, including backed artefacts, tulas and the comparatively more abundant non-formal retouched implements. It is argued that the results of these measurements can be used in conjunction with a suite of other assemblage variables to reliably differentiate between the provisioning strategies that formed the Puritjarra stone artefact assemblage.

A Geometric Index of Unifacial Reduction

The first technique that is used to measure retouched flake reduction at Puritjarra is Kuhn's (1990) Geometric Index of Unifacial Reduction (GIUR). As the name suggests, the measure is exclusive to unifacial, dorsally retouched flakes. The GIUR calculates the amount of reduction incurred on the dorsal surface of a retouched flake from its lateral margins. Hiscock and Clarkson (this volume) have demonstrated the robustness of this technique as a measure of flake reduction. The measure assumes that flakes, in general, are triangular shaped in cross-section (Figure 3). The thickness of the flake (T) is measured perpendicular from the ventral surface to the dorsal ridge. An additional measure of retouch scar thickness (t) is measured perpendicular from the ventral surface to the termination of retouch scar. The formula t/T calculates a result between 0 and 1. This scale represents the intensity of reduction that has been incurred from the lateral margin to the thickest (usually midline) of the flake. For example, a GIUR result such as 0.12 indicates very little reduction while a GIUR result of 0.86 suggests intensive reduction from the point of retouch.

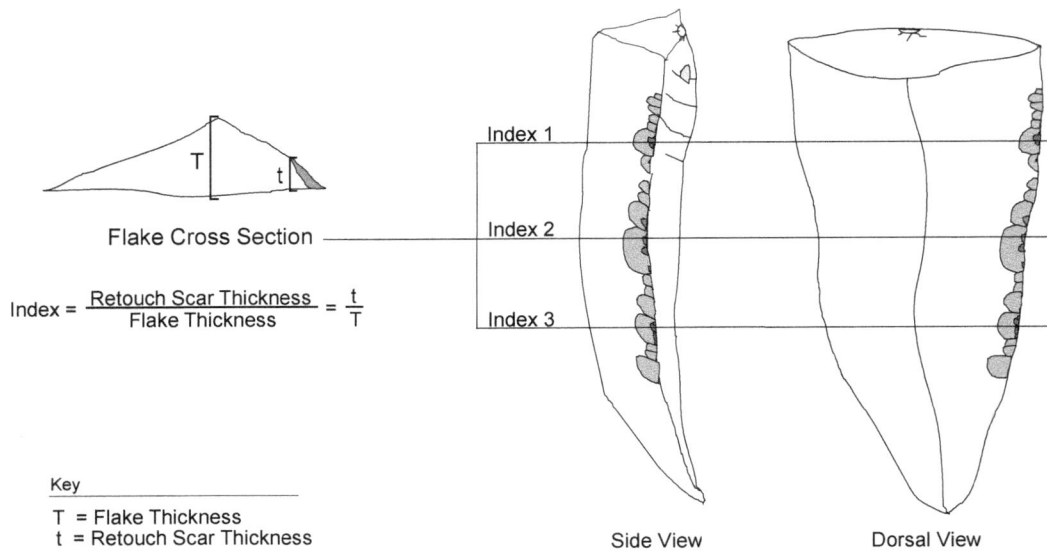

Figure 3. An illustration of the retouched flake attributes measured for Kuhn's (1990) Geometric Index of Unifacial Reduction (GIUR). The geometrical index is based on a triangular flake cross section. The index is calculated by dividing the retouch scar thickness (t) by the flake thickness (T) resulting in a score between 0.00 and 1.00.

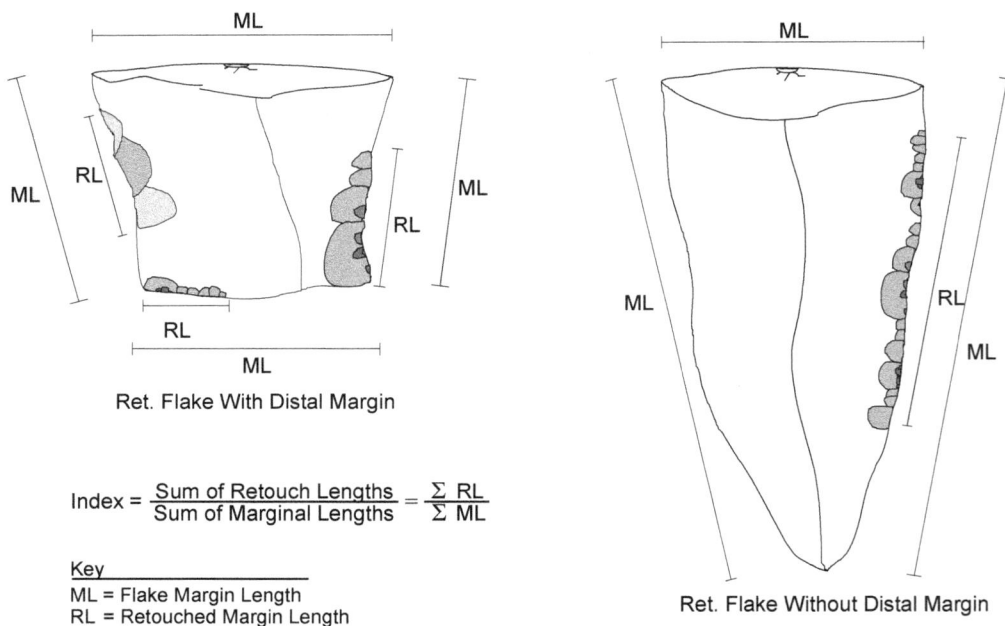

Figure 4. Two examples of the retouched flake attributes measured for the Perimeter Reduction Index (PRI). The PRI is calculated by dividing the sum of the perimeter retouch lengths (RL) by the sum of the flake margin lengths (ML) resulting in a score between 0.00 and 1.00.

As Kuhn points out, this measurement is not suitable for all retouched flakes. To prevent generating erroneous results the following criteria are therefore considered for each retouched flake specimen:

1. The specimen must be unifacially retouched onto the dorsal surface from a lateral margin.
2. The dorsal ridge must be located near the flake midline.
3. The dorsal surface lacks features that may interfere with measurement (ie. multiple dorsal ridges, cortex, or overhang removal scars).
4. The ventral surface lacks an unusually large bulb of percussion.
5. For best results, an average index should be calculated from three locations along the retouched margin.

Unfortunately, the GIUR cannot calculate unifacial reduction directed from the distal margin of a retouched flake. Retouched flake geometry prevents an accurate measure of distal reduction. It is possible, however, to consider reduction along the distal margin by utilising the Perimeter Reduction Index.

A Perimeter Reduction Index
The Perimeter Reduction Index (PRI) calculates the proportion of retouch that has occurred along the edge of the retouched flake. The measure is similar to that used by Barton (1988). The PRI is measured by dividing the total sum of the retouched margin lengths (RL) by the total sum of margin lengths (ML) (Figure 4). The formula $\Sigma RL / \Sigma ML$ therefore calculates the proportion of flake perimeter that has been modified.

The PRI assumes two forms of retouched flakes—a four-margin retouched flake and a three-margin retouched flake. A retouched flake with four margins has one proximal margin, two lateral margins, and one prominent distal margin. The three-margin retouched flake has one proximal margin and two lateral margins. The main difference between the two forms concerns the measurement of the distal margin. If the distal margin is pronounced, or near perpendicular to the lateral margins, four marginal measurements are used to calculate the PRI. However, if the lateral margins converge at the flake termination, only three measurements are required. Figure 4 illustrates the difference between these two retouched flake forms.

Like the GIUR, the results represent an approximate score of perimeter reduction that also ranges between 0 and 1. A PRI index of 0.15 suggests little perimeter reduction while a PRI index of 0.91 indicates considerable perimeter reduction. The PRI can be used on unifacial or bifacial retouched flakes. The only criteria for appropriate use of the index is that the retouched flake must be complete.

The GIUR and PRI measure different kinds of flake reduction. The GIUR measures the intensity of lateral margin reduction from the point of retouch. The PRI measures the proportion of the retouched flake margins that have been reduced. Because both measures differ greatly in the kind of reduction they measure, an interpretation of the two measurements together provides the best approximation of overall retouched flake reduction.

Results
The results of the GIUR are PRI analysis are presented below using a system of raw material classes and a series of broad temporal units employed by Smith for Puritjarra rockshelter (1988, Smith *et.al.* 1997). Smith's analytical units represent blocks of time that roughly coincide with the terminal Pleistocene (Unit 2a) as well as the early (Unit 1c), middle (Unit 1b), and late Holocene (Unit 1a) levels of the site. Unit 2a is estimated to begin shortly after the last glacial maximum (18,000 B.P) and to terminate around 7,500 years ago (Smith *et.al.*1997, 2001). Unit 1c spans the early Holocene period from

7,500 to 3,500 B.P, while Unit 1b relates to mid-Holocene between 3,500-800 B.P. The late Holocene Unit 1a is estimated to be no older than the last 800 years.

Retouched flakes are grouped into three raw material classes—local, intermediate, and distant. These classes indicate the approximate distances over which raw materials have been transported to Puritjarra. Local raw materials can be procured immediately within and around the rockshelter and are composed primarily of silicified sandstone. Intermediate raw materials consist of silcrete and quartzite and can be obtained at a distance of less than 30km from the site. Distant raw materials are cryptocrystalline cherts that derive at sources more than 30km from the site.

In total, 431 retouched flakes were recovered from the Puritjarra excavations. Of these, 288 are complete specimens. The GIUR and PRI were measured only on the 288 unbroken retouched flakes to avoid problems associated with broken retouched flake specimens. The GIUR was measured in 130 instances on 101 retouched flakes that exhibited the appropriate range of criteria (see above) to accurately calculate the GIUR. 29 of these retouched flake specimens are unifacially reduced on both lateral margins, and these specimens yielded two GIUR results accordingly. Since the accuracy of the PRI is only limited by retouched flake breakage, all complete retouched flake specimens were eligible for measurements (*n*=288).

Table 1 lists the overall GIUR and PRI results by analytical unit. Results that are highlighted and in bold indicate a significant chronological change in reduction. Only the GIUR data returned significant results at the .05 level. Student's *t*-test scores indicate a significant increase in the intensity of retouched flake reduction that begins in analytical unit 1b and this higher level of reduction is sustained in analytical unit 1a. The PRI shows no broad scale chronological changes in the overall intensity of retouched flake reduction.

Tables 2 and 3 summarise the GIUR and PRI results by analytical unit and raw material origin. These results show that there is a considerable difference in the treatment of retouched flakes manufactured from non-local raw materials. Retouched flakes made from raw materials of intermediate and distant origin are significantly more reduced than those made from locally procured materials (GIUR *t*-tests—local vs intermediate t=-3.68, df=89, p=.000, local vs distant t=-4.59, df=93, p=.000; PRI *t*-tests—local vs intermediate t=3.52, df=188, p=.000, local vs distant t=3.74, df=226, p=.000). However, this pattern is not consistent chronologically. The GIUR results in Table 2 show that retouched flakes from intermediate and distant raw material origins are more reduced than local retouched flakes, but only for the past 3,500 years. Student's *t*-test results comparing raw material classes also support this observation (see Table 2).

Table 1: Geometric Index of Unifacial Reduction (GIUR) and Perimeter Reduction Index (PRI), Puritjarra rockshelter. Summary statistics* by analytical unit.

Analytical Unit	GIUR				PRI			
	Mean	Median	sd	n	Mean	Median	sd	n
1a (0.8-0.0kya)	**.42**	**.39**	**.18**	**55**	.41	.41	.21	132
1b (3.5-0.8kya)	**.50**	**.50**	**.27**	**43**	.37	.38	.21	87
1c (7.5-3.5kya)	.39	.39	.14	15	.37	.34	.18	29
2a (18-7.5kya)	.32	.28	.16	17	.36	.37	.17	40
Summary Stats	.43	.40	.21	130	.39	.38	.20	288

*Statistically significant results highlighted. Significant t-test results (95% Confidence):
GIUR Analytical Unit 2a:Analytical Unit 1b t=2.54, df=70, p=.014, significant.
GIUR Analytical Unit 2a:Analytical Unit 1a t=1.99, df=58, p=.049, significant.

Table 2: Geometric Index of Unifacial Reduction (GIUR) results.
Summary statistics* by analytical unit and raw material class, Puritjarra rockshelter.

Analytical Unit	Raw Material Class											
	Local Origin				Intermediate Origin				Distant Origin			
	Mean	Median	sd	n	Mean	Median	sd	n	Mean	Median	sd	n
1a (0.0-0.8kya)	.34	.35	.11	19	**.46**	**.44**	**.20**	**18**	**.46**	**.43**	**.21**	**18**
1b (0.8-3.5kya)	.28	.21	.14	9	**.51**	**.54**	**.28**	**16**	**.60**	**.67**	**.25**	**18**
1c (3.5-7.5kya)	.40	.39	.15	11	.47	.47	.	1	.32	.31	.12	3
2a (7.5-18.0kya)	.32	.28	.16	17	.	.	.	.	.	.	.	.
Summary Stats	.34	.34	.14	56	.48	.48	.23	35	.51	.50	.24	39

*Statistically significant results highlighted. Significant t-test results (95% Confidence):
Analytical Unit 1a; local:intermediate t=-2.23, df=35, p=.032; local:distant t=-2.22, df=35, p=.033.
Analytical Unit 1b; local:intermediate t=-2.24, df=23, p=.035; local:distant t=-3.51, df=25, p=.002.

Table 3. Perimeter Reduction Index (PRI) results.
Summary statistics* by analytical unit and raw material class, Puritjarra rockshelter.

Analytical Unit	Raw Material Class											
	Local Origin				Intermediate Origin				Distant Origin			
	Mean	Median	sd	n	Mean	Median	sd	n	Mean	Median	sd	n
1a (0.0-0.8kya)	.33	.32	.18	47	**.49**	**.50**	**.23**	**35**	**.43**	**.45**	**.18**	**50**
1b (0.8-3.5kya)	.31	.28	.22	26	.40	.38	.23	24	.41	.42	.19	37
1c (3.5-7.5kya)	.38	.34	.19	20	.17	.17	.	1	.37	.38	.16	8
2a (7.5-18.0kya)	.36	.34	.16	36	.05	.05	.	1	.55	.60	.11	3
Summary Stats	.34	.31	.18	129	.44	.42	.24	61	.42	.43	.18	98

*Statistically significant results highlighted. Significant t-test
Analytical Unit 1a; local:intermediate t=3.53, df=80, p=.000; local:distant t=2.73, df=95, p=.008.

The PRI reports a similar pattern for only the last 800 years of occupation. Retouched flakes made of intermediate and distant raw materials are significantly more reduced around the perimeter than the local retouched flakes from this period. Student's t-tests confirm that this pattern is statistically significant (see Table 3). A combined interpretation of the specific PRI and GIUR data suggest an increased overall intensity of reduction for non-local derived retouched flakes during the last 800 years, but not for local raw materials. This trend can be observed by the error bar plots (95% confidence interval) in Figure 5.

An issue of concern for these results is whether the increased reduction of non-local retouched flakes simply reflects the advent of the new technologies such as backing and tula manufacture in the mid-Holocene. While backed artefacts and tulas compose only a small portion (<10%) of the total retouched flake assemblage, their manufacture nevertheless typically involves a considerable degree of retouching. Furthermore, at Puritjarra these forms appear around 3,500B.P. and are almost entirely manufactured from intermediate and distant raw materials (99%). To test the proposition that backed artefacts and tulas are responsible for this increase, these formal implements were omitted from the GIUR and PRI results presented in Tables 4 and 5. Since the removal of these backed artefact and tulas decreases the sample size of intermediate and distant raw material classes, artefacts made from these non-local classes are combined in Tables 4 and 5. Student's t-test results (see Tables 4 and 5) indicate that that the trend toward increasing reduction in the middle to late Holocene is equally reflected in the reduction of non-formal retouched flakes which compose 90% of the retouched flake assemblage.

Table 4. Geometric Index of Unifacial Reduction (GIUR) results (backed artefacts omitted).
Summary statistics* by analytical unit and raw material class, Puritjarra rockshelter.

	Raw Material Class							
	Local Origin				Intermediate and Distant Origin			
Analytical Unit	Mean	Median	sd	n	Mean	Median	sd	n
1a (0.0-0.8kya)	.34	.35	.11	19	.43	.42	.18	33
1b (0.8-3.5kya)	.28	.21	.14	9	.48	.51	.24	26
Summary Stats	.32	.32	.12	2	.46	.45	.21	59

*Statistically significant results highlighted. Student's t-test results (95% Confidence):
Analytical Unit 1a; Local:Intermediate/Distant t=-2.3, $d.f.$=50, p=.027, significant. Analytical Unit 1b; Local:Intermediate/Distant t=-3.1 $d.f.$=33, p=.005, significant.

Table 5: Perimeter Reduction Index (PRI) results (backed artefacts omitted).
Summary statistics* by analytical unit and raw material class, Puritjarra rockshelter.

	Raw Material Class							
	Local Origin				Intermediate and Distant Origin			
Analytical Unit	Mean	Median	sd	n	Mean	Median	sd	n
1a (0.0-0.8kya)	.33	.32	.18	47	.45	.43	.22	61
1b (0.8-3.5kya)	.31	.28	.22	26	.39	.39	.22	47
Summary Stats	.32	.31	.20	7	.42	.41	.22	108

*Statistically significant results highlighted. Student's t-test results (95% Confidence):
Analytical Unit 1a; Local:Intermediate/Distant t=-3.01, $d.f.$=106, p=.003, significant.

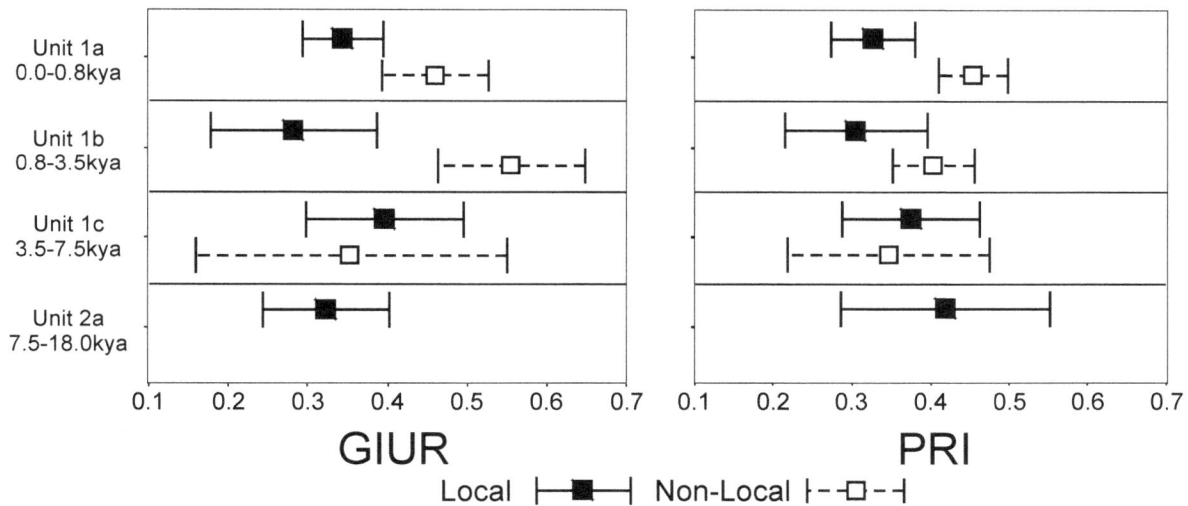

Figure 5: Error bar plots (95% confidence interval) of the Geometric Index of Unifacial Reduction (GIUR) and the Perimeter Reduction Index (PRI). Error bars are chronologically illustrated for local and non-local retouched flakes by analytical unit at Puritjarra rockshelter.

Provisioning Strategies at Puritjarra

Both the GIUR and PRI measures have proved useful in identifying chronological changes in flake reduction, but can these changes be attributed to changing patterns of residential mobility, and if so, in what ways do they support competing models of arid zone settlement? To answer these questions the GIUR and PRI results will be compared with general technological trends described by Smith for the Puritjarra sequence. This exercise will help determine whether changes in provisioning strategies are evident.

Smith (1988, 1996) has identified several stone artefact trends within the Puritjarra assemblage. His research

points to an increase in chipped stone artefact densities, discard rates, and core reduction throughout the Holocene period, but particularly in the late Holocene after 800BP. Smith (1988, 1996) attributes this pattern to a "late Holocene intensification" where desert populations became more sedentary over the past 1,500 years.

Certainly, one could interpret the changes in GIUR and PRI to indicate increasing sedentism at Puritjarra if the reasoning were followed that sedentary populations have less opportunities to "embed" lithic procurement in long-distance foraging activities (Binford 1979). If populations have less opportunity to reprovision with non-local raw materials, it follows that such populations

Table 6: The frequency and proportion of retouched flakes by analytical unit and raw material class, Puritjarra rockshelter.

| Raw Material Class | All Retouched Flakes | | | | |
	Unit 2a 18-7.5kya	Unit 1c 7.5-3.5kya	Unit 1b 3.5-0.8kya	Unit 1a 0.8-0.0kya	Total
Local	47 (90%)	25 (58%)	37 (30%)	65 (30%)	174
Intermediate/Distant	5 (10%)	18 (42%)	86 (70%)	146 (70%)	255

| Raw Material Class | Complete Retouched Flakes | | | | |
	Unit 2a 18-7.5kya	Unit 1c 7.5-3.5kya	Unit 1b 3.5-0.8kya	Unit 1a 0.8-0.0kya	Total
Local	36 (89%)	20 (69%)	26 (30%)	47 (30%)	129
Intermediate/Distant	4 (11%)	9 (31%)	61 (70%)	85 (70%)	159

might therefore employ reduction strategies that extend the utility of more valuable exotic stone rather than mount costly expeditions to resupply with favoured raw materials.

One way it may be possible to test for an increase in late Holocene sedentism is to examine the proportion of artefacts made from non-local and local raw materials through time. If residential mobility has decreased, as Smith (1988, 1996) claims, then the opportunities to reprovision the rockshelter with non-local raw materials should also have reduced, and consequently we would expect a decrease in the number of artefacts manufactured from non-local raw materials in the Puritjarra assemblage. Unfortunately Smith's (1988) data does not break down stone artefact numbers by raw material classes and relative time units, so this information is not presently available for the entire stone artefact assemblage. It is however available for the retouched flake assemblage. Table 6 shows that the numbers of non-local retouched flakes and stone tools increases throughout the Holocene and the proportion of artefacts manufactured on non-local raw materials composes 70% of the retouched flake assemblage from the mid-Holocene onward. This trend is not suggestive of reduced mobility. On the contrary, the pattern suggests groups were frequently mobile and had many opportunities to reprovision with non-local raw materials.

A second test of Smith's late Holocene intensification model involves examining changes in the size and composition of artefact assemblages through time to detect provisioning strategies. Kuhn (1995) has suggested that infrequently mobile populations will employ a strategy of provisioning of places. Stone artefacts with "tool making potential" such as large cores, large flakes, and unmodified non-local raw materials are expected to characterise the provisioning of places strategy. An increase in sedentism at Puritjarra might therefore be indicated by an increased discard of large cores and large flakes through time. At Puritjarra, the average size of cores (both local and non-locally derived) and other artefacts does not increase during the middle or late Holocene (Smith 1988:119). In fact, the evidence

suggests that the mean weight of late Holocene cores and artefacts are 10-20 times smaller than terminal Pleistocene/early Holocene specimens and 2-10 times smaller that mid-Holocene samples (Smith 1988:119).

Smith (1988) implies that the increased core reduction can be attributed to an increasingly sedentary late Holocene population. However, a chronological reduction in mobility may not be established by increased core reduction alone. Based on Kuhn's (1995) provisioning model, the artefact assemblage of sedentary populations will be marked by a proportional increase of core provisioning. Smith (1988:108) reports that the size of Puritjarra assemblage increases exponentially throughout the Holocene (Table 7), but the number of cores deposited within the rockshelter remains quite small. A total of 15, 16, and 13 cores were recovered from the early, middle, and late Holocene (Smith 1988:119). These numbers indicate that there is not a proportional increase of cores accompanying the increasing assemblage size. Thus, it does not appear that increased core reduction alone can unambiguously be linked to increased sedentism.

Another strategy that Kuhn (1995) argues may be employed in the provisioning of places is the stockpiling (or caching) of functional stone tools. This activity has been recorded in arid western Queensland by Hiscock (1988) who has documented the caching of functional tulas (see Figure 2). Though Hiscock's research demonstrates that functional tulas may have been cached in some instances, this appears not to have been the case at Puritjarra where all (100%) recovered tula specimens were severely reduced to the point of discard, as indicated by exhausted "slug" forms (Figure 2).

I argue that the most consistent interpretation of the Smith's (1988, 1996) technological trend may not be one of increased sedentism, but rather the contrary—increased mobility. The evidence presented thus far suggests that the middle and late Holocene stone artefact technologies of Puritjarra are best characterised by increases in artefact reduction and increases in the transport of non-locally derived artefacts. Both of these features are characteristic

Table 7. Smith's (1988:108) comparative analysis of chipped stone artefact densities from Puritjarra rockshelter, grid squares N9 and N10 only. Estimated ages have undergone extensive revision since this table was first published. For recent age estimates refer to Smith et.al. (1997, 2001).

Estimated Age	Vol (m³)	No.	Wt. (g)	No./m³	No/kya	No./m³/kya
0-600BP	0.26	1252	1981.8	4815	2087	8025
600-6,500BP	0.64	860	2888.9	1344	146	228
22,000-6,500BP	0.55	92	2575.2	167	6	11
Total	1.45	2204	7445.9	6326	2239	8264

of the technological planning of provisioning individuals. Small artefacts (<5cm) and stone tools are easily transported and when manufactured from high quality raw materials, have long lasting durability. The increase of non-local retouched flakes within Puritjarra suggests that frequent long range movements allowed for opportunity to reprovision. Therefore the reduction of stone artefact and stone tool size along with their increased manufacture from high quality non-local raw materials most likely indicates the utilisation of a mobile toolkit that emphasised portability and multifunctionality in its design.

The demonstration that retouched flake reduction increases in the mid-Holocene for both non-typologically regular artefacts and formal implement classes, suggests that the strategy of retouching flakes to conserve and extend their use-life is an important strategical component of middle and late Holocene artefact technologies. This argument assimilates well with Hiscock's (1994) "risk reduction" model which proposes backed artefacts, tulas, and points—formal implements which commonly exhibit extensive retouch—are part of a mobile toolkit that reduced the risk of foraging failure in an uncertain environment. Non-typological regular artefacts made from high quality raw materials could easily be transported alongside these formal implements by provisioning individuals. Thus the transport of non-typologically regular retouched flakes to Puritjarra presumably forms part of an overall strategy to manufacture portable artefacts and stone tools from raw materials of superior quality that both perform better and are more amenable to extended reduction than local materials.

Holocene Mobility and Arid Zone Settlement Patterns
Although the reduction evidence from Puritjarra suggests that provisioning individuals have continuously utilised a risk reducing mobile toolkit since the mid-Holocene, this is not to say that no changes in desert settlement and resource use have occurred. As mentioned earlier, the middle and late Holocene climates are notably different and are important variables that must be considered alongside provisioning strategies when modelling desert settlement. The technological trends discussed so far point to a high degree of parity between technological changes (including increased reduction and transport of non-local raw materials) at a time of deteriorating climate in the mid-Holocene. Palaeoclimatic research has recently shown that the dry, climatically unpredictable period

beginning in the mid-Holocene may have lasted until 1,000-2,000 years ago in many parts of the arid zone (Cupper et.al. 2000, Cupper 2002, McCarthy and Head 2002). The infrequent rainfall events experienced during the mid-Holocene dramatically affected the predictability and accessibility of watering points in the arid zone which most likely affected the nature of human mobility and settlement in this region. If mid-Holocene populations were expanding into previously unused or poorly utilised territories at this time (as suggested by Hiscock (1994) and Veth (1993)), then it is likely that there would have been only a limited knowledge of the location and nature of regional resources—including water. The increased reliance on well-known dependable permanent waters at this time would therefore likely have narrowed the foraging area over which populations could effectively procure resources.

During the late Holocene, an improved rainfall regime over the last 1,500 years more frequently recharged ephemeral water sources. Thorley (1998b, 2001) proposes that at this time people began exploiting ephemeral water holes as a "risk minimisation" settlement strategy and this allowed populations to more fully exploit the previously untapped resources of the arid zone, while reserving the resources around permanent waters for stressful times.

A large permanent water source called Murantji rockhole is located 3km north of Puritjarra. A small ephemeral rockhole is also located just 200 metres south of the rockshelter. If mid-Holocene populations centred their mobile foraging activities around permanent waterholes (such as Murantji) throughout this much drier period, this might explain the significant increase in stone artefact density, artefact discard, core reduction, and retouched flake reduction recorded at Puritjarra during the mid-Holocene. Likewise, if ephemeral water sources like the one at Puritjarra were widely utilised during the late Holocene, as suggested by Thorley (1998b, 2001), then the increased activity within and around the rockshelter at this time would remain consistent with the further increases in artefact density, discard, and core reduction over the last 800 years.

Because the ephemeral rock pool located immediately adjacent to Puritjarra was more regularly recharged in the late Holocene, it is suggested that frequently mobile populations had more opportunities to utilise the rockshelter and local resources during the last 800 years

91

than at any time previously. This appears to explain the increase in artefact densities and discard rates in late Holocene deposits. At first glance these increases might seem to indicate that residential mobility decreased (Smith 1988, 1996), but in actual fact, the frequency of residential moves more likely increased at this time. Late Holocene populations continued to rely on the technological strategies of mobile provisioning individuals rather than switching to a strategy of provisioning places as would be expected if any move toward decreasing residential mobility had occurred at this time. The increased size of the artefact assemblage from the last 800 years suggests that populations were occupying the rockshelter more frequently, if not for longer periods. The continued presence of "risk reduction" technologies and the more intensive reduction of non-locally derived retouched flakes at this time suggest visiting groups continued to utilise a portable and multifunctional mobile toolkit.

The late Holocene patterns documented in this paper are consistent with Thorley's (1998b, 2001) "risk minimisation" settlement model, and suggest that groups visiting Puritjarra during the last 800 years were foraging over a much greater area than was exploited during the drier mid-Holocene period. Late Holocene groups maximised their opportunity to forage over this much larger area by employing a settlement strategy that allowed them to successfully exploit the natural resources surrounding ephemeral waters. Consequently, populations became more residentially mobile than in the past and utilised a larger number of sites as they foraged across the landscape.

Conclusion

The GIUR and PRI have proved effective measures that are helpful in characterising prehistoric provisioning strategies. Although encouraging, these results are limited to a single site (Puritjarra) within the arid zone. The application of these techniques at other regional sites may help to further establish the residential mobility of Holocene arid zone populations and test the applicability of regional models of residential mobility. For example, it would be particularly interesting if the approach adopted here could be applied to arid zone assemblages from the early Holocene, when Smith (1998) argues that populations became less mobile as climate ameliorated. Another potential area where this research may be applied is to sites within the Palmer River catchment where Thorley (1998b) demonstrates that Smith's (1988b, 1998) late Holocene artefact trends are not entirely consistent across the central Australian region.

At Puritjarra, I suggest the stone artefact record best follows both Hiscock's (1994) mid-Holocene and Thorley's (1998b, 2001) late Holocene risk reduction models. These models suggest that middle and late Holocene populations were frequently mobile and utilised a mobile tool kit that consisted of backed artefacts, tulas, points, and high quality retouched flakes to counteract the

risk of being unsuccessful in procuring resources. The biggest difference between the mobility demonstrated by middle and late Holocene populations concerns the size of the foraging area available to these mobile populations. Mid-Holocene groups were less familiar with entire arid zone landscape and subsisted within narrow foraging range dictated by permanent waters. Late Holocene populations were able to forage over a much larger and wider area due to the increased availability of ephemeral waters.

Acknowledgements

I would like to thank the continuous support of friends and staff from the School of Archaeology and Anthropology at the Australian National University. Specifically, I thank Chris Clarkson and Lara Lamb for having the ambition to organise the papers in this monograph. My thesis supervisor, Dr. Peter Hiscock, has provided immeasurable support and inspiration for this research. A big thank you is warranted to Dr. Mike Smith of the National Museum of Australia for access to unpublished materials on Puritjarra. The Central Land Council and community members of Mt. Liebig generously granted permission to visit Puritjarra and provided invaluable assistance during fieldwork. I also express gratitude to the Museum and Art Gallery of the Northern Territory for access to the Puritjarra collection. Finally, I thank my wife, Sarah B. Strong-Law, for loving and tolerating her utterly mad husband.

References

Bamforth, D.B. 1986 Technological Efficiency and Tool Curation. *American Antiquity* 51:38-50.

Bamforth, D.B. 1991 Technological organization and hunter-gatherer land use: a California example. American Antiquity, 56(2):216-234.

Bamforth, D.B., and P. Bleed 1997 Technology, flaked stone technology, and risk. In G. Clark and M. Barton (eds.) *Rediscovering Darwin: Evolutionary Theory and Archaeological Explanation.* Archaeological Papers of the American Anthropological Association, no. 7, pp. 109-139.

Barton, C.M. 1988 *Lithic Variability and Middle Paleolithic Behaviour: New evidence from the Iberian Peninsula.* Oxford: British Archaeological Reports.

Behr, M.E. 1990 More Often or Longer? Site Use and Function during the late Holocene at Puritjarra Rockshelter. Unpublished Honours Thesis, The Australian National University: Canberra.

Binford, L. 1979 Organization and formation processes: Looking at curated technologies. *Journal of Anthropological Research* 35:255-273.

Binford, L. 1980 Willow Smoke and Dogs' Tails: Hunter-Gatherer Settlement Systems and Archaeological Site Formation. *American Antiquity* 45:4-20.

Bleed, P. 1986. "The Optimal Design of Hunting Weapons: Maintainability or Reliability?" *American Antiquity* 51.

Bleed, P. 2002 Obviously sequential, but continuous or staged? Refits and cognition in three late paleolithic assemblages from Japan. *Journal of Anthropological Archaeology* 21:329-343.

Bowdery, D. 1998 *Phytolith Analysis Applied to Pleistocene-Holocene Archaeological Sites in the Australian Arid Zone.* BAR Series 695.

Clarkson, C. 2002 An Index of Invasiveness for the Measurement of Unifacial and Bifacial Retouch: A Theoretical, Experimental and Archaeological Verification. *Journal of Archaeological Science* 29: 65–75.

Cupper, M., Drinnan, A., and Thomas, I. 2000 Holocene palaeoenvironments of salt lakes in the Darling Anabranch region, south-western New South Wales, Australia. *Journal of Biogeography* 27:1079-1094.

Cupper, M. 2002 Late Glacial and Holocene Environments of Playas in Southeastern Australia. *Conference Abstract from The Geological Society of America Annual Meeting and Exposition*, Denver, October 27-30.

Dibble, H. 1995 Middle Palaeolithic Scraper Reduction: Background, Clarification, and Review of the Evidence to Date. *Journal of Archaeological Method and Theory* Vol.2. No. 4:299-368.

Dimitriadis, S. and P.S. Cranston. 2001. An Australian Holocene climate reconstruction using Chironomidae from a tropical volcanic maar lake. *Palaeogeography, Palaeoclimatology, Palaeoecology* 176:109-131.

Goodyear, A.C. 1989. A hypothesis for the use of cryto-crystalline raw materials among Paleoindian groups of North America, in Ellis, C.J. & J.C. Lothrop (eds.). *Eastern Paleoindian lithic resource use.* Boulder (CO): Westview Press. 1-9.

Gould, R.A. 1969 Subsistence behaviour among the Western Desert Aborigines of Australia. *Oceania* 39:253-274.

Gould, R.A. 1977 Puntutjarpa Rockshelter and the Australian Desert Culture. *Anthropological Papers of the American Museum of Natural History* 54.

Gould, R.A. 1978 James Range East Rockshelter, Northern Territory, Australia: a summary of the 1973 and 1974 investigations. *Asian Perspectives* 21:85-125.

Gould, R. A. 1980 *Living Archaeology.* Cambridge: Cambridge University Press.

Hiscock,P. 1986 Technological change in the Hunter River Valley and the interpretation of Late Holocene change in Australia. *Archaeology in Oceania* 21 (1):40-50.

Hiscock, P. 1988 A cache of tulas from the Boulia District, Western Queensland, *Archaeology in Oceania* 23(2):60-70.

Hiscock, P. 1994 Technological responses to risk in Holocene Australia. *Journal of World Prehistory* 8(3):267-292

Hiscock, P. and V. Attenbrow 2003 Early Australian implement variation: a reduction model. *Journal of Archaeological Science* 30(2): 239-249.

Hiscock, P. and Kershaw, P.A. 1992 Palaeoenvironments and prehistory of Australia's tropical Top End. In Dodson, J. (ed.), *The Naïve Lands*, Longman, Cheshire, pp.43-75.

Kershaw, A.P. 1995 Environmental change in Greater Australia. *Antiquity* 69:656-675.

Kelly, R.L. 1992 Mobility/Sedentism: Concepts, Archaeological Measures, and Effects. *Annual Review of Anthropology* 21:43-66.

Kelly, Robert L. (1995) *The foraging spectrum: diversity in hunter-gatherer lifeways.* Washington, D.C.: Smithsonian Institution Press.

Kuhn, S. 1990 A geometric index of reduction for unifacial stone tools. *Journal of Archaeological Science* 17:583-593.

Kuhn, S. 1995 *Mousterian Lithic Technology.* Princeton: Princeton University Press.

Lambeck, K. and Chappell, J., Sea Level Change through the last Glacial Cycles, *Science*, **292**, 679-686.

McCarthy, L. and Head, L. 2002 Holocene variability in semi-arid vegetation: new evidence from *Leporillus* middens from the Flinders Ranges, South Australia. *The Holocene* 11:681-689.

Nelson, M. 1991 The Study of Technological Organisation. In M. Schiffer (ed.) Archaeological Method and Theory. Vol. 3. pp. 57-100.

Shott, M.J. 1986. Technological organization and settlement mobility: an ethnographic examination, *Journal of Anthropological Research* 42:15-51.

Smith, M.A. 1986 The antiquity of seedgrinding in central Australia. *Archaeology in Oceania* 21:29-39.

Smith, M.A 1988 The pattern and timing of prehistoric settlement in central Australia. Unpublished Ph.D. thesis, The University of New England, Armidale.

Smith, M.A. 1989 The case for a resident human population in the central Australian ranges during full glacial aridity. *Archaeology in Oceania* 24:93-105.

Smith, M.A. 1996 Prehistory and human ecology in central Australia: an archaeological perspective. In S.R. Morton and D.J. Mulvaney *Exploring Central Australia: Society, the environment, and the 1894 Horn Expedition,* pps. 61-73. Norton: Surrey Beatty and Sons Pty. Ltd.

Smith, M.A., Bird, M.I., Turney, C.S.M., Fifield, L.K., Santos, G.M., Hausladen, P.A. and di Tada, M.L. 2001 New Abox AMS-14C ages remove dating anomalies at Puritjarra rock shelter. *Australian Archaeology* 53:45-47.

Smith, M.A., Fankhauser, B., and Jercher, M. 1998 The Changing Provenance of Red Ochre at Puritjarra Rock Shelter, Central Australia: Late Pleistocene to Present. *Proceedings of the Prehistoric Society* 64:275-292.

Smith, M.A., Prescott, J.R. and Head, M.J. 1997 Comparison of C14 and Luminescence Chronologies at Puritjarra Rock Shelter, Central Australia. *Quaternary Science Reviews* 16:299-320.

Thorley, P. 1998a Pleistocene settlement in the Australian arid zone: occupation of an inland riverine landscape in the central Australian ranges. *Antiquity* 72:34-45.

Thorley, P. 1998b Shifting *Location, Shifting Scale: A Regional Landscape Approach to the Prehistoric Archaeology of the Palmer River Catchment, Central Australia.* Unpublished Ph.D. thesis, Northern Territory University: Darwin.

Thorley, P. 2001 Uncertain supplies: water availability and regional archaeological structure in the Palmer River catchment, central Australia. *Archaeology in Oceania* 36:1-14.

Torrence, R. 1983. Timebudgeting and hunter-gatherer technology, in G. Bailey (ed.), *Hunter-gatherer economy in prehistory: a European perspective*:11-22. Cambridge: Cambridge University Press.

Torrence, R. 1989. Retooling: towards a behavioural theory of stone tools. In *Time energy and stone tools,* (ed.), R. Torrence, pp. 57-66. Cambridge University Press.

Veth, P. 1989 Island in the Interior: a model for the colonisation of Australia's arid zone. *Archaeology in Oceania* 24:81-92.

Veth, P. 1993 *Islands in the Interior: The Dynamics of Prehistoric Adaptations Within the Arid Zone of Australia.* International Monographs in Prehistory. Archaeological Series 3. Michigan: Ann Arbor.

Veth, P. 2000 Origins of the Western Desert language: convergence in linguistic and archaeological space and time models. *Archaeology in Oceania* 35:11-19.

Wyrwoll, K.H. and Miller, G.H. 2001 Initiation of the Australian summer monsoon 14,000 years ago, *Quaternary International*, 83-85: pp 119-128.

9 | Informal Movements: Changing Mobility Patterns at Ngarrabullgan, Cape York Australia

Alex Mackay

Abstract

This paper explores variability in artefact assemblages at a series of open and rockshelter sites on and around a mountain (Ngarrabullgan) in northeastern Australia. Assemblage variability through time and space is explored and explained in terms of changing group mobility. In the process, it is demonstrated that theoretical models usually used to explore change through formal assemblage components can usefully be applied to informal components. Such an approach allows inferences to be drawn about changing subsistence-settlement systems from relatively small assemblages lacking recognised implement types. The case study produces results that challenge existing models of occupation in the region.

Introduction

Interest in the role of mobility in subsistence strategies has increased in recent years. This has been consistent with a move towards complex mechanistic explanations of variation in human settlement organization, its causes and material consequences. Theoretical literature has been developed relating the organization of technology to a number of variables in past land use practices, among which mobility has featured prominently (Hiscock 1996; Kelly 1988, 1983; Kelly and Todd 1988; Kuhn 1995, 1994, 1992, 1989). Characteristic of the literature has been the development and application of interpretative schema to deal with tools and / or tool design (Bleed 1986; Bamforth 1986; Kelly 1988; Kelly and Todd 1988; Nelson 1991; Shott 1986; Torrence 1989). There is no reason, however, why many of the theoretical postulates which underpin tool-oriented schema should not be equally useful in interpreting those non-formal, non-used assemblage components – commonly referred to as debitage – that constitute the overwhelming bulk of artefact assemblages.

Specifically, this paper explores the effects of variable mobility from the viewpoint of provisioning (*sensu* Kuhn 1992, 1995). Transported tool kits are considered in broad terms of utility and opportunity potential within the constraints imposed by a mobile land use system. The approach adopted here does not differ significantly from existing theoretical bases, however, it explores the implications of organizational constraints on assemblages as a whole, rather than on small subsets of formal implements. This approach has three distinct advantages. First, it places the analytic focus on the largest assemblage component. Second, as not all assemblages necessarily contain formal components, this approach broadens the potential application of provisioning models. And third, there is less reliance on assumed and demonstrably problematic form-function associations (Kelly 1988:717; Hiscock and Attenbrow, this volume).

In this paper a suite of open and rockshelter sites in northeastern Australia is examined in relation to the provisioning model. All of the assemblages examined lacked formal tool components. Nevertheless, an examination of spatial and temporal variation in debris demonstrates that important inferences can be drawn about changing subsistence and land use.

Aspects of Mobility, Subsistence and Technology
Mobility and Subsistence Organisation

A growing body of literature exists exploring the relationship between technology and subsistence organization (Bamforth 1986, 1991; Bleed 1986; Hiscock 1994; Kelly and Todd 1988; Parry and Kelly 1988; Kelly 1992; Kuhn 1992, 1994, 1995; Nelson 1991; Shott 1986). Mobility has been identified as one important variable in subsistence organisation, the material consequences of which have been explored both theoretically and empirically. Briefly, being mobile allows populations to exploit an array of resources over a broad spatial range. In consequence, reliance on any one resource or resource-harvesting location is reduced and the relative significance of failure to harvest a key resource at a time of access is lessened. Following Binford (1980), two broad kinds of mobility, *residential* and *logistical,* are distinguished. The crux of the distinction is that groups can either move residential locations proximate to specific resources at different times (residential movements), or can use small parties to harvest resources and return with them to residential camps (logistical movements). These strategies are not exclusive and may be used in concert (Binford 1980:19). However, while being mobile helps to resolve problems of access to subsistence resources, it poses a number of problems for the organization of stone artefact technology.

Uneven distributions of stone raw materials, the rapid consumption of stone during reduction, the lack of a

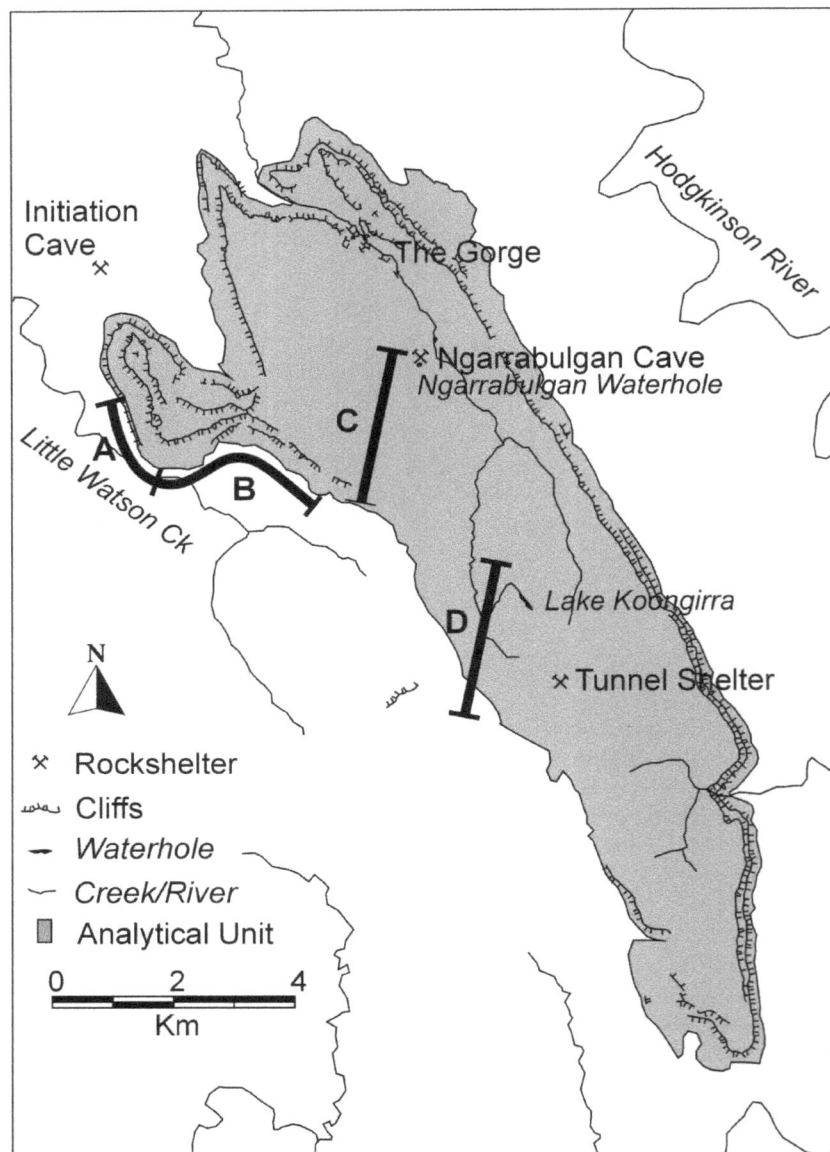

Figure 1. Location of survey units used in spatial analysis.

necessary correlation between the locations of usable stone and the locations of subsistence tasks, the qualitative unsuitability of certain materials to certain tasks and the frequent impracticality of making tools as subsistence opportunities arise (Torrence 1989; Kuhn 1992:188) all effect the relationship between mobility and technology. These factors necessitate the existence of problem solving strategies to ensure both that technology is always at hand when needed and that it is adequate to those needs. Provisioning is the term given to the systems by which tool-using groups reconcile these spatial, temporal and qualitative inconsistencies (Kuhn 1995).

Technological Provisioning: Aspects and Implications
The problems that provisioning must solve result primarily from the mobility of the group and the predictability of the subsistence environment. Being mobile continually alters the spatial relationship between the tool-using group and stone raw materials. Thus, mobility necessitates the transportation of items, in turn limiting the group to the use of a finite number of portable items. This is commonly referred to as the toolkit. The predictability of the subsistence environment affects the nature of those stone items that will be procured at a given time of access. As procurement necessarily precedes the tasks in which the resultant tools will be used, a provisioning system must involve predictions about the location, timing and nature of impending tasks, what technology is suitable, where and when it will be possible to acquire replacement materials, and the cost of transporting procured items from point of acquisition through to point of discard and / or replacement. Whether a provisioning strategy is specific or generalised (probabilistic) will depend on how effectively future tasks can be predicted.

Kuhn (1992:188, 1995) distinguishes two forms of provisioning – the provisioning of places and the provisioning of individuals. Place provisioning may be understood as the bringing of artefact-making potential to a strategic point in space, such that artefacts can be made to suit impending needs. The provisioned place is likely to be a residential base from which subsistence activities are to be undertaken. Alternatively, individual provisioning focuses on ensuring that individuals have at hand immediately useful items capable of effectively meeting such needs as might arise. Thus, the two strategies may be seen as extremes of a spectrum with the provisioning of potential utility at one end and the provisioning of immediate utility at the other, between which lie tool-kits comprised of varying combinations of potential and immediate utility. As with the distinction between logistical and residential mobility, Kuhn's provisioning systems may be employed in concert across space and time and need not be seen as mutually exclusive (Kuhn 1995:26).

Both individual and place provisioning have a number of advantages and disadvantages which can be brought into play by varying aspects of mobility and predictability. For example, the individually provisioned toolkit is easily transported and may be geared to meet both specific and general tasks as they are encountered. Such a strategy is ideal for highly mobile populations, however, extended or less mobile occupation of an area would lead to over-reliance on the limited number of preprepared items transported. Thus, the flexibility, and ultimately the functionality of the toolkit may be compromised. Such circumstances are more likely to favour place provisioning of a spatial locus (Kuhn 1995:25). Such a strategy allows the group to manufacture the broadest range of items, and thus to respond effectively to the broadest array of tasks. Place provisioning necessitates, however, that the duration of occupation is both extended and broadly predictable. Highly mobile groups are unlikely to recoup the energy expended in stocking materials at a locus, nor are groups whose residential movements are unpredictable (Kelly and Todd 1988; note also Gould 1991:19). Kuhn's "paradigmatic" example of place provisioning, drawn from Parry and Kelly (1987), involves near sedentary landuse.

Kuhn's provisioning models appear likely to be useful in distinguishing patterns of mobility over time. It remains to explore the specific material consequences of variable provisioning strategies, starting with individual provisioning.

The chief constraints on individually provisioned items arise from continued transportation (Kuhn 1995:25). Thus, portable implements capable of fulfilling a variety of roles are expected to be favoured, creating an inverse correlation between mobility and toolkit weight and diversity (Shott 1986). Consequently, those few items transported must be suited to extended use-lives through on-going maintenance. (Bleed 1986; Shott 1986). Aspects

of suitability may include the selection of high quality raw materials which fracture predictably and maintain a sharp working edge (Torrence 1989:64; Bleed 1986). Predictability of fracture also helps to mitigate the probability of tool failure, which takes on particular significance when a limited array of tools is being transported.

The risk of tool failure may be further mitigated by the use where possible of locally available raw materials (Kelly 1988; Kuhn 1995). Over-reliance on, or too frequent maintenance of a transported tool increases the probability of exhaustion or breakage, compromising the technological capacity of the group. Edge rejuvenation on transported tools may be considered an alternative method of conservation when suitable local materials are not available (Bamforth 1986:40). Tools made from opportunistically acquired local materials are likely to be abandoned soon after the completion of tasks, thus they need not be of high quality, beyond that needed to perform requisite tasks. Comparatively, transported, rejuvenated items are only likely to be discarded when exhausted, broken or when replacement materials of comparable quality are available.

Given these considerations, assemblages resulting from individual provisioning are expected to contain relatively high percentages of locally available materials. Transported items can enter the record in one of two ways; through on-site manufacture or through discard. Cores will be uncommon given the emphasis on immediate utility, thus on-site manufacture is likely to be limited to retouch events. Discard of transported items will be relatively infrequent, unless the item is broken or exhausted, or suitable replacements are available. Under such circumstances discarded items are expected to display conservation in the form of retouch. Consequently, the assemblages will be dominated by small, thin flakes with few to very few large items. As mobility increases, the weight and diversity of transported items is expected to decrease. Thus higher mobility is expected to result in increased use of local materials and the decreased probability that transported items will be discarded.

Alternatively, effective place provisioning largely negates the need for raw material conservation. Portability and immediate utility become less relevant than manufacturing potential, increasing the ratio of cores to tools. This strategy creates greater flexibility in the manufacturing process and places fewer constraints on tool design. Relatively "casual" reduction of raw materials has been observed under such circumstances (Parry and Kelly 1987), with little flake retouch and the discard of artefacts prior to exhaustion. Such assemblages are expected to contain a greater range of artefacts sizes than assemblages resulting from individual provisioning, including a relatively high proportion of large, unused and unretouched flakes. Furthermore, there is less need to conserve transported items through the supplementary use of poor quality expediently gathered raw materials. Consequently, high quality provisioned materials should dominate assemblages.

While individual and place provisioning are presented as essentially distinct, strategic intermixing is not logically precluded. Toolkits composed of small cores and formal tools would support a highly mobile subsistence regime featuring some extended occupation of certain loci. Such a strategy would result in a greater range of discarded flakes than provisioning with immediately useful items alone, while retaining an emphasis on raw material conservation.

This section has reviewed key aspects of the relationship between technology and variable population mobility. It has also considered ways in which modelling of technological organisation can be applied to assemblages lacking formal implements. These principles are applied in the following sections to sites on and around the mountain known as Ngarrabullgan (Mt Mulligan) in southeast Cape York Peninsula, Australia. The objective is to explore and explain changes in technological provisioning and mobility over the last 10,000 years.

Ngarrabullgan

Ngarrabullgan is a sandstone plateau 18km long and 6.5km wide. It is bounded to the north, south and east by cliffs up to 400m high, and much of the western side is too steep for travel. Terrestrial access to the mountain is most effectively gained along three sections of variable lengths along the western side – 500m long in the northwest, 2km long in the central west, and 700m long in the southwest. Ngarrabullgan is depauperate in workable stone and many plant and animal food resources, though it is well supplied with water and with various other kinds of resources (e.g. ochre and *Xanthorrhoea johnsonii* plant resins).

The most common stone material suited to flaking that is available on the mountain is quartz – which is broadly ubiquitous throughout the research area – and less common nodules of chert. Quartz occurs as medium to small pebbles with abundant incipient fracture planes. This combination of features places heavy constraints on its size, utility and predictability of fracture. Conversely, it has the advantage of being widely available. Alternatively, reasonably high quality volcanic rocks (mainly rhyolites) are highly available off the mountain, although these are concentrated along its western side. The constraints of size and fracture predictability associated with quartz are less applicable to the volcanic raw materials, which are available as large reasonably homogeneous blocks. Between them, quartz and volcanics account for about 90-95% of the artefacts in the archaeological assemblages to be examined at Ngarrabullgan.

The mountain supports a suite of endemic plants and plant communities distinct from those surrounding the mountain (Shaw and Wason 1998:92). Mammalian fauna are poorly represented on the mountain; surveys indicate that large mammals, relatively common on the surrounding plains, are absent from the mountaintop. Excavations on and around the mountain suggests that this absence is not a recent development, and likely dates to 30,000 BP or earlier (David and Wilson, 1999:165).

Ngarrabullgan provides good, concentrated and relatively consistent supplies of fresh water. Seasonal creeks and permanent waterholes are relatively common on the mountain; permanent water is concentrated in the gorge at the north of the mountain, and at Lake Koongirra, a 350m by 50m waterhole located towards the centre of the mountain. Although fluctuating in size, the lake is believed to have been permanently filled since at least 6000 BP (Butler 1998), providing a "generally good" supply of water until the present.

Initial occupation of Ngarrabullgan began at approximately 35,500 BP, at Ngarrabullgan Cave (David 2002). Five rockshelters are known to have been occupied on and around the mountain prior to 5500 BP, increasing to 15 between 5500 BP and 700 BP. The number of artefacts discarded in all sites also shows an increase in the period after 5500 BP. This pattern of increased site occupation, and increasing numbers of discarded artefacts during the mid-Holocene is consistent with that observed throughout Cape York Peninsula and indeed across much of Australia. This has often been interpreted as symptomatic of increases in population sizes, densities and degrees of territoriality (David 2002). Some researchers have suggested these changes to be indicative of decreased residential mobility with a possible transition to sedentism being "nipped in the bud" by European colonization ~ 200BP (eg. Lourandos 1983, 1997; also Morwood and Hobbs 1995). Interestingly, in the case of Ngarrabullgan, occupation of the mountain appears to have largely ceased in the last 700 years, with few cultural materials evident after this date (David and Wilson 1999).

Spatial Patterns in Provisioning at Ngarrabullgan

The first data sets examined here are used to explore spatial differences in the technology of discarded items on Ngarrabullgan. The objective is to distinguish patterns that may reflect differences in provisioning on and around the mountain. These data are drawn from artefact assemblages recorded in open contexts on and around the mountain. Surveying methods involved systematic non-site surveys within survey quadrats. 'Sites' were identified as individual or groups of stone artefacts separated by more than 25m from nearest neighbouring artefacts (Bruno David pers. comm.). The transects formed by the survey quadrats along which these artefacts were recorded are shown in Figure 1. For analytic purposes, the surveyed areas are divided into 4 units:

A – This unit, containing 1289 artefacts, lies off the

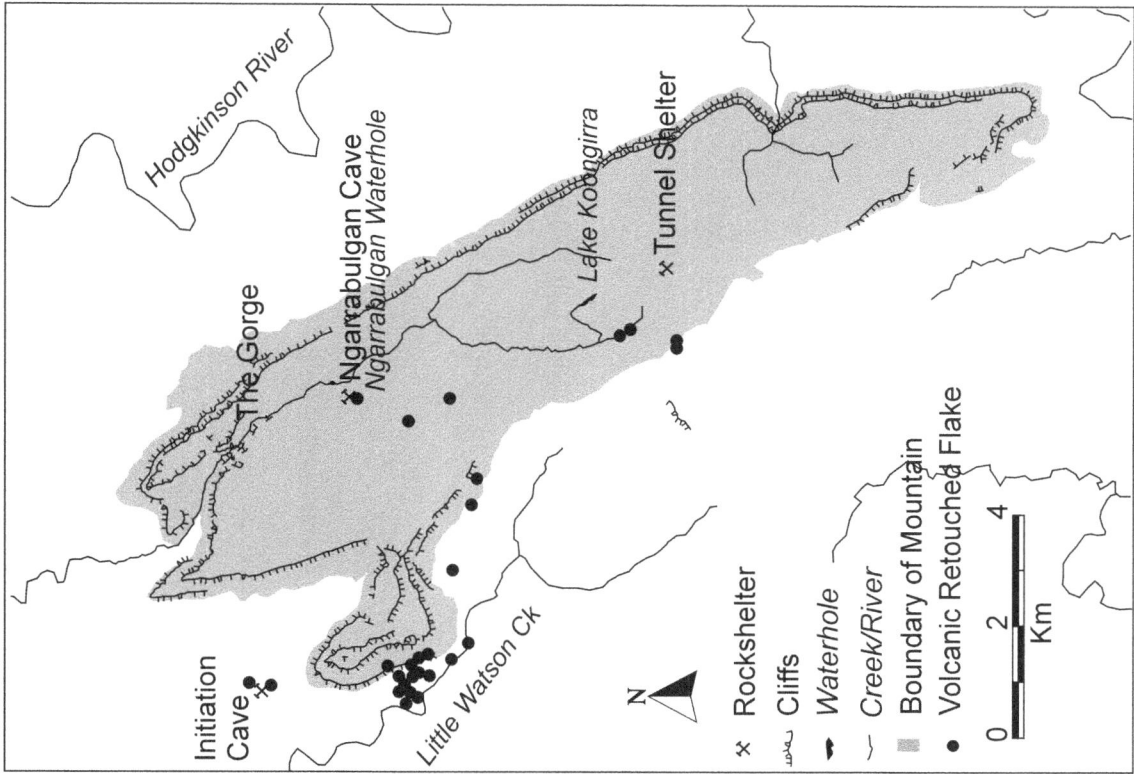

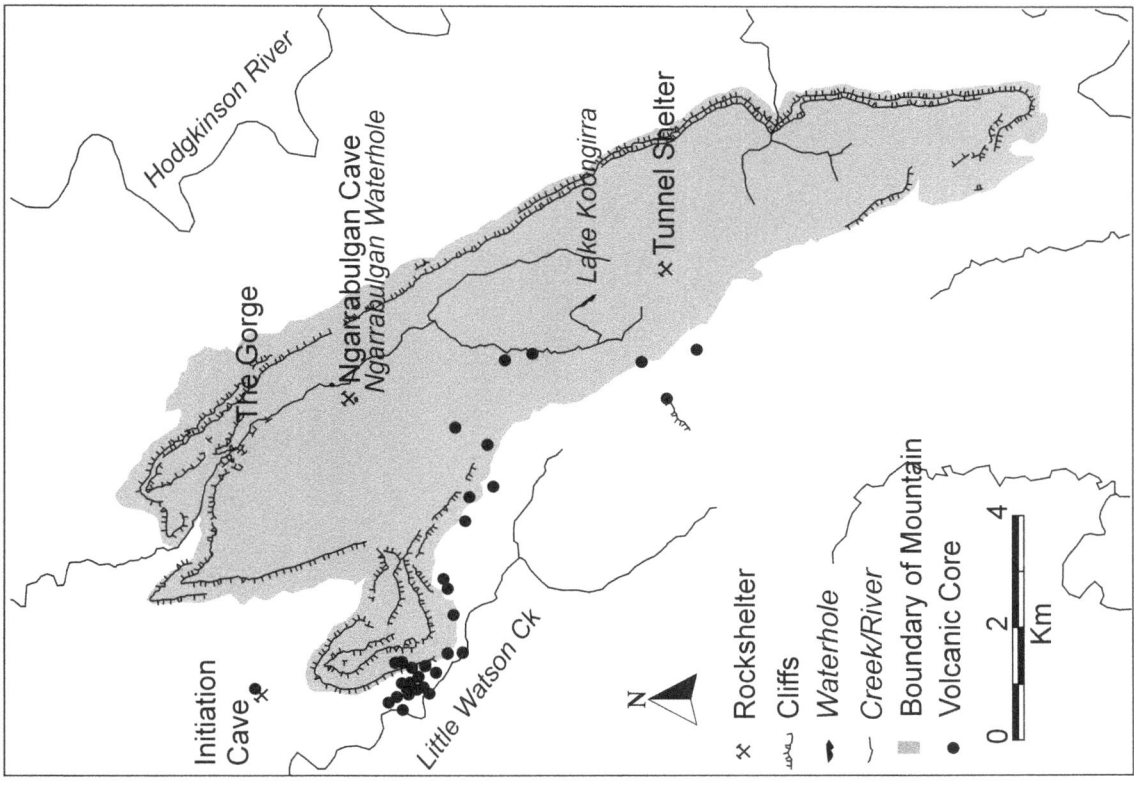

Figure 2. Spatial variation in the location of assemblage components. A: Location of volcanic cores, and B: location of retouched volcanic flakes.

mountain only, stretching around the base at the western side.

B – This unit, containing 38 artefacts, includes both a stretch at the base of the mountain on the western side and the northern access ridge to the mountain top.

C – This unit, containing 100 artefacts, runs from the top of the northern access route onto the mountain to Ngarrabullgan Cave and associated waterholes.

D – This unit, containing 234 artefacts, stretches from just north of Lake Koongirra south to the southern access route onto the mountain.

Patterns in Spatial Distribution of Artefacts
This section focuses on the way in which the mountain, rich in water but depauperate in high quality stone raw materials, was provisioned by past Aboriginal populations. As assemblages on and off the mountain are dominated by quartz and volcanic artefacts, these two materials form the focus of analysis. The first spatial patterns considered are the distributions of volcanic cores and retouched flakes.

Figure 2 and Figure 3 show the locations of sites in which volcanic cores and retouched volcanic flakes were found. Several points are worth making. Volcanic rocks do not occur on the mountain, thus their presence on the mountaintop necessarily relates to transportation. Volcanic cores were located in all units, both on and off the mountain, with particular concentration off the mountain in Unit A. Of the units on the mountain, volcanic cores were recorded through Unit D, but were not recorded in the northern section of Unit C. This complements the distribution of quartz cores (not shown), which were recorded in the northern part of Unit C (n=4) and not at all in Unit D. There are also differences in the size and reduction of the volcanic cores, as noted in Table 1.

While sample numbers are very small, the data suggest that of the volcanic cores transported onto the mountain, (i.e. those in central section of the mountain - Unit D) are on average larger at point of discard than those in the north of the mountain (Unit C). Furthermore, the low mean number of flake scars on volcanic cores in Unit C suggests that the small size of these cores is not a result of extensive reduction, but is more likely the result of small initial size. In contrast, the large size of cores at discard in Unit D, combined with the large number of flake scars implies that these cores were relatively large when selected for transportation. The very large number of cores in Unit A reflects the presence of a material source in this Unit.

In contrast to the distribution of volcanic cores, retouched volcanic flakes, though also located in all units, occur in that part of Unit C where volcanic cores are absent. These differences in distribution may imply differences in the nature of materials provisioned to the north and south of the mountain. Differences between the two units located off the mountain (Unit A and Unit B) are likely to be

strongly influenced by the procurement of volcanic stone near to or within Unit A (eg., differences in raw material access) making the relationship between landuse and provisioning in this area ambiguous.

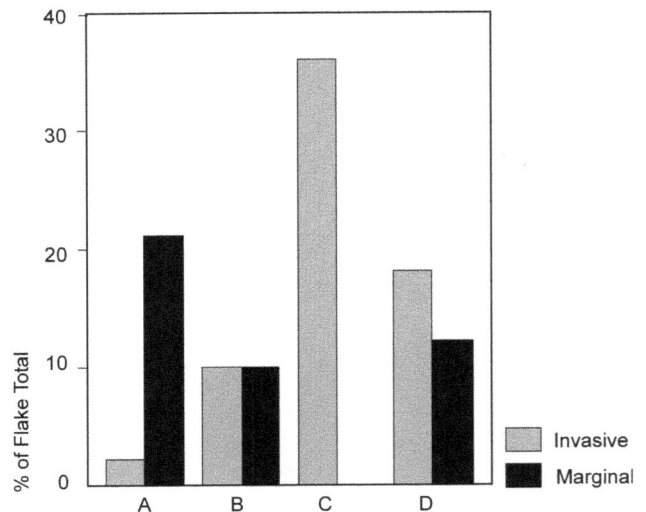

Figure 3. Percentages of flake retouch in survey units.

From the data above it might be suggested that different kinds of volcanic artefacts are following different movement trajectories once on the mountain top. Support for this is provided by an examination of trends in retouch and platform preparation on volcanic flakes (Figure 3 and Figure 4).

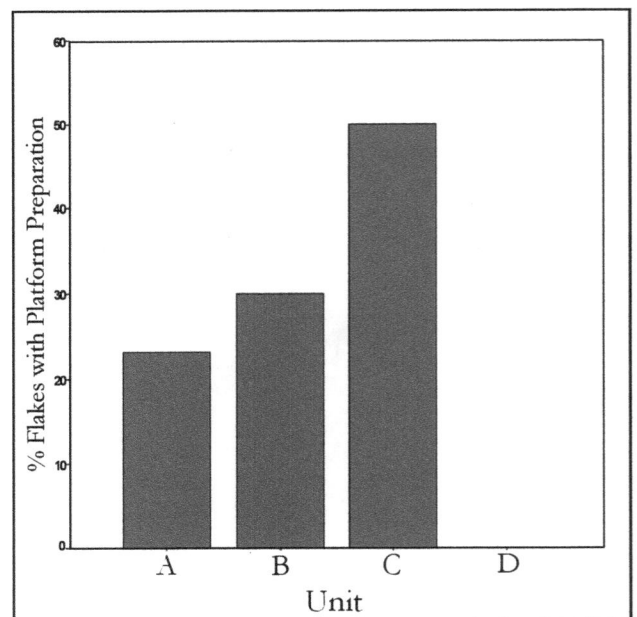

Figure 4. Percentages of flakes with prepared platforms in survey units.

Table 1: Mean volcanic core dimensions and flake scars by unit.

Unit	Number of Cores	Mean Maximum Dimension (mm)	Mean Number of Flake Scars
A	148	38.6	7
B	8	45.5	9.5
C	4	27.3	4.5
D	5	53.4	12.6

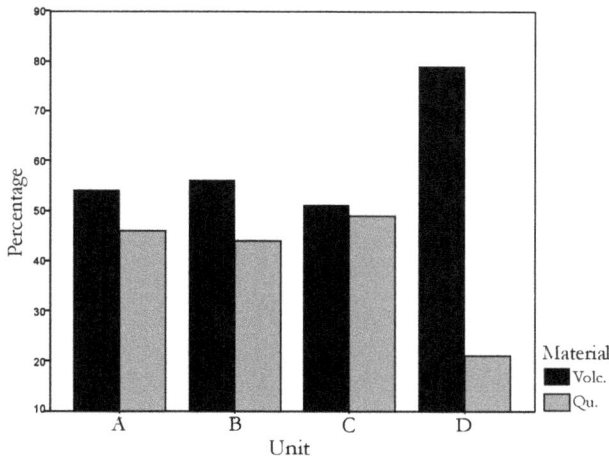

Figure 5. Ratio of quartz to volcanic artefacts in survey units.

Retouched flakes are divided into marginal and invasive forms (following Clarkson 2002). These nominal distinctions provide a rough guide to the amount of retouch to which flakes were subject prior to discard. Figure 3 shows that as distance from Unit A increases, the percentage of invasively retouched flakes increases, and the percentage of marginally retouched flakes decreases. Insufficient data preclude further exploration of this pattern through changes in flakes size (eg., the possible existence of a distance/decay relationship). The amount of invasive retouch in Unit D conforms with the trend established in the other three units (reduction increasing with distance from source), though the amount of marginal retouch is somewhat higher than would be anticipated were Unit D on a direct trajectory from Unit A.

From Figure 4 it can be inferred that flakes with prepared platforms (both overhang removal and faceting) were preferentially selected for transport from Unit A to Unit C. This figure may help to explain the marginal retouch rates in Unit D. The complete absence of flakes with platform preparation in this unit makes it possible to suggest that flakes in this area were not a transported subset of flakes occurring in Units A – C, but were rather transported from a different source, possibly immediately adjacent to Unit D at the western side.

A final distinction between the spatial units is found in the use of raw materials. While in all units volcanic artefacts are more prevalent than quartz artefacts, the

ratio of volcanic to quartz is by far the highest in Unit D (Figure 5). The comparatively low ratio (~1:1) of quartz to volcanic stone in Unit C is partially explained by the distance from volcanic sources and the presence of quartz cores noted earlier. The high ratio (4:1) of volcanic to quartz in Unit D is at odds with a distance to source relationship, but is consistent with the presence of volcanic cores in the area and the absence of quartz cores. The combination of these factors suggests that Unit D was provisioned with high quality raw materials both in the form of flakes and flake-making potential.

Summary of Spatial Patterns

On the mountain, at least two provisioning systems appear to have been employed. The north of the mountain appears to have been supplied with volcanic flakes, which were conserved through retouch and by the supplementary use of locally available quartz. Artefacts in this area appear to have been transported and reduced along a trajectory from Unit A, through Unit B, and into Unit C, possibly with some limited movement south into Unit D (Figure 6). These patterns appear to correlate with a signature of individual provisioning, and by inference, high residential or logistical mobility. Alternatively, provisioning in Unit D seems to have involved the transportation and reduction of both volcanic cores and flakes, with local quartz comparatively under-exploited. The cores in this area were comparatively large, moderately well reduced and discarded prior to exhaustion. This appears consistent with the anticipated signature for a degree of place provisioning. The relatively small number of cores, and the presence of a relatively high frequency of retouched flakes suggests, however, that if such a strategy pertained it was either intermixed with individual provisioning, or did not occur throughout the entire occupational history of this part of the mountain. Existing theory about the occupation of this part of Australia suggests that place provisioning is most likely to have occurred in the latter part of the sequence. Changes in artefact assemblages through time at Ngarrabullgan are considered in the following section.

Temporal Patterns in Provisioning at Ngarrabullgan

This section focuses on changes in the period 5500 – 700 BP, during which the number of sites occupied and the number of artefacts discarded on the mountain both show significant initial increase, prior to systematic abandonment. Three sites are used in this analysis, one from survey Unit A (Initiation Cave), one from Unit C (Ngarrabullgan Cave) and one from Unit D (Tunnell Shelter). Initiation Cave is the only site to be examined

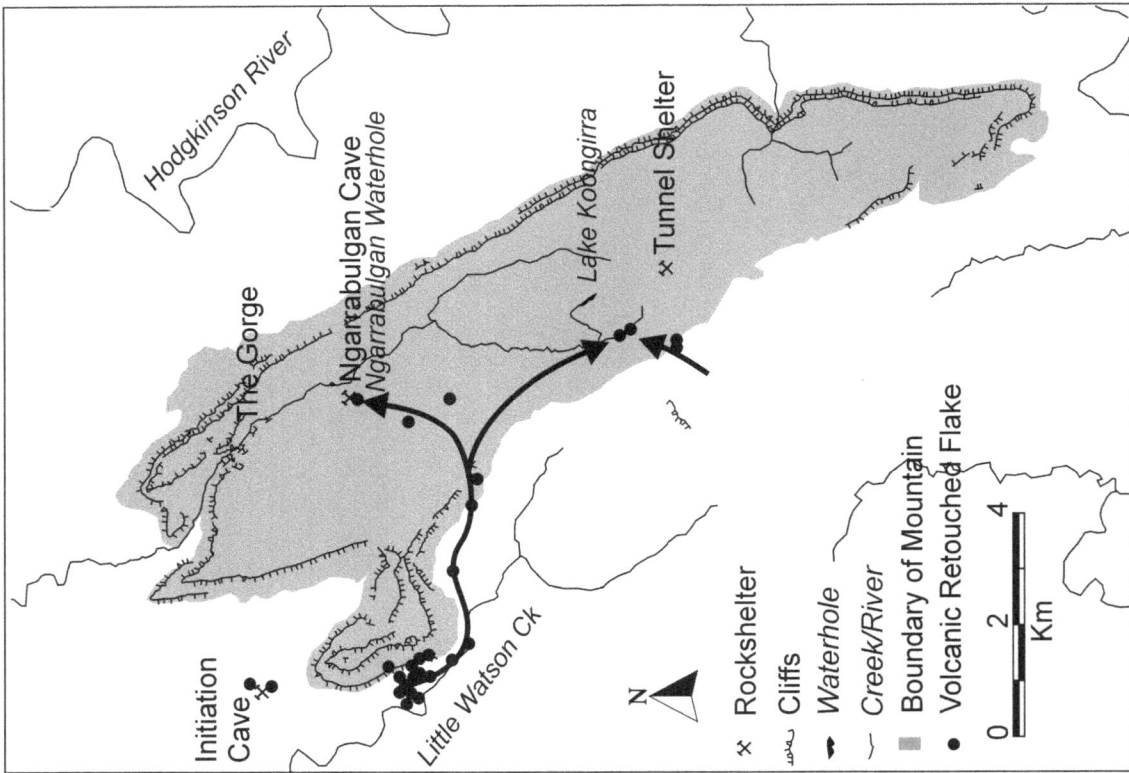

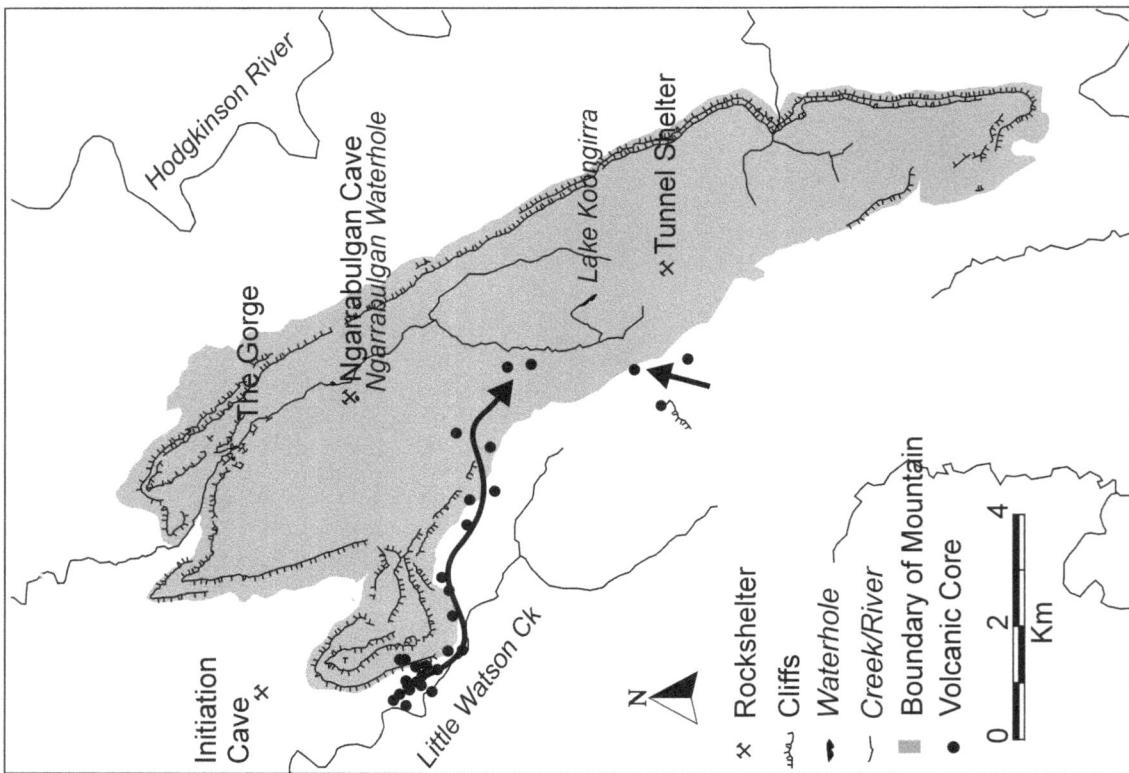

Figure 6. Inferred provisioning trajectories at Ngarrabullgan.

which is located off the mountain near a source of volcanic stone. Ngarrabullgan Cave is located in the far north of the mountain in the area suggested to have been exploited through individually-provisioned forays, while Tunnell Shelter is located towards the centre of the mountain in the area in which some place provisioning is suggested to have occurred. The sequences used from each site are roughly as follows:

- Ngarrabullgan Cave from 5400 to 700 BP
- Tunnel Shelter from 5400 to 700 BP
- Initiation Cave from 5300 to 2400 BP.

For analytic purposes, and due to the small number of artefacts in many spits, the study period is divided into three temporal units based on changing environmental conditions. Period 3 covers the time between about 5500 and 3500 BP, during which rainfall appears to have been higher than present. Estimates from surrounding regions suggest the difference in rainfall to have been substantial (Kershaw, 1983; Nix and Kalma, 1972). Period 2 is from 3500 to 2000 BP, during which rainfall decreases. Period 1 covers the time from 2000 BP to the cessation of occupation. During this period the supply of water in Lake Koongirra fluctuated, becoming increasingly uncertain, although it always appears to have held water (Butler, 1998).

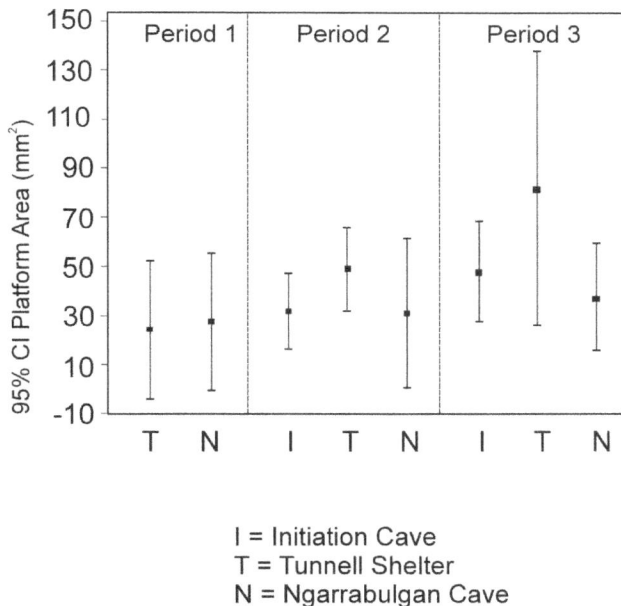

I = Initiation Cave
T = Tunnell Shelter
N = Ngarrabulgan Cave

Figure 7. Error bars of changing volcanic flake platform area by period.

These periods prove useful in the analysis of the excavated assemblages from the study region. However, Period 1 is absent from Initiation Cave, which was last occupied at approximately 2400 BP. Occupation commences more or less simultaneously at all three shelters, and ends more or less simultaneously at Tunnell Shelter and Ngarrabullgan Cave.

The first issue to be considered is whether the spatial variation in provisioning inferred from the open site data is reflected in the excavated assemblages. Support for a degree of place provisioning in the central part of the mountain is provided by the presence of a single volcanic core in both Periods 2 and 3 at Tunnell Shelter. Volcanic cores are absent at both Initiation and Ngarrabullgan Caves. If the presence of these cores is indicative of a provisioning strategy involving cores, then we would expect to see an assemblage comprising a population of relatively large, thick flakes. We might also expect a broader range of flake platform sizes, assuming that core reduction will result in more flakes with broad, thick platforms than flake reduction (i.e retouching). A final expectation is for comparatively relaxed discard thresholds. What is considered useable will depend on what is available, thus when the range of transported items is limited, the probability of relatively large, useful flakes being discarded will be low.

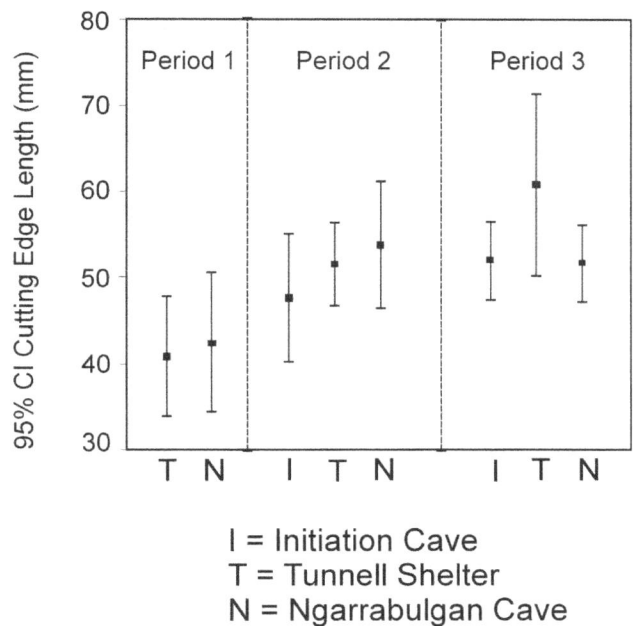

I = Initiation Cave
T = Tunnell Shelter
N = Ngarrabulgan Cave

Figure 8. Error bars of changing volcanic flake cutting edge by period.

Due to the fragmented nature of the assemblages, the number of complete flakes is too small to allow meaningful statistical comparisons of mean length and weight between sites. Alternatively, flake thickness is not expected to change significantly as a result of flake breakage, allowing a greater sample to be used. Differences in flake thickness support the timing of and nature of those differences suggested by the presence of volcanic cores. In Period 3, t-tests demonstrate significant differences in mean flake thickness (volcanic flakes only) between Tunnell Shelter and Ngarrabullgan Cave and between Initiation Cave and Ngarrabullgan Cave (Table 2). In both instances, mean flake thickness is significantly greater in those sites around which cores were located.

Table 2. Period 3 variation in mean volcanic flake thickness between sites.

Site	N	Mean	Std Dev.	t-Test	
				df	Sig.
Ngarrabullgan Cave	51	3.3	1.8	80.8	0.060
Tunnell Shelter	57	4.4	3.9		
Ngarrabullgan Cave	51	3.3	1.8	146.1	0.098
Initiation Cave	112	4.0	2.9		
Tunnell Shelter	57	4.4	3.9	88.5	0.420
Initiation Cave	112	4.0	2.9		

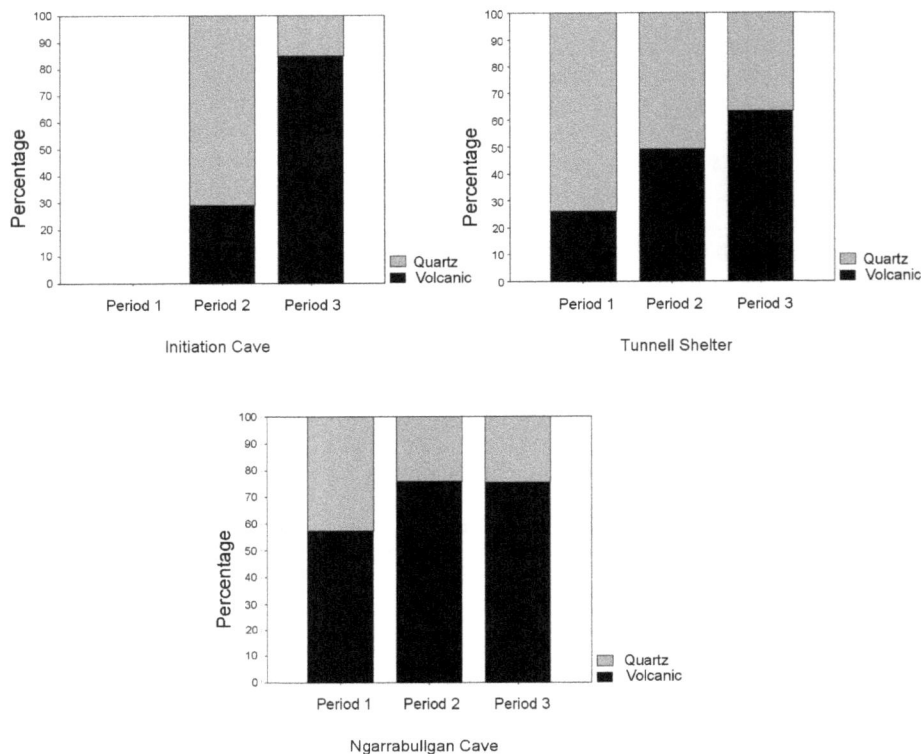

Figure 9. Ratios of quartz to volcanic artefacts by site.

Differences between Tunnell Shelter and Initiation Cave were not found to be significant.

Subsequently in Period 2, mean flake thickness decreases at both Tunnell Shelter (mean = 4.0, s.d. = 2.6) and Initiation Cave (mean = 3.4, s.d. = 2.7), while increasing at Ngarrabullgan Cave (mean = 3.8, s.d. = 1.7). Consequently, all means are relatively similar in this period and no significant differences are displayed. Initiation Cave is not occupied in Period 1, while at the remaining two sites mean thickness continues to decrease. Differences between sites are not significant, but differences within sites from the preceding period are. At Ngarrabullgan Cave, the significance of differences between mean flake thickness in Periods 2 and 1 is 0.049 (df = 42). At Tunnell Shelter, significance is 0.034 (df = 94.7). At all sites, lowest mean thickness is recorded in the period immediately preceding abandonment.

Changes to platform area (platform width x platform thickness) mirror those seen in flake thickness (Figure 7). While no significant differences are recorded within or between periods, both mean and standard deviation are notably greater at Tunnell Shelter in Period 3 ($\mu_{Tunnell}$ = 82.3, s.d. = 123.1) than at the other sites ($\mu_{Initiation}$ = 48.3, s.d. = 73.0; $\mu_{Ngarrabullgan}$ = 37.7, s.d. = 49.8). In Period 2 at Tunnell Shelter both mean and range are reduced ($\mu_{Tunnell}$ = 48.7, s.d. = 47.3), though mean remains greater than at the other two sites ($\mu_{Initiation}$ = 31.7, s.d. = 40.5; $\mu_{Ngarrabullgan}$ = 30.8, s.d. = 41.8). The lowest means are recorded in the final period of occupation at all sites, though sample numbers in Period 1 at Tunnell Shelter and Ngarrabullgan Cave are very small.

Directional changes paralleling those in volcanic flake thickness and platform area are found in two further measures; changes in cutting edge length at discard, and changes in raw material use.

Cutting edge length refers to the length of sharp edge remaining on a flake at the time of discard. Sharp edges on a broken flake are assumed to be no less useful than those on a complete flake, thus relevant sections of all flakes are incorporated (excluding platforms). Changes in cutting edge length over time are expected to be influenced both by manufacturing behaviour and discard thresholds.

Error Bars (95% Confidence Interval) of changing cutting edge length at all sites are shown in Figure 8. Changes follow the preceding trend of general decrease in mean and range over time, with a significant drop in the period preceding abandonment at each site. The reduction in mean cutting edge length is significant between periods 3 and 1 at Ngarrabullgan Cave (p = 0.05, df = 65) and Tunnell Shelter (p = 0.00, df = 74). Differences at Tunnell Shelter are also significant between periods 2 and 1 (p = 0.00, df = 96). These differences cannot be ascribed to increased rates of flake breakage, as the percentage of broken flakes does not vary greatly between periods at any site. Only at Initiation Cave is the percentage of broken flakes highest in the final period.

Changes in the proportions of quartz and volcanic artefacts over time are shown in Figure 9. At all sites, the relative frequency of volcanic items follows the established trend. Both Tunnell Shelter and Initiation Cave exhibit a consistent decrease through time. Ngarrabullgan Cave increases between Period 3 and Period 2, and then decreases sharply in Period 1. The general trend is of a decrease in the proportion of volcanic artefacts over time, with the lowest proportion occurring at each site in the period immediately preceding abandonment.

Given the consistency of the trend through time towards small range and size of artefacts across all sites, it is worth testing for a general pattern of reduction in flake size across the study area as a whole. Conflating the data from all excavated sites provides sufficient sample numbers to allow complete flakes to be used. Weight is used to approximate total flake size.

Table 3. Mean weight (g) of complete flakes by period for all sites combined.

Period	Mean	N	Std Dev
1	0.25	37	0.35
2	0.74	119	1.55
3	1.22	158	3.26

Table 3 reveals the anticipated trend of reduced overall weight of complete flakes over time. Significance tests reveal that the difference in weight is significant overall (ANOVA, p = .01) and between Periods 1 and 2 (t-test, p = .003, df = 454) and between Periods 2 and 3 (t-test, p = .05, df = 723). At the same time there is comparatively little fluctuation in the mean weight of quartz artefacts, which remain small throughout the sequence (ANOVA, p = .90). Although a few large sized quartz and volcanic

outliers exist, the vast majority of artefacts made from quartz and volcanic stone weigh less than 1g (80%). In all periods the median weight of complete flakes is 0.1g. This suggests that very small flakes predominate throughout time, with the distinction between periods largely resulting from changes to the range of artefacts manufactured and/or discarded at sites.

Summary of Temporal Patterns
The data presented above appear to reflect broadly directional changes in artefact assemblages in sites both on and off the mountain. The observed trend toward size reduction in the study area is argued to result from a combination of changes to manufacturing behaviour and artefact discard thresholds. As outlined earlier, a change from core to flake reduction is likely to result in the contraction of the range of manufactured flakes towards the small end of the spectrum. Compounding this is the decreased probability that large flakes will be discarded, given the increased need to conserve transported materials. The dominance of small thin flakes at these sites in all time periods therefore appears best explained by a high frequency of flake reduction as the source of flake debris. Most flakes weigh less than 1g, and are unlikely to have been brought to the site as part of a transported tool-kit. They are therefore assumed to have been manufactured on-site. Thus, the data do not appear to support "paradigmatic" place provisioning at any stage, but rather a combination of core and flake reduction limited to Period 3, and to a lesser extent Period 2, at Tunnell Shelter. Through time, larger items increasingly drop out of assemblages, culminating in the almost total absence of large flakes in the final stages preceding abandonment. At all other sites, on-site reduction appears to have been limited to flake reduction only.

Consistent with the reduction in size and range of volcanic flakes is the increased use of locally procured items. Given the small size of quartz pebbles and the difficulty in controlling fracture on this material, the desirability of quartz as a raw material must have been reasonably limited. Its use therefore suggests the conservation of higher-quality imported items through supplementation.

These changes are taken to suggest decreased diversity of transported items through time as well as increased conservation of transported raw materials. As such, they appear to represent an increasingly mobile use of Ngarrabullgan through the mid to late Holocene. Increased mobility would have placed greater restrictions both on the size and range of transported artefacts, decreasing the probability of core transportation in favour of items conferring greater immediate utility, such as flakes (both retouched and unretouched). Consequently, on-site manufacturing of new artefacts would have relied increasingly on flakes from retouch events and the supplementary use of locally available, poor quality stone.

Discussion

Land use at Ngarrabullgan is argued to have been variable through space and time, with variation in assemblage structure implying different strategies of mobility and subsistence. Spatial patterns suggest that parts of Ngarrabullgan at the central western edge were occasionally provisioned with flake making potential in the form of volcanic cores, the largest of which occur in the area around Lake Koongirra. The relatively large size of these items at discard suggests that the useable potential of raw material need not have been maximized. This is taken to represent a degree of place provisioning and thus, comparatively low residential mobility in this part of the mountain. This would appear consistent with the location of relatively less mobile camps close to the largest source of permanent water on the mountain.

The combination of cores and heavily retouched flakes in this area may be explained by changes in provisioning through time, as demonstrated by the assemblage at Tunnell Shelter. Initial mid-Holocene occupation of this site suggests some on-site core reduction as indicated by the relatively high mean thickness, platform area and cutting edge length for discarded flakes. At this time, most technological demands appear to have been met with volcanic stone. Over time, the relative use of quartz increases and the range and size of volcanic items decreases, suggesting either an increase in residential mobility or a shift to logistical use of the area, and a concomitant shift from a combination of place and individual provisioning to individual provisioning only.

In the north of the mountain, the absence of cores is complemented by the presence of retouched volcanic flakes and the relatively high ratio of quartz to volcanic artefacts, suggesting transportation of flakes to this location and their conservation through the use of local raw materials. From this it is inferred that subsistence in the north of the mountain was undertaken either as episodes of brief residential occupation or as logistical movements from a base either near the lake or possibly off the mountain. At both Ngarrabullgan Cave and Initiation Cave a pattern of increased group mobility is inferred from the decreased size, constrained range and low prevalence of volcanic artefacts leading up to the abandonment of those sites. The patterns demonstrated at all sites are in contrast to existing models of the occupational history of northeastern Queensland, which suggest decreases in mobility through time. This model does not appear to be supported at Ngarrabullgan

Changes in provisioning and mobility also correlate reasonably well with changes in water availability through the study period. Changes from Period 3 to Period 2 follow a decrease in annual precipitation, while the change from Period 2 to Period 1 appears to correlate to changes in water reliability in waterholes on the mountain. Some caution needs to be exercised in regard to this final change, however, given that permanent water is still common on the mountain-top today. It is beyond the scope of this data to explain the final abandonment of the study area (but see David and Wilson 1999).

Conclusion

The objective of this paper has been to demonstrate that meaningful conclusions about settlement and subsistence behaviour can be drawn from manufacturing debris without recourse to tools or tool design. It has been shown that existing theory makes such conclusions possible without requiring major changes or novel developments. The approach taken here has a number of advantages over formalized approaches to stone artefacts and assemblages, the most significant being the capacity to interpret small assemblages lacking in formal components or even large numbers of retouched flakes. Given that the debitage component will vastly outnumber the tool component of any complete assemblage, it would seem worthwhile exploring the informative potential of these frequently underutilized artefact populations.

Acknowledgements

I would like to extend my thanks to Chris Clarkson for help, encouragement and critical comment in the preparation of this paper; to Bruno David for allowing me to work on the Ngarrabullgan assemblages and for insight, assistance and critical comment thereafter; to Peter Hiscock and Cheyla Samuelson for critical comment, and to W. Boone Law for consideration and politeness. Also thanks to my previous employers, Umwelt Australia, for providing me with time and facilities to work on an earlier version of this paper. The survey data used in this paper was collected in the field by Bruno David, Chris Clarkson and Catriona Murray between 1995 and 1997, while the excavations of the three analysed rockshelters were undertaken by Bruno David and Chris Clarkson.

References

Bamforth, D. 1991 Technological organization and hunter-gatherer land use: A California example. *American Antiquity* 56:216-234.

Bamforth, D. 1986 Technological efficiency and stone tools curation. *American Antiquity* 51: 38-50.

Binford, L. R. 1979 Willow smoke and dogs' tails: Hunter-gatherer settlement systems and archaeological site formation. *American Antiquity* 45:4-20.

Binford, L. R. 1980 Organisation and formation processes: Looking at curated technologies. *Journal of Anthropological Research* 35:255-273.

Bleed, P. 1986 The optimal design of hunting weapons. *American Antiquity* 51:737-747.

Butler, D. 1998 Environmental change in the Quaternary. In David, B. (ed.) *Ngarrabullgan: Geographical Investigations in Djungan Country, Cape York Peninsula.* Pp.78-97. Melbourne: Monash Publications.

Clarkson, C. 2002 An index of invasiveness for the measurement of unifacial and bifacial retouch: A theoretical, experimental and archaeological verification. *Journal of Archaeological Science* 29:65-75.

David, B. 2002 *Landscapes, Rock-art and the Dreaming: An Archaeology of Preunderstanding.* London: Leicester University Press.

David, B., and M. Wilson 1999 Re-reading the landscape: Place and identity in NE Australia during the Late Holocene. *Cambridge Archaeological Journal* 9:163-188.

David, B., McNiven, I., Bekessy, L., Bultitude, B., Clarkson, C., Lawson, E., Murray, C., and C. Tuniz 1998 More than 37000 years of aboriginal occupation. In David, B. (ed.) *Ngarrabullgan: Geographical Investigations in Djungan Country, Cape York Peninsula.* Pp.78-97. Melbourne: Monash Publications.

Gould, R. 1991 Arid-land foraging as seen from Australia: Adaptive models and behavioral realities. *Oceania* 62:12-33.

Hiscock, P. 1993 Bondaian technology in the Hunter Valley, New South Wales. *Archaeology in Oceania* 28:65-76.

Hiscock, P. 1994 Technological responses to risk in Holocene Australia. *Journal of World Prehistory* 8:267-292.

Hiscock, P. 1996 Mobility and technology in the Kakadu coastal wetlands. *Bulletin of the Indo-Pacific Prehistory Association* 15:151-157.

Hiscock, P. and V. Attenbrow 2003 Morphological and reduction continuums in eastern Australia: measurement and implications at Capertee 3. *Tempus* 7:167-174.

Kelly, R. 1983 Hunter-gatherer mobility strategies. *Journal of Anthropological Research* 39:277-306.

Kelly, R. 1988 The three sides of a biface. *American Antiquity* 53:717-734.

Kelly, R. and L. C. Todd 1988 Coming into the Country: Early Palaeoindian hunting and mobility. *American Antiquity* 53:231-244.

Kershaw, A. P. 1983 The vegetation record from northeastern Australia 7+2KA. In *CLIMANZ*, Chappell J. and A. Grindrod (eds). Pp.100-101. Canberra: Research School of Pacific Studies, ANU.

Kuhn, S. L. 1992 On planning and curated technologies in the Middle Paleolithic. *Journal of Anthropological Research* 48:185-213.

Kuhn, S. L. 1994 A formal approach to the design and assembly of mobile toolkits. *American Antiquity* 59:426-442.

Kuhn, S. L. 1995 *Mousterian Lithic Technology.* Princeton University Press.

Lourandos, H. 1997 *A Continent of Hunter-Gatherers.* Cambridge: Cambridge University Press.

Lourandos, H. 1983 Intensification: a late Pleistocene-Holocene archaeological sequence from southwestern Victoria. *Archaeology in Oceania* 18:81-94.

Morwood, M., and D. Hobbs 1995 Themes in the prehistory of tropical Australia. *Antiquity* 69:747-768.

Nix, H., and J. Kalma 1972 Climate as a dominant control in the biogreography of northern Australia and New Guinea. In *Bridge and Barrier: The Natural and Cultural History of Torres Strait.* Pp.61-92. Canberra: Research School of Pacific Studies, ANU.

Parry, W. and R. Kelly 1987 Expedient core technology and sedentism. In J. Johnson and C. Morrow (eds) *The Organisation of Core Technology.* Pp.285-309. Boulder, Co.: Westview Press.

Torrence, R. 1989 Re-tooling: Towards a behavioural theory of stone tools. In R. Torrence (ed.) *Time, Energy and Stone Tools.* Pp57-66. Cambridge: Cambridge University Press.

Shaw, J. D., and Wason, S. 1998 Appendix 6.1. Useful plants. In David, B. (ed.) *Ngarrabullgan: Geographical Investigations in Djungan Country, Cape York Peninsula.* Pp.78-97. Melbourne: Monash Publications.

Shott, M. 1986 Technological Organisation and Settlement Mobility: an ethnographic examination. *Journal of Anthropological Research* 42:15-51.

10 | The Reduction Thesis and its Discontents: Overview of the Volume

Michael J. Shott

Introduction

Archaeologists study stone tools to learn about the people who made and used them. In their abundance and diversity, tools pattern in virtually infinite ways that analysis might reveal. Whether patterns detected reveal what archaeologists wish to know -how tools were designed and used and how their cultural context influenced both, for instance - depends upon whether they mean what we suppose they do. By their nature or circumstances of use, many objects do not change in size and form during use. Like other people, archaeologists conclude from this trivial fact that objects' size and form are constants in use and that they bear some necessary relationship to function.

No matter how true this is generally, it is demonstrably untrue of commonplace things like pencils. Nor is it true of stone tools, perhaps the most abundant and therefore informative archaeological material. No one ever doubted that stone tools were reduced as they were fashioned, but until recently few archaeologists assimilated the extension or corollary that many stone tools continued to be reduced during use, such that their original size and form were much changed.

This is the reduction thesis, and it has far-reaching implications for ontological fundamentals like the nature and identity of types and how tool assemblages form. Most dictionaries define 'discontents' as something like 'restless aspiration to improve'. The reduction thesis's aspiration, demonstrated throughout this volume, is to improve the quality and expand the breadth of lithic analysis by accounting for systematic patterns of reduction before interpreting variation in tool size and form as the result of cognition, design or use.

The reduction thesis had independent Old World and New World origins. In recent years Australian archaeology emerged as an innovator in lithic analysis, partly due to the efforts of Peter Hiscock and his students at Australian National University. This volume assembles some of their latest and best work, and simultaneously establishes Australia as an independent centre of the reduction thesis. Collectively, these papers use experiments and original analysis of empirical data to explore the reduction thesis's implications for Australian taxonomy and assemblage analysis.

Types as Essences, Types as Populations

Archaeologists know that classification is important but most treat it as a tiresome chore, not an intrinsically fascinating intellectual exercise. No one who has attempted it would doubt that classification of stone tools is difficult, but even biological classification, which seems straightforward, is more problematic than many suppose. Consider species, a fundamental biological unit of observation and inference. "Species" is a fundamental taxon - the unit of evolution - in a higher-order body of theory. It is not, however, easily defined. Biologists work with living taxa, difficult enough to classify, paleontologists with their fossil remains. Trivially, to identify reproductive boundaries requires observing reproduction. This is not always easy, so biologists sometimes rely upon gross differences in size and anatomy to distinguish species. But paleontologists cannot observe reproduction, so rely entirely upon such differences to distinguish fossil species. For them, classification is even less straightforward, their dilemmas more akin to archaeology's. Unable to observe living organisms, paleontologists must order the great diversity of evidence into meaningful units like species but must not confuse them with other sources of variation like individual difference, growth from birth to maturity and taphonomic distortion. When contemplating two or more specimens that broadly are similar but that differ in some respects, paleontologists must decide if the fossil individuals were conspecifics that document the taxon's range of variation or members of two or more taxa separated by time, selection, and evolutionary change.

To pursue the paleontological analogy, archaeologists must define types from the great variation expressed in stone tools. But they cannot observe in use the tools that they classify, and must remember that some stone tools were only parts of larger wholes, not wholes themselves. Like paleontologists, archaeologists must accommodate systematic variation that occurs within, not just between, taxa. Types are Platonic ideals that specimens only approximate, so there is ordinary variation within them. Stone tools do not grow but, on the contrary, become smaller with use. Reduction is an archaeological analogue of biological growth that works in the opposite direction. Finally, tools can be broken after deposition, so suffer some taphonomic effects. As in biology, so in archaeology: classification can be complicated.

Assuming that we distinguish accurately, tools can be classified into groups like bifaces and unifaces and then more finely by specific type. Among finished bifaces, classification sometimes is easy. No one would confuse a Clovis fluted biface, for instance, with an Acheulean handaxe. But depending on how and how finely we classify, and mindful of the complicating effects of raw material, technology, reduction and other factors, classification can be very difficult, and archaeologist can disagree on type definitions and the assignment of specimens among them.

Bifaces and some other tools are so extensively modified by hafting and use to be impossible to mistake for other types. North American fluted bifaces, for instance, are a relatively homogeneous type that requires no sophisticated methods to recognize, but the definition of specific fluted-biface types like Clovis and Gainey is much disputed. Ancient people only hafted some stone tools and used many, hafted or otherwise, that were not constrained in size or form by their manner of use. Most lithic classification is by size and form, but these properties are ill-suited to flake (and some core) tools that vary widely in those respects but perhaps less in the characteristics of their use and retouch. For every biface, archaeologists might encounter dozens of unmodified or slightly modified flake tools, especially in places like Australia.

Whatever its problematics in use, classification traditionally started from two related premises. First, their size and form was essential to the definition of tool types. Any type defined differed from any other in these respects, and all tools belong unambiguously to one or the other. There is no continuum of variation between types. There is no continuity, metrically or otherwise, between knives and forks, wrenches and hammers, Middle Palaeolithic single, double and convergent scrapers, or Australian steep-edge scrapers and flat scrapers. These beliefs are archaeological variants of essentialism, the view that types are discrete Platonic essences and that their boundaries are marked by gaps or discontinuities in size and form however measured or categorized. Circles and squares are different essential types separated by the chasm of categorical difference; you can't square a circle by degree.

The second premise is that the size and form in which archaeologists find tools are the size and form in which they were used, excepting of course the fracture experienced by many specimens. It is equivalent to supposing that we find short stubs of pencils in trash cans because that is the size at which people used pencils or, for that matter, that cigarettes were smoked only for fleeting moments because usually they are found as short, crushed butts.

Unlike metal, pottery and other important materials, stone is a reductive medium; no one assembles stone tools. From original cobble to finished tool and beyond, size

change occurs only in one direction. However trite it may seem, this observation has deceptively profound implications for both typological premises. Taking them in reverse order, the undeniable fact of reduction means that many tools are found at whatever their size and form not because they were designed for use that way but because they were reduced during use and then discarded. They were not designed for use at that size and form, but thrown away precisely because that diminished size and perhaps changed form rendered them useless. The second premise therefore is compromised by reduction.

Reduction itself occurs retouch flake by retouch flake, so in a sense is a discrete process. But it is better understood as a continuous process, both because the incremental units - retouch flakes - ordinarily are very small relative to the tool and because reduction is measured by continuous variables or dimensions like length and width. If tools are reduced and reduction is continuous, then tools vary in continuous terms (Hiscock and Attenbrow 2002). Things that vary so cannot approximate Platonic essences. Any types formed among the complex variation in stone-tool size and form are empirical tendencies; they are populations, not essential types.

This is not to deny the validity of typological concepts nor the reality of many stone-tool types. Even empirical tendencies sometimes are discretely different from one another. It is, however, to deny the necessity of essential types and to acknowledge the possibility that much variation in stone-tool size and form owes to continuous reduction combined with modes of use and retouch. In recent decades, therefore, archaeologists around the world have reimagined the nature of lithic types and nature of variation within and between them.

Antipodean Typology
Archaeologists may indulge Platonic notions about stone tools, but the people who made and used them were more practical. Australia and New Guinea have a long tradition of flake-tool use and comparatively little formal structure in lithic industries, so archaeologists there turned to people who still used stone (e.g., Gould *et al.* 1971; White *et al.* 1977). Those people cared little for the distinction between core and flake so important to archaeologists; they bashed cores freely to produce flakes and sorted through the debris for specimens suitable for particular, often momentary, tasks; they chose those specimens for the properties of their edges, not overall size or form; and they often discarded tools after short use, the edges acquiring neither use-wear nor retouch.

Australian aborigines surprised Hayden (1977) by using whatever stone was at hand, indifferent to its size or form. Tindale (1965) showed how one tula - an unmodified flake hafted to the end of a spearthrower and used as a general cutting-scraping tool -was resharpened, changed in form and much reduced in size in two weeks' use. The resulting 'slug' was a depleted discard, not a designed original type. From comparison of many tulas,

Cooper (1954, Figures 1-6) deduced the same process. New Guinea flake tools varied sufficiently in size, form and technology to defy classification into discrete, mutually exclusive types (White 1969). Instead of the dozen or so flake-tool types defined in traditional typology, White's (1969:41) analysis revealed fascinating if complex patterns of variation between attributes, and only several ambiguous functional types defined by use-wear. Traditional typology dislikes such ambiguous results, but they are more faithful to the true patterns of variation in used-flake assemblages.

Recent Australian research systematizes these perspectives. "Capertian" industries occupy the early phases of Australian prehistory, preceding "Bondaian" ones. Capertian types are defined by combinations of tool size and the placement and kind of retouch. Types are presumed to be distinct from one another in form and function, so that differences in type proportions between assemblages reflect differing proportions of the activities in which types were used. But many Capertian types are linked in a continuum defined by tool size and measures of reduction (Hiscock and Attenbrow 2002), including Kuhn's (1990) edge-profile inflection index or "Geometric Index of Unifacial Reduction," used extensively in this volume, and number, length and form (concave vs. convex) or retouched edges. Thus, Capertian types differ in average reduction measures. As reduction proceeds, the mean edge-profile index and the number and length of retouched edges rise, and edges become progressively convex. To Hiscock and Attenbrow "the difference between perceived implement types is largely related to differences in the extent of reduction" (2002:247). Variation is by continuous reduction; Capertian types lack integrity as markers of function or style. They are not distinct types, merely arbitrary subdivisions of a continuum of size reduction by retouching.

Paleolithic Typology
Flake tools dominate Old World Paleolithic industries, and elaborate typologies arose to classify them. Most emphasize object form and pattern of flaking; Bordes's (1961) widely used Middle Paleolithic typology is the best known such approach. However they differ in details, Paleolithic flake-tool typologies treat types as distinct from one another in form and, usually, in function. By implication, all specimens approximate the ideal or template of their type. During their use lives, specimens do not change substantially in size or form.

In the past 20 years, however, archaeologists have questioned these assumptions in two respects. First, some reject the view that flake-tool form was fixed in users' minds, either for functional or stylistic reasons, instead linking formal types to one another within reduction sequences. Essentially, they question the integrity of formal types that Bordean systematics presumed. Second, following White's lead, archaeologists emphasize retouched and used edges rather than the flakes on which

they occur. Bisson (2000), for instance, proposed replacing Bordean Middle Paleolithic typology and its focus on flakes with an edge-based approach.

Dibble (1995) summarized revisions to various Paleolithic typologies and industries that were inspired by the reduction thesis. From Lower Paleolithic Oldowan industries through Middle Paleolithic Acheulian and Mousterian ones to Upper Paleolithic ones, from Oldowan cobbles and spheroids to Acheulian bifacial handaxes to varieties of Mousterian scrapers and notches to Aurignacian burins and late Paleolithic microliths, much variation in tool size and form once attributed to template, index fossil, or design instead can be attributed to reduction effects. Because typological assignment of flake tools is partly a result of degree of reduction, even type proportions in Paleolithic European and African assemblages partly are products of reduction mediated by time-averaging (Shiner *et al.*, Chap. 7; Shott 2003, in press). Type proportions are a fundamental property of assemblages because they determine assemblage composition. Bordes interpreted those proportions in cultural or iconic terms, Binford in functional ones (Shott 1996b), but this perspective reinterprets them, in part, in terms of reduction.

North American Bifaces
Flake tools abound in Old World Paleolithic assemblages. In the New World, bifaces were used from the start. So were flake tools, but the abundance and diversity of bifaces drew most attention. Frison's (1968) refitting of resharpening flakes and tools fragments showed the changes in tool size and form that reduction caused. Wheat (1975) demonstrated that the "San Jon" type was merely a reduced version of Firstview bifaces. Thus, one type was linked to another by reduction. Changes experienced by specimens were in size, of course, but also in blade form and proportion. Simultaneously, Goodyear (1974) showed that several southeastern Dalton tool types were merely various degrees of reduction of a single original form, thereby linking not just one but several derivative types to an original prototype. Granger (1978) echoed this judgment for Great Lakes Meadowood assemblages, showing the relationship between Meadowood blanks and their typological "descendants," previously considered distinct types. In these cases, differences were not only of size and proportion but also variables like edge shape and treatment (e.g., bevelled or not, orientation to tool long axis), and number of notches. Truncer (1990:11-13) did the same for eastern Perkiomen bifaces, which ranged from large-blade point to drill to transverse bifacial scraper.

Hoffman's (1985) definitive study of biface reduction's typological effects linked no fewer than 12 Southeastern biface types, as well as unnamed scraper and drill types, to a single stemmed prototype. The types differed in blade size and form but little in the stem; they were not truly distinct types, merely variously reduced forms of one original type. Hoffman demonstrated that biface

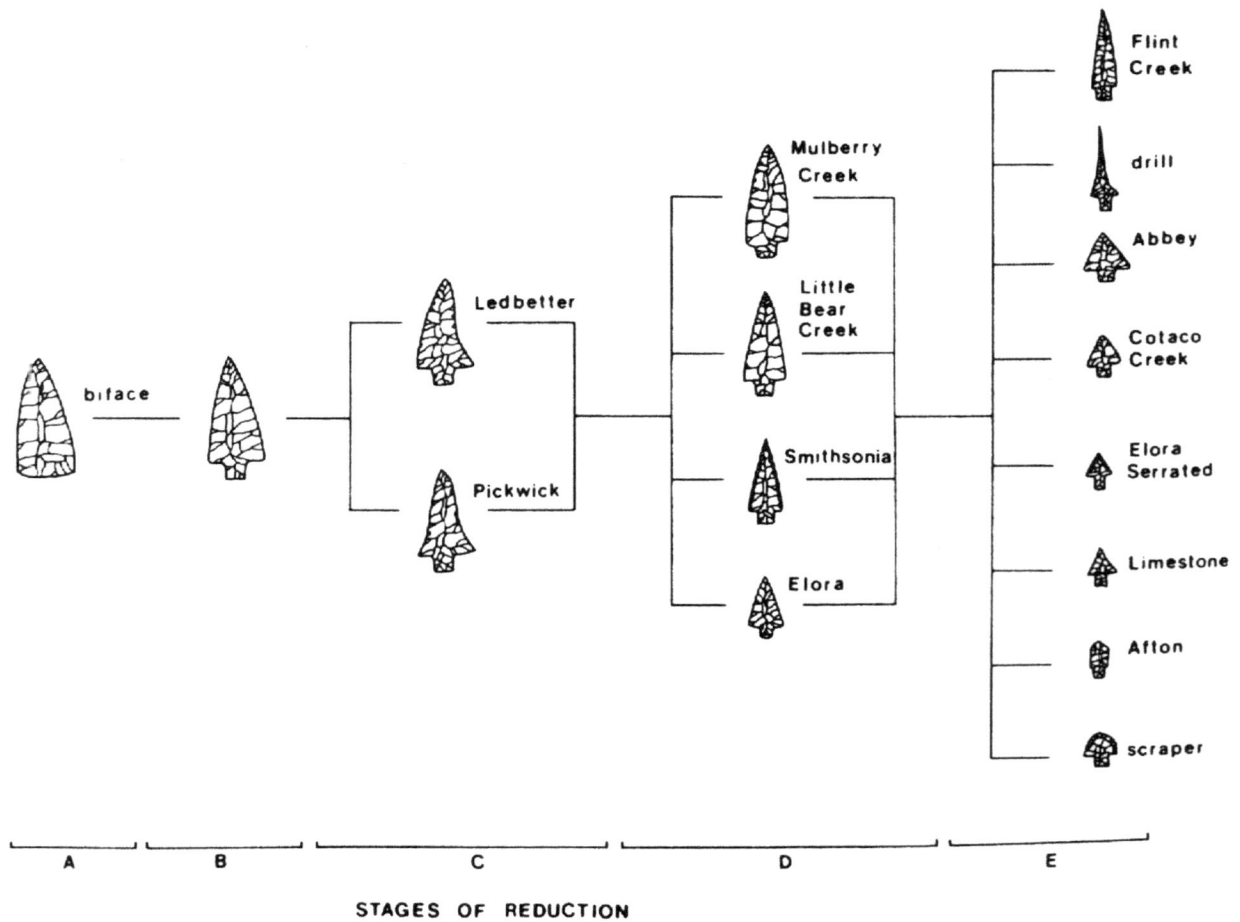

Figure 1. Reduction continuum that links apparently distinct biface types in the American Southeast (Source: Hoffman 1986, Figure 18.5).

blades were more variable in size and, to some extent, form than were their stems. The essential similarity of what previously were considered distinct types was revealed graphically (Figure 1). Aftons were reduced Eloras were reduced Ledbetters or Pickwicks, not distinct types. Yet analytically, when specimens were reduced to orthogonal dimensions like length and width, their similarities were obscured until Hoffman separated stem and blade variables. Only then were the types shown analytically to be reduction variants of the same prototype.

Summary of Reduction Effects
Reduction and its effects on tool size and form—and therefore on typologies based on these properties— register clearly in Paleolithic tools, North American stemmed bifaces, Australian tulas and other flake tools, even in contemporary Ethiopian (Weedman 2000, 2002) and ancient Paleoindian (Shott 1995) hidescrapers. That is, reduction effects are recognized in many tool types of many ages from many parts of the world. Flake tools always have been used in myriad ways. In use, specimens passed through degrees or stages of reduction. The types defined in these reduction trajectories lack integrity (but

may retain descriptive validity); defining types in these industries and tools is like slicing a piece from a stream.

In biology, species enjoy at least a measure of integrity, both in the sense that, say, lions never become giraffes and that the two are not easily confused. Once a lion, always one. But in evolutionary time, species evolve into descendants by various modes, so typological integrity is breached over long spans or at higher taxonomic levels than species. In different ways, lithic reduction compromises the integrity of tool types. Lions never become giraffes but Oldowan cobbles become discoids become scrapers and Meadowood points become Meadowood scrapers.

The typological implications of the reduction thesis are difficult to exaggerate. Traditionally, much variation observed in tool assemblages is attributed to cultural affinity, activity variation or other factors. Indeed, Paleolithic archaeologists record affinity or activity almost entirely in different type proportions. If the reduction thesis is correct, these conclusions are illusory. There are no Developed Oldowan industries, no distinct notched-tool types, no Quina Mousterian facies. There is instead complex and fascinating assemblage variation to explain. More than any other recent development, the reduction thesis shows that how we classify determines what we perceive about the past. Erosion is a natural process that no geologist can ignore. Reduction is a cultural practice that no lithic analyst can ignore.

Reduction and Curation

In Australia and around the world, the reduction thesis explains some variation in tool size and form better than do traditional approaches. But the reduction thesis reveals more than just each tool's path through one formal type to another. Trivially, each tool entered the archaeological record by being discarded for some reason. At the higher level of assemblages as sets of tools, variation in degree of reduction identifies both the amount of reduction that tools experienced and the processes that led to discard.

Besides its typological implications, therefore, reduction engages the theoretical question of curation. This quantity is the relationship between realized and maximum utility of tools, i.e., how used up tools become (Shott 1996b). So defined, curation itself engages the additional concept of utility. "Utility" has several meanings (Elston 1992:40-42; Kuhn 1994:430-432; Shott 1996b:269-271; for practical purposes, it signifies the amount of use that a tool can supply, equivalent to Elston's (1992:41) "use-life utility," Schiffer's (1976:54) "number of uses," DeBoer's (1983:26) "remnant uselife," and Macgregor's (Chapter 6) "reduction potential." Practically, maximum utility is approximated as the greatest amount or degree of reduction that a tool can undergo, realized utility as the reduction (less than or equal to maximum utility) that it actually experiences. Therefore, measuring utility requires knowing the amount of usable material that a tool contained originally (Kuhn 1994; Shott 1996:270). This abstract quantity is approximated by object mass, size or volume; Kuhn (1994:429) added edge length for some purposes. Obviously, to estimate either utility value requires knowing original size of specimens, a subject discussed above. Thus, reduction measures curation and the amount or degree of reduction measures amount or degree of curation. Curation itself is a variable linked in models of activity and assemblage formation to important characteristics of ancient cultures. Indirectly, then, reduction registers cultural properties and practices that are worth knowing.

As defined, curation is not the same thing as use life, which is simply the longevity of tools in time, number of uses or other units. Each tool type can be characterized by its mean curation from 0 to 100% of maximum utility, and its mean use life in whatever units (e.g., time, number of uses, number of strokes). Curation and use life are measured in different units on different scales. Tools in any type are apt to vary around the means of both curation and use life, yielding distributions of values in both quantities. For individual tools, curation and use life must correlate, because curation rises only as use life does. But at the assemblage level, curation and use life

are independent not only because they are measured differently but because specimens in a tool type can be highly curated even if the type's mean use life is short or, conversely, curated at low rates even though the type's mean use life is high. Also, the rate of tool reduction and therefore curation can vary with use life at different rates in different types.

For individual tools, curation is the ratio of two utilities noted above. It can suggest the discard processes (Schiffer 1976:30-34; Shott 1989) by which tools entered the archaeological record. Tools that were cached or abandoned in production cannot be curated at all, and those lost or abandoned in use cannot be extensively curated. Only depleted tools can have high curation values. Knowing how tools entered the archaeological record still seems esoteric and therefore unimportant to many archaeologists, yet is vital to grounded inference from the record. Measurement of reduction and therefore curation aids this vital task.

Like use-life, curation can be measured by central tendency (e.g., mean, median) (Schiffer 1976:54). Unless all specimens had identical histories, however, the distribution of curation values is as important as central tendency (Shott 1996b; Shott and Sillitoe 2004). Two artifact categories can be equal in mean curation but very different in their distributions, one showing little variation around the mean, the other a great deal. Consider an analogy to pencils. Two sets of discarded pencils both average, say, 50% reduction of original length. In one, all pencils are reduced to that figure. In the other, pencils are discarded in equal proportions from slight reduction of 1% to practically complete reduction to stubs at 99%. The populations are identical in mean curation but very different in the distribution of curation values.

At the assemblage level, degree or amount of curation is distributed across specimens to form curation distributions or curves. Curation distributions may seem esoteric, but actually influence how the regional archaeological record forms. To appreciate why, consider hypothetical distributions (in arbitrary units) for one artifact class. Curation mean is identical among them, but curation distributions differ. In one case, all specimens are curated to exactly the same degree, like the first set of hypothetical pencils. There is no distribution, only a single value. Other distributions are progressively wider and more dispersed, like the second set of pencils. In the first case, each specimen found represents about the same degree or amount of use, at least as this quantity is measured by curation. Specimens from progressively wider distributions represent more variable curation rates, and are not equivalent in degree or amount of use experienced. Inferring amount of tool use represented in the assemblages is confounded by curation's distribution independently of its mean (Shott and Sillitoe 2004). This hypothetical illustration is simplified, but it shows how curation distribution affects archaeological inference and assemblage formation. The same use of the same number of specimens in curation distributions can yield very different assemblage size and composition (Shott and Sillitoe 2004, Table 1).

Cumulative survivorship is one way to characterize the distribution of curation values among specimens in or between tool types and assemblages. For instance, a tool class called "flakeshavers" differed in degree of curation between two North American Paleoindian assemblages (Grimes and Grimes 1985; Shott 1996b, Figure 1) (Figure 2). Specimens in the Vail assemblage were curated more extensively than those from Bull Brook. Why this should be is a matter for Paleoindian scholars to determine; perhaps it owed to lower raw-material supply at Vail, or to more extensive mobility and the need it created to use tools more thoroughly. He did not compile curation curves but Cooper (1954:94-96) described variation in the lengths of discarded tulas and in the average lengths between assemblages, attributing this variation in part to toolstone supply effects.

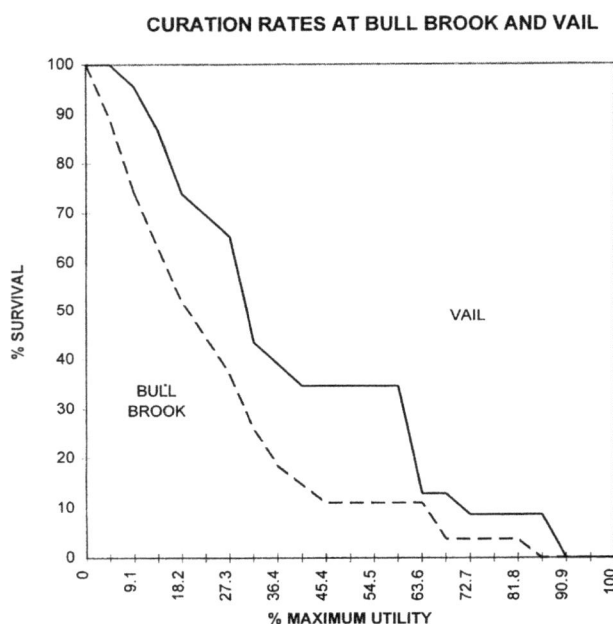

Figure 2. Curation curves for flakeshavers in two North American Paleoindian assemblages (Source: Shott 1996, Figure 1).

Curation curves can be compared between assemblages, but they also can be analyzed. Depending on their forms and the distribution of values that comprise them, curves fitted to the Weibull and other theoretical models may implicate the effects of chance versus attrition in tool failure (e.g., Shott and Sillitoe 2004), with far-reaching implications for assemblage formation. In North American Paleoindian assemblages, for instance, fluted bifaces and end scrapers have different characteristic cumulative-survivorship curves and failure distributions (Shott and Sillitoe 2004). Biface discard is governed by

chance, which is no surprise considering that bifaces ("points") are thin for their size and in use are subjected to many physical stresses from striking objects at high speeds. End-scraper discard is governed by attrition, again no surprise considering that scrapers are thicker and more robust for their size and in use are subjected to fewer and less variable stresses. Perhaps discard of Australian tulas, like end scrapers, is governed by attrition while discard of, say, Kimberley points is governed by chance.

Measuring Reduction

As important as it is for typology and curation analysis, reduction has proven difficult to measure. Until accurate and precise reduction indices were devised, tool reduction could only be approximated qualitatively. With some qualifications, Dibble's (1987) Middle Paleolithic reduction thesis similarly equated reduction stage with typological status (i.e., if a flake tool was reduced so much, it became a Type A tool, if so much more a Type B tool, and so on). Essentially, reduction approximated this way is a nominal variable, a necessary status in the absence of reduction measures. Lancashire (2000) measured reduction on an ordinal scale. But only reduction indices grounded in estimates of tools' original size can measure reduction and curation as ratio-scale, continuous variables. This point is much more than academic, because continuous measurement of reduction is faithful to the continuous nature of the reduction process (e.g., Bradbury and Carr 1999; Hiscock and Attenbrow 2002; Shott 1996a). As above, ratio-scale reduction can be analyzed in ways that nominal- or ordinal-scale reduction cannot be. So measuring reduction requires comparing the end result—the tool as discarded to enter the archaeological record and thus found by archaeologists—to its original size and form. Measuring reduction thus requires estimating original size and/or form.

Reduction and Original Size
This section briefly describes the various methods used to estimate the original size and form of flake blanks that were used and retouched. It starts with the index that proved so popular in chapters of this volume, then considers measures based on kind, amount or patterning of retouch, then "allometry" measures (Blades 2003), and concludes with measures based on distinctions between tool haft element and blade and that use contextual evidence.

Geometry
Kuhn's (1990) "Geometric Index of Unifacial Reduction" (GIUR) is the most popular reduction measure used in chapters in this volume, which will serve as a handbook for its application. Like all methods, the GIUR has limitations, some of which are inherent and others depending on mode or pattern of tool use. Because it is so popular in Australia, as these papers show, the limitations bear careful consideration, not to question the index but to promote its intelligent use. GIUR has certain minor

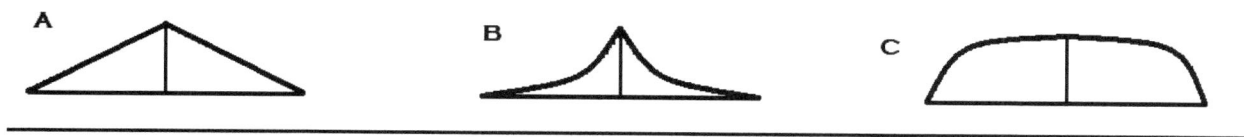

Figure 3. Idealized flake-blank cross-section forms.

limitations engaged by its assumptions about the nature or pattern of retouch. As Hiscock and Clarkson's chapter notes, it is complicated somewhat by the angle or steepness of retouch and by retouch on the interior surface. GIUR has other limitations as well.

1. GIUR assumes that sections are triangular, as Law (Chapter 8) emphasized. If a flake's faces are nearly parallel over much of the section, then t/T reaches its maximum value after little resharpening and remains constant as resharpening continues. This is the "flat flake" problem (Dibble 1995, Figure 12)

2. Between the GIUR's ideal triangular section and the near-parallel sections of flat flakes are incurvate and excurvate sections (Figure 3), the latter of which approximates the flat-flake condition and its problems. In these cases, t/T rises slowly (incurvate sections) or rapidly (excurvate sections) with unit increases in invasive resharpening. That is, the same amount of use, resharpening, and reduction yield a range of t/T values depending on sectional geometry. In fact, these problems are not so grave as they may seem. First, they are acknowledged by GIUR's advocates. Second, comparison of t/T values can be confined to specimens of similar sectional geometry or corrections can be calculated mathematically.

3. Another geometric limitation of GIUR involves variation in angle that separates each flake's interior and exterior surfaces. The specimens in Figure 2 are identical in thickness T but different in width so therefore in edge angle. Acute angles on relatively thin flakes (e.g., Figure 4a) require absolutely more reduction to reach the same t/T value than do steep angles on thicker flakes (Figure 4b). The cross-section area resharpened to reach a t/T value of .5 in Figure 4a is twice as large as in Figure 4b. Because it is a three-dimensional measure, difference in volume despite equal t/T value would be even greater. Again, index value and amount of reduction are partly independent. On specimens resharpened along both section edges, different amounts of reduction yield identical t/T values if the section is not symmetrical (Figure 5).

4. Geometric limitations are simultaneously limitations of scale. As tool size and sectional area increase, absolutely more resharpening is needed to reach any given t/T value. In Figure 5, for example, two specimens have identical t/T values but the larger one, twice the smaller one's size, requires twice the absolute amount of reduction. GIUR shares this scale effect with reduction measures like the allometric methods discussed below.

5. Hiscock and Clarkson's (Chapter 2) experiment shows that GIUR increases as a nonlinear function of weight loss in flake-tool reduction. As they note, this means that "not all increments in the Kuhn index are equivalent." It is a rubber, not a rigid, yardstick. Again, GIUR may share this quality with other measures, and the absence of such evidence in others is not evidence of absence, merely our ignorance of their properties. Documentation for the GIUR is a testimony to the careful design of Hiscock and Clarkson's experiment. Still, the GIUR is not an arithmetic or interval-scale variable but one whose magnitude or rate of change varies along its range. Hiscock and Clarkson also note that the GIUR's nominal range of 0-1 actually is only 0.1- or 0.2-1. Because reduction continues considerably beyond the maximum GIUR value in their experiment, that maximum does not span the full range of reduction. As a result, the GUIR might exaggerate reduction in early stages and underestimate it in later ones.

6. Finally, interpretation of GIUR values can be complicated depending on the pattern of edge use and resharpening. A notched flake not only can differ in t/T values on different notches along the same edge, but the edges separating notches could have a t/T value of 0 because t = 0. This complication is a quibble more than a major problem, both because notching is not particularly common and because it is conspicuous. No one should compare notched flakes and those resharpened continuously along an edge, nor is anyone likely to try.

Most prehistoric Australian flake tools presumably were hand-held or hafted in mastic. Many if not most hand-held tools apparently were used on their lateral margins; morphologically, they are sidescrapers. Hafted tools may have been worked and resharpened on any suitable edge (e.g., Tindale 1965), making them either sidescrapers, endscrapers or some combination. In either case, mastic hafts accommodate tools without requiring modification for hafting. There is little doubt that the GIUR works well on flake sidescrapers, subject to the limitations noted above. To judge from his illustration, for instance, the tula whose reduction Tindale (1965, Figure 19) documented was used first on one lateral edge, then rehafted and used on the other. GIUR should be a valid measure of its reduction.

115

A

B

A

A

B

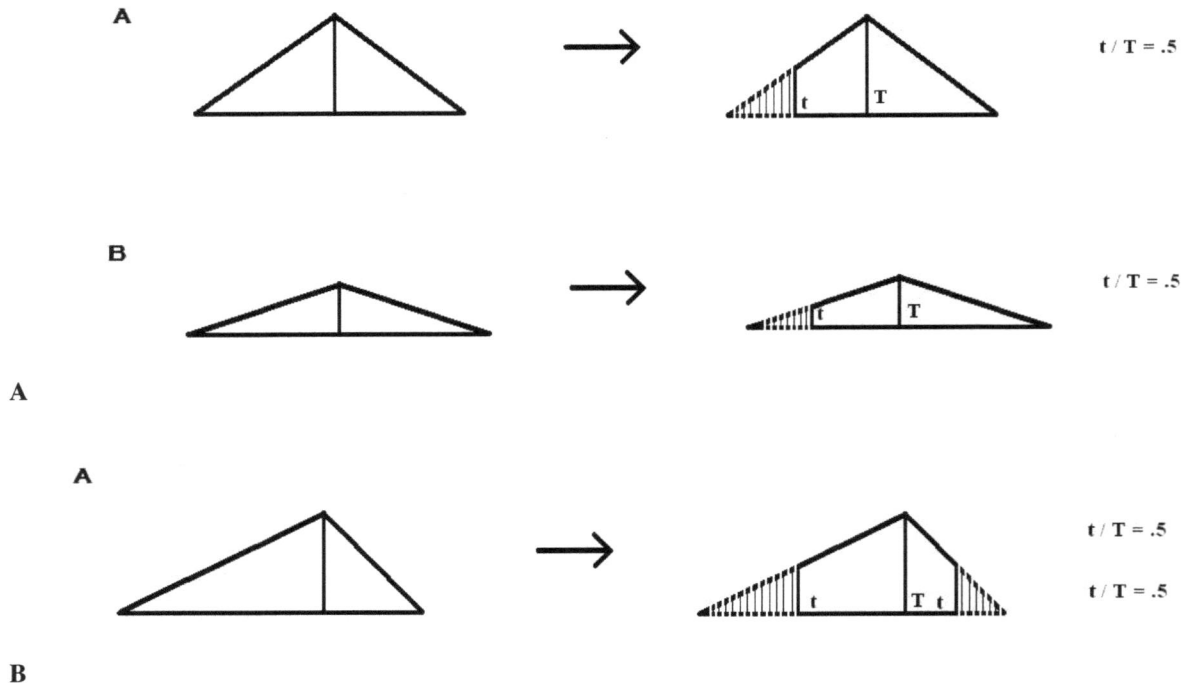

Figure 4. Effects of cross-section Form on the GIUR. A: Flake thickness and cross-section form, B: cross-section symmetry.

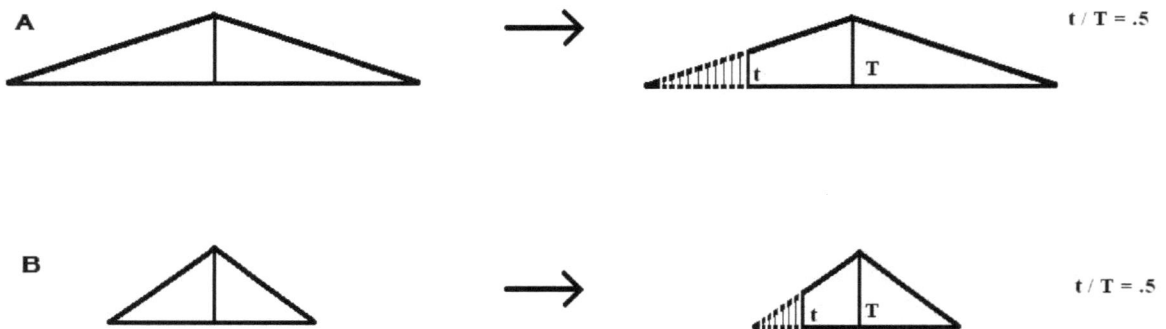

Figure 5. Effects of scale on the GIUR.

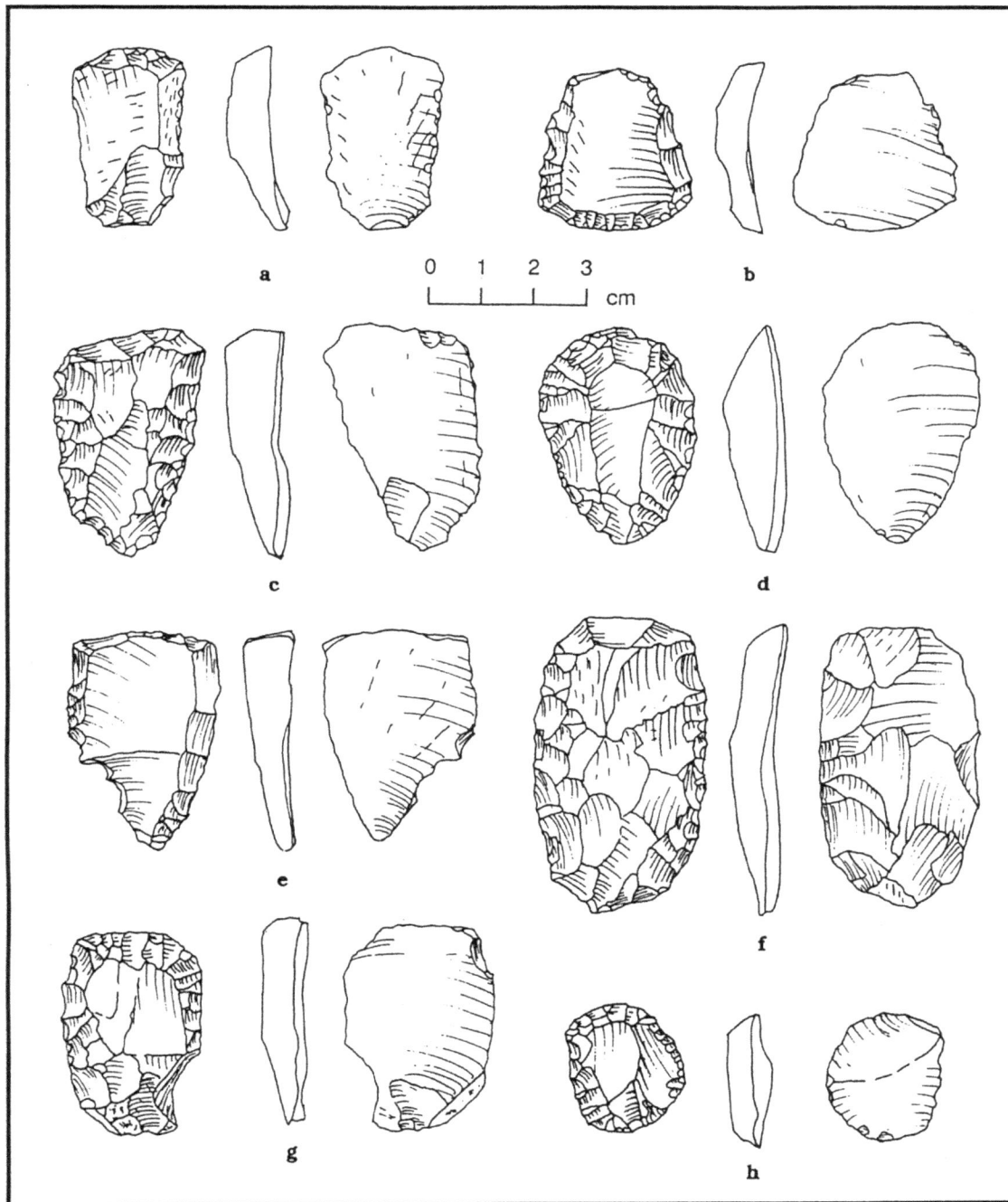

Figure 6. Leavitt Paleoindian endscrapers.

Similar flake tools are not uncommon in assemblages anywhere, but endscrapers also are common. Many endscrapers were fashioned from relatively thick blanks struck from polyhedral, prismatic or even biface cores. Their interior and exterior surfaces are subparallel for most of their longitudinal sections, abruptly converging only near the distal edge. Figure 6 shows typical endscrapers from the Leavitt Paleoindian assemblage in North America (Shott 1995). Among them, only Figure 6d possesses the triangular longitudinal section that the GIUR assumes. In other specimens, thickness t on the retouched biface is practically constant over a wide range of use, resharpening and reduction. On their longitudinal sections, along which they were worked, endscrapers are Dibble's "flat flakes." The GIUR does not work on them. Lest anyone doubt that original, unreduced flakes from which endscrapers were made had the triangular sections that the GIUR requires, Figure 7 (Shott 1995:Fig. 4) shows a Paleoindian endscraper blank compared with a depleted specimen nearly identical in the attributes it retains. The blank has subparallel faces for most of its longitudinal section. After one or two resharpenings, t and therefore t/T would reach their maximum values, yet much more reduction could occur.

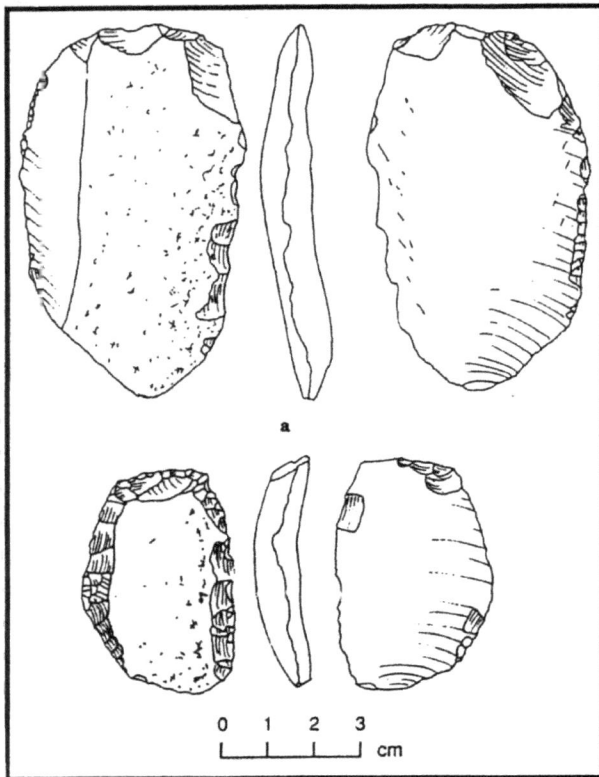

Figure 7. Leavitt Paleoindian endscraper blank
and resharpened endscraper.

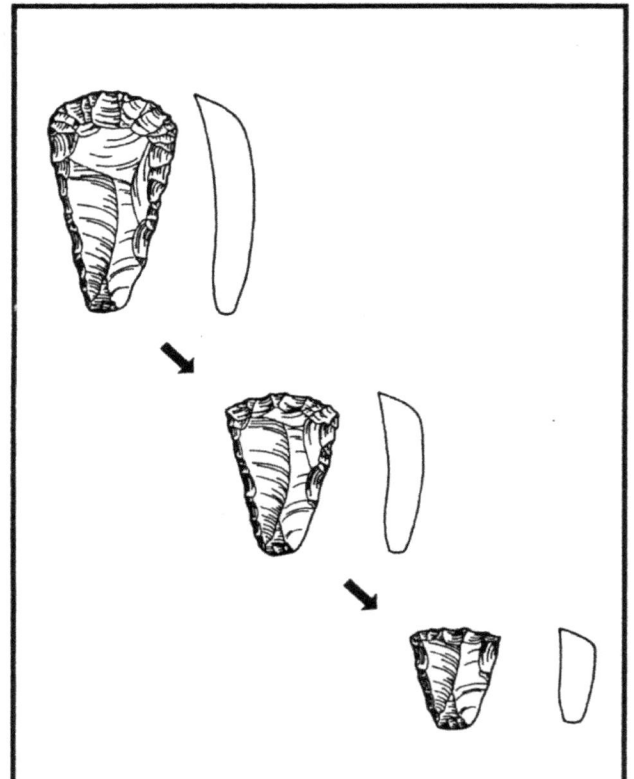

Figure 8. Resharpening of replicated endscraper showing
that the GIUR does not change as reduction progresses.

Lest even this example be doubted, consider Morrow's (1997) resharpening and reduction of endscrapers. Morrow did not measure t/T (essentially, it would be the ratio of bit thickness to maximum thickness) but the progressive reduction of specimens showed little change in what would amount to t/T over as many as 25 resharpening episodes and a wide range of length reduction (Morrow 1997, Table 4). Figure 8 (Morrow's Figure 10) shows clearly the extensive reduction of an endscraper without significant change in its t/T ratio. Not only Paleoindian endscrapers show this resistance to the GIUR; some ethnographic Ethiopian hidescrapers also possess subparallel faces and trapezoidal or rectangular longitudinal sections along with much reduction can occur with little if any change in t/T (e.g., Weedman 2000:Fig. 4-4). In all such cases, T is little affected by resharpening, and t is little changed after the first resharpening episodes. Although specimens could experience much resharpening and reduction thereafter, t/T and therefore GIUR would change little if at all.

The conclusion is inescapable: GIUR does not work on endscrapers. It works, subject to other limitations noted above, on sidescrapers that are triangular in cross-section. This is scarcely an original observation (Kuhn 1990:586, 591). Hand-held sidescrapers are common in Australia, and many have the cross-section that GIUR assumes. In these circumstances, GIUR is a sensible reduction measure.

GIUR's advocates must forgive skepticism, not of its considerable value but of its general superiority. Hiscock and Clarkson's own experiment, impressive in its design and implementation, nevertheless leaves nagging doubts. The single best reduction measure there must be number of blows, because each one caused reduction. Yet the GIUR correlated ambiguously with this measure (Chapter 2's Figure 6). GIUR's distribution might be left-skewed, because Hiscock and Clarkson's Table 2 shows that its mean is much nearer its maximum than its minimum value, such that most values are crowded to its upper range. This is precisely where number-of-blows varies most widely, suggesting that much reduction occurred after the GIUR reached its maximum value.

Retouch
Clarkson (2002; see also Chapter 3) devised a reduction index that involves type of invasive retouch and its distribution around a flake tool's perimeter. Shiner *et al.* (Chapter 7) use a simpler variant. Like the Kuhn Index, Clarkson's was tested in controlled experiments. Still, it seems more complicated to measure than others. Each tool is divided into eight segments per face, six of which are equal in size (Clarkson 2002, Figure 1). Proximal and distal segments vary in size. A perimeter zone then cross-cuts the segments, yielding a total of 16 per face, each of which is coded for dichotomous amount of invasive retouch. Standard templates cannot be used to measure the index because each tool's size determines the size of

its constituent segments. The index also equates amount of faceting with amount of reduction, but strictly measures only the former. A tool that originally was very large but that was resharpened minimally along its edge many times may yield a similar value to an original small tool. Finally, why does the procedure require a tool's subdivision into eight or 16 zones? On what theoretical or practical ground are those numbers preferable to, say, four or 29 or any other numbers chosen at random? Clarkson (2002:72) is aware of and acknowledges these and other limitations; no measure is a panacea, and this one should prove its value among others.

Law (Chapter 8) noted that the GIUR is not a good reduction measure for flakes retouched on their distal margins. He proposed instead a perimeter reduction index (PRI) found as the ratio of the length of retouched edge segments to total edge length or perimeter. This measure has the virtue of making no assumptions about cross-section geometry or the pattern of edge retouch. But its own limitations include reaching a maximum value of 1 when the entire perimeter is retouched, while the flake could continue being used, retouched and reduced long past that point. A related limitation concerns hafted flake tools, again illustrated by North American endscrapers. Those tools are fashioned, hafted and used such that only one edge, usually the distal one, is fully exposed. It is the only edge retouched and used, and the entirety of that edge is retouched and used. As endscrapers are used, retouched and reduced, length of retouch does not change while reduction progresses.

Flake "Allometry"
Allometry concerns how the proportions of components of things vary with the sizes of those things. As reduction progresses some dimensions are much reduced, others little reduced. Their proportions change accordingly. In reduction studies, allometry (Blades 2003) refers chiefly to the relationship between attributes of flake blanks that change little with reduction (e.g., flake thickness, and platform area and thickness) and those that do, particularly surface area and mass. Hiscock and Clarkson (Chapter 2) identified these as ratios of flake surface area to thickness or platform area, but they also include the ratio of platform area to mass (Dibble and Pelcin 1995).

Hiscock and Clarkson's chapter discusses the relevant literature at some length. Briefly, ratios of platform dimensions or area to any measure of flakes' original sizes are statistically significant almost everywhere studied. But assemblage-level correlations accommodate sufficient variation to have little predictive value for individual flakes. Moreover, most correlations are better for hard-hammer than soft-hammer or certainly pressure flakes, so these estimates of original size and, by extension, reduction are limited by technology. Blades (2003) estimated original size (i.e., surface area) of flake blanks used for Upper Paleolithic endscrapers from thickness, because thickness correlated better with size in experimental studies than did platform dimensions. In Hiscock and Clarkson's experiment, allometric estimates of surface area from platform area performed poorly but estimates from flake thickness were fairly accurate (Chapter 2, Table 4).

Haft-Blade Ratio
Many flake tools were not hafted. But tools like bifaces are common outside Australia, at least in North America, and they were modified as much for hafting as for intended use. Even slightly retouched flake tools like endscrapers can be designed and partially modified for hafting (e.g., Morrow 1997; Shott 1995). When hafts can be distinguished from blades, bits or other functional segments, the relative size of haft and functional elements can be a reduction measure. In tools designed for hafting, especially in lashed or socketed hafts, as opposed to the mastic hafts common in Australia (e.g., Tindale 1965), haft elements tend to be relatively standardized in both size and form. Excluding broken or recycled specimens, haft elements of little reduced and much reduced tools are similar. Tools not reduced at all sometimes are found in caches or at quarries and workshops, and little reduced ones can be found in some assemblages. Subject to these qualifications, measures like the ratio of haft to blade (or other functional segment) length, area or mass estimate amount of reduction experienced by tools. Grimes and Grimes (1985) used this logic to calculate measures of reduction and, by extension, curation and to plot their distribution among specimens in an assemblage of North American Paleoindian flakeshavers.

Table 1. Reduction measures.

Index	Basis	Source/Example
GIUR	Section geometry	Kuhn 1990
Invasiveness	retouch	Clarkson 2002
Typology	retouch	Dibble 1987
Platform:surface area	flake allometry	Dibble & Pelcin 1995
Platform: weight	flake allometry	Dibble & Pelcin 1995
Thickness:surface area	flake allometry	Blades 2003
Ratio	haft-blade	Grimes & Grimes 1985
Context	comparison finished but unused specimens	Hiscock 1988

Context

A similar reduction measure derives from contextual data. Unused specimens from caches, whether modified for hafting or not, indicate the original size of tools. Used tools found discarded can be similar to cache specimens in unreduced dimensions (e.g., thickness, platform area). Their differences from cache specimens in measures like length or mass, which reduction obviously affects, are measures of reduction. Hiscock (1988) used this reasoning to estimate amount of reduction experienced by used and discarded tulas by comparison to a cache of unused ones. Like Grimes and Grimes, Hiscock (1988, Figure 5) compiled a distribution of reduction values.

Comparing Reduction Measures

By now archaeologists have devised several reduction measures and tested several of them (Table 1). GIUR is the sole measure that exploits section (usually cross-section) geometry. Clarkson's (2002; see also Barton 1990, Figure 2; Law, Chapter 8) invasiveness index and, to some extent, Dibble's (1987) approaches exploit kind and extent of retouch to gauge reduction. Allometry measures exploit the correlation between dimensions of original, unretouched flake blanks that are affected and unaffected by reduction. Form of manufactured tools, as opposed to form or size of original flake blanks, can yield reduction estimates by, for instance, calculation of haft-blade ratios.

Thus, archaeologists have at least eight reduction measures based on form, retouch characteristics, the allometry of original size and form, and archaeological context. All have some value, which might vary by tool type, industry, toolstone, context or other factors. All are inherently limited, but in different respects; no biface-reduction measure, for instance, can be grounded in the cross-section geometry of flakes or in platform allometry because bifaces lack these features. Even some flake tools like endscrapers are modified extensively before use by trimming or removing features like their platforms. But several indices can be measured on the same specimens, so there are opportunities, some taken in Hiscock and Clarkson's chapter, to compare them. Comparisons can involve any two or more indices. They should be attempted in a range of assemblages that differ in tool types and industry, toolstone, geography and other salient respects.

Comparisons will be complicated because measures do not scale identically. The GIUR is a ratio that varies nominally between 0 and 1 and measures reduction in two-dimensional cross-section form of three-dimensional objects. Clarkson's Invasiveness Index varies over the same range but measures reduction by the sum of interval scores of retouch extent. Flake allometry measures also are ratios, one between two two-dimensional ratio measures (platform area and surface area), another between one such measure (platform area) and mass, and a third between a one-dimensional (thickness) and two-dimensional (area) ratio variable.

No matter their differences in scale, reduction measures are worth comparing further in controlled experimental context like Hiscock and Clarkson's and also in archaeological evidence. A good test in the latter would compare cached and depleted tulas from western Queensland. The two sets of artifacts differ greatly in length, the chief dimension reduced by resharpening, somewhat in width, and insignificantly in platform dimensions (Hiscock 1988, Table 3). This is expected in a tool class used and resharpened distally and that retains the flake platform. The distribution of the ratio of length to width also differs between cache and depleted tulas (Hiscock 1988, Figure 5) as predicted in Ahler's (1975, Figures N-5, N-6) reduction argument and documented in tool classes as different as North American Paleoindian flakeshavers (Grimes and Grimes 1985, Figure 7) and Neolithic Swedish shaft-hole axes (Lekberg 2000, Figure 2). Based on Hiscock and Clarkson's results, I would expect the GIUR to be a better estimator of reduction in tulas than allometric measures, but the comparison should be made.

But reduction is best measured using all means available, and no single estimator is likely to be best for all purposes or in all tool types. Several estimators are apt to correlate with one another, as did GIUR and length of retouch in the Capertree assemblage that Hiscock and Attenbrow studied. Generally, which ones are best under which conditions? Paleodemographers encounter similar questions in estimating age-at-death in skeletal populations. They use morphological and histological estimators like fusion of cranial sutures, pubic symphysis, and tissue age to estimate age-at-death. Resulting estimates do not always agree. In a controlled study, Meindl et al. (1983:75-76) calculated an average from each estimator's value weighted by its score on the first component of a principal-components analysis of all estimators. They argued that "the first component of a principal components analysis of the correlation matrix of the individual estimators of age is actual age" (Meindl et al. 1983:76), and found that the several estimators varied in their intercorrelations and component loadings. All estimators were not equal. Archaeologists might do the same in controlled or experimental studies like those described by Hiscock and Clarkson (Chapter 2). Across a range of tool types or industries, the best individual reduction estimators should emerge, and their fidelity both to Meindl et al.'s concept of "summary age" or reduction and to experimental knowns can be determined.

Comments on Individual Papers

Clarkson writes on reduction continua in north Australian scrapers, showing how defined types partition a complex continuum of metric and technological variation. The paper is a good example of the reduction perspective's typological implications. Clarkson's measures or correlates of reduction include edge angle and shape, and characteristics of the retouched edge. As a small point, he might have included overall flake size among them. One surprising conclusion is that north Australian scrapers often have concave edges when unmodified and convex ones once retouched. In many North American industries, particularly among hafted endscrapers, edges before retouch were convex (they probably were fashioned deliberately so, unlike the Australian scrapers that had this unmodified form) and were progressively flattened with retouch. That is, the trend in retouched north Australian flake tools is toward convex edge form, in North American endscrapers away from convexity.

Hiscock and Clarkson compare the GIUR to other proposed reduction measures. The chapter is a good example of the kind of comparison between measures advocated above; it would be interesting to apply Meindl et al.'s methods to the comparison. Hiscock and Clarkson conclude that variants of the GIUR and the simple ratio of flake area to thickness are the best measures, the ratio of flake area to platform area the poorest. All of us who have advocated other measures should reconsider our positions in light of these conclusions. At the same time, Hiscock and Clarkson might consider the limitations of GIUR noted above and elsewhere (e.g., Dibble 1995). In this respect, they acknowledge but finesse the limitations, arguing that their effect "has not been established." This is not the same thing as saying that they cannot be established nor that they did not influence experimental results. Moreover, Hiscock and Clarkson argue that the GIUR works as well on "flat flakes" (e.g., their Figure 5, Specimen 21) as on those possessing triangular cross-sections. There are simple and, to my mind, conclusive reasons why it cannot work on such flakes, so I look forward to the demonstration to the contrary. Finally, their well controlled experiments show that the GIUR itself reaches its theoretical maximum value considerably before flakes are depleted, a corollary of the "flat flake" problem. That is, they continue to be used and reduced even though their GIUR values do not continue to increase. In 40% of flakes, about 24% of reduction occurred after the GIUR ceased to register it. This does not prove that other reduction measures are any better, but it certainly suggests limitations to GIUR. Hiscock and Clarkson find their best result when plotting and correlating the GIUR with reduction measured by loss of weight. This is both interesting and surprising, because the GIUR itself measures change in cross-section geometry, not mass. If the GIUR correlates so well with mass reduction, then measures based on estimates of original mass also should perform well.

It is easier to question experiments for what they might have done than to do them in the first place, but the importance of Hiscock and Clarkson's experiment justifies the effort. Weight was their measure of specimen size, and all indices compared were correlated with weight reduction. Unfortunately, Hiscock and Clarkson did not include the only estimator of original weight, the various platform methods developed by Pelcin and others (e.g., Dibble and Pelcin 1995). Also, the only two measures that Hiscock and Clarkson did not transform for

correlation with weight reduction were allometry measures based on platform dimensions. The poor performance of the area:platform estimator is surprising. Because this allometry measure correlated fairly well with flake area in other experiments (e.g., Dibble and Pelcin 1995), its low r value in this case seems anomalous. More detailed study of this measure's failure seems warranted. It is a poor estimator in soft-hammer percussion flakes (Shott et al. 2000:892); if experimental specimens were knapped that way, then a strong correlation was virtually precluded at the outset. To test this possibility, it would have been interesting to correlate platform area with flake area *before* specimens were reduced. If that correlation was high, as in many previous experiments, the low correlation found following reduction supports Hiscock and Clarkson's view that the estimator is a poor reduction measure. If it was low, then with respect to just the area:platform measure, the results can be questioned. Another possibility is that outliers perhaps reduced the correlation which otherwise might have been higher. A cross-plot of this measure against weight reduction might be examined for any such outliers.

Several papers apply the GIUR to archaeological assemblages. Hiscock and Attenbrow take the reduction perspective to the iconic Capertree assemblage from which Australian flake-tool typology originated. Their skepticism about form-function identities presumed there echoes Odell's (1981) judgment from use-wear analysis of European tools and, among others, Hayden's (1977) ethnographic observations from Australia itself where individual flake tools were used in several tasks and where some passed through several morphological types in the course of a single use. No form-function identities there. Hiscock and Attenbrow's rhetorical question, "How can implements be designed for, and be efficient in, a specific use if their morphology is continuously changing?", contains the false premise of form-function identity that they legitimately question, so cannot be answered at face value. In part it can be answered by citing White's (1969) observation that New Guinea flake-tool users were concerned much less with overall shape of the flake than with its edge. Morphology or form is not necessarily a functional attribute. Form-function identities sometimes are valid, but to assume them generally is a mistake. Hiscock and Attenbrow make a strong case for the continuous-reduction perspective. My only (slight) reservation about their thorough analysis is that they use the GIUR as an unequivocal, independent measure of degree of reduction by which to study the correlation with reduction of other measures. Some first decline and then rise with GIUR values (e.g., percentage of retouched edged notched), but this pattern is valid only on the assumption that the GIUR itself is an unequivocal reduction measure. Following Meindl et al.'s approach to age estimation in paleodemography, the form and degree of intercorrelation between all estimators should be studied.

Controlled experiments in fracture mechanics, the subject of Macgregor's chapter, are vital to progress in lithic analysis. Macgregor's "reduction potential" seems more akin to "utility" than to use-life or the "maintainability" with which he equates it. Maintainable tools or industries were defined as those that, if "broken or not appropriate for the task at hand…can quickly and easily be brought to a functional state" (Bleed 1986:739). The concept has more to do with whether or not tools can be repaired than with how long they are used or the rate at which they are used up. But Macgregor's main point is an apt one that is worth emphasizing: a tool's remnant utility is a function of not just its gross size but also its condition. Edges marred by step or hinge fractures can ruin a flake tool no matter how much or little it was used or how much more service it might have provided without those defects.

Shiner et al.'s well controlled surveys in interior southern Australia reveal how the sparse archaeological record of hunter-gatherers formed. Their chapter here expands their treatment by comparing surface records to the Burkes Cave assemblage. Controlling reasonably well in empirical data for location, age, and material supply, they analyze and compare assemblages to reconstruct patterns of site and landscape use. This chapter uses a broader set of analytical methods than just the reduction indices that are the subjects of most chapters. Ingeniously, Shiner et al. expand an argument (Shott 2003; in press) on the relationship between occupation span and assemblage size and composition to the technology of flake-tool reduction. In the process, they demonstrate that Burkes Cave was not a semi-permanent camp but a complex palimpsest whose assemblage formed over many occupations of varying span, nature and size. The chapter is a nice illustration of the implications that a reduction perspective has not only for typology but for assemblage analysis and the inference of occupation modes.

Most chapters explore reduction's implications for typology, curation rates or assemblage formation. Law expands the scope of application of reduction measures, using them to test models of hunter-gatherer technological organization. Large-scale land use and the mobility that it entails are conspicuous characteristics of many hunter-gatherer cultures. Since the 1980s, archaeologists in Australia and elsewhere have considered how people accommodated their need for tools with conflicting needs imposed by the constraints of movement, access to supply and other factors. Law emphasizes the exigencies of residential mobility, what elsewhere I called "mobility frequency" to distinguish it from "mobility magnitude" (Shott 1986). How often people move is their frequency, how far they move in the aggregate their magnitude. Mobility frequency and magnitude have somewhat different effects; it would be interesting to consider the latter's in organizational models for later Australian prehistory. One of Law's substantive findings is that two reduction measures, GIUR and his Perimeter Reduction Index patterned differently over time. This is further evidence that different reduction indices do not always agree, partly because they measure different things. This partial independence of measures is all the more reason to use several when possible, and to rank them against external controls as did Hiscock and Clarkson or against one another as in Meindl et al.'s approach.

Mackay's chapter resembles Cowan's (1994) North American study. Cowan was perhaps the first to extend organizational analysis to debris, noting differences in tool assemblages between phases and corresponding differences in the debris from producing the tools (1994:158-159). Where, for instance, bifaces were common so was debris from biface production. As Mackay notes, debris is abundant even when tools are not; inferring kinds and amounts of tools produced from debris (e.g., Shott 1997) enables the study of technological organization even when tools are lacking. Mackay's approach follows Kuhn in distinguishing between place and person. Most organizational models and applications assume individual "provisioning," but Kuhn's alternative is either to use what is available locally (risky when places are poorly known, precluded when they are known not to contain usable toolstone) or somehow to supply stone to places, presumably by caching. Each strategy has its advantages, and Mackay emphasizes that they are not mutually exclusive. Generally, "place provisioning" is best when transport costs are prohibitive for individuals, and is limited in value to contexts where occupations are both fairly long and predictable; it does no good to "provision" a place for three weeks, say, with expendable stone when you might have to stay there for four.

Mackay's reasoning is unassailable. My only reservation about the Kuhnian approach that he follows concerns its somewhat low opinion of "individual provisioning." This view rests upon an equation between tool size and multifunctionality (i.e., the bigger the tool the more multifunctional it is), which is plausible but untested. That is, supplying people rather than places is considered inadvisable because people can only carry so many small tools, and small tools cannot be multifunctional. People run the risk of not having the proper tool for the vital task at hand. Leaving aside the question of ingenuity, no such relationship between size and functionality appeared in, for instance, Odell's (1981) functional study; there, small and large knives were equally multifunctional and small axes were more, not less, multifunctional than large ones. Similarly, Pumé metal knives were smaller than arrows but experienced more types of use on average (Greaves 1997:306-309). On this evidence, size is not obviously related to function, and concluding that small size precludes multiple functions is questionable. "Place provisioning" also incurs its own costs—hauling quantities of blanks, cores or unworked cobbles to places where they might possibly be used at some future time—that the approach does not clearly take into account.

Backed flakes are common in lithic industries around the

world. Like other classes, traditionally they were defined by one or few criteria and the type that resulted were treated as homogeneous entities. Lamb's work with the assemblage from the South Molle Island quarry shows that backed and non-backed artifacts can be linked, not separated, by a reduction continuum and that amount of reduction partly is a function of flakes' original size. Yet another Australian tool type is revealed as a segment or range of complex reduction continua.

Broader Implications of the Reduction Thesis

Australian archaeology is a late arrival to the reduction thesis but its acceptance was foreshadowed by Mulvaney, who abandoned a pure typological approach in favor of a metric one (Holdaway 1995:785). Whatever the reason, Australia may achieve the most comprehensive assimilation of the reduction perspective. European Paleolithic archaeology remains divided on the relative importance of reduction and original design in stone tools. Most reduction-thesis advocates are from North America or Australia (e.g., Hiscock 1996), most traditionalists Europeans. Similar disagreements in the Levant have similar geographic correlates (e.g., Neeley and Barton 1994; cf. Goring-Morris 1996), although the American Henry (1996) is among the traditionalists. Most North American archaeologists now seem to accept the reduction thesis's implications for biface classification, but a substantial minority retains the traditional view. No doubt there are traditionalists everywhere but, to judge from this volume and other recent studies, Australian lithic analysis now is dominated by those who accept the reduction thesis.

For reasons that mystify me, there is a linguistic dimension to the reduction thesis. Most advocates are English-speaking Antipodeans and North Americans, most traditionalists continental Europeans who speak other languages, principally French, or those trained at continental universities. Thus, Clark (1996) legitimately could call Israeli traditionalists more French than the French. The exception to this pattern is Britain, but less obviously than it may seem. In Paleolithic archaeology Britain substantially is a French colony, so it illustrates more than violates the pattern.

Besides its obvious implications for lithic typology and curation, the reduction thesis has a deceptively profound implication for the meaning to attach to tool assemblages. The traditional archaeological view identifies tool size and form with templates and thereby constructs types. It associates types with activities, whether broad ("scraper") or narrow ("dry-hide scraper"). The traditional premises are that variation in tool size and form is essential (i.e., forming sets of discrete formal types) and that types bear some relationship to activity or function. The view accepts a measure of uncertainty; some types are more distinct, have more formal integrity than others, and some types might be more multifunctional than others. Substantially, though, both premises are qualitative. Traditional lithic classification identifies kinds of

activities or uses. The presence of a cleaver in an assemblage indicates butchering, the presence of a scraper scraping. In the same way, the presence of a hammer in a modern toolkit identifies hammering as an activity (itself surprisingly broad in subjects hammered [e.g., nails, boards] and context [e.g., construction, repair, carpentry]), but not the amount of hammering done.

The reduction thesis has different premises. It views variation in tool size and form as continuous, i.e., forming complex patterns of variable association and distribution but not discrete, essential types. It does not so much reject as moot the traditional view's form-function identities. However tools were used, much of their size-form variation owes to amount of use and pattern of retouch. Substantially, the reduction thesis has quantitative, not qualitative, premises. In its view, the presence in an assemblage of, say, a tula slug is not evidence of a kind of activity, unless that activity is defined broadly as scraping-planing-cutting. Instead, its presence registers an amount of reduction that attended some kind and amount of tool use. That is, a type's presence in an assemblage no longer means "Kind of Tool or Activity X" but instead "Amount of Reduction Y."

Conclusion

In years to come, Australian archaeologists will view this volume as a landmark of intelligent reduction analysis. But it deserves the attention of archaeologists everywhere who are concerned about how the record formed and how our classification methods comport with the sources of variation in artifacts. Whatever its past importance to the discipline, today lithic analysis is regarded by many archaeologists as an esoteric pursuit of limited value to the larger scholarly enterprise. This view is tragic not merely because of how it consigns stone-tool studies but because other archaeologists miss the opportunity to see the unique contribution that lithic analysis makes to the study of the past.

Acknowledgements

Christopher Clarkson of the University of Queensland solicited this contribution. He and the various authors deserve thanks for the quality of their scholarship, which made my job easy. Thanks go to Jonathan Hutchins of the University of Northern Iowa as well, who drafted Figures 3-5.

References

Ahler, S.A. 1975 Extended coalescent lithic technology: supporting data: Part II, appendices K-O. Report on file, Midwest Archaeological Centre, National Park Service. Lincoln, Nebraska, USA.

Barton, C.M. 1990 Stone tools and paleolithic settlement in the Iberian Peninsula. *Proceedings of the Prehistoric Society* 56:15-32.

Bisson, M. 2000 Nineteenth Century tools for Twenty-First Century archaeology? Why the Middle Paleolithic typology of François Bordes must be replaced. *Journal of Archaeological Method and Theory* 7:1-48.

Blades, B.S. 2003 End scraper reduction and hunter-gatherer mobility. *American Antiquity* 68:141-156.

Bleed, P. 1986 The optimal design of hunting weapons: maintainability or reliability. *American Antiquity* 5_:737-747.

Bordes, F. 1961 *Typologie du Paleolithique Ancien et Moyen*. Bordeaux: Institut de Quaternaire, Université de Bordeaux.

Bradbury, A.P. and P.J. Carr 1999 Examining stage and continuum models of flake debris analysis: an experimental approach. *Journal of Archaeological Science* 26:105-116.

Clark, G.A. 1996 Plus Français que les Français. *Antiquity* 70:138-139.

Clarkson, C. 2002 An index of invasiveness for the measurement of unifacial and bifacial retouch: a theoretical, experimental and archaeological verification. *Journal of Archaeological Science* 1:65-75.

Cooper, H.M. 1954 Material culture of Australian Aborigines: Part 1. Progressive modification of a stone artefact. *Records of the South Australian Museum* 11:91-97.

Cowan, F.L. 1994 *Prehistoric Mobility Strategies in Western New York: A Small Sites Perspective*. Unpublished Ph.D. Dissertation, Department of Anthropology, State University of New York-Buffalo.

DeBoer, W.R. 1983 The archaeological record as preserved death assemblage. In Keene, A. and J.Moore (eds) *Archaeological Hammers and Theories*. Pp.19-35. New York: Academic Press.

de Sonneville-Bordes, D. and J. Perrot 1953 Essai d'adaptation des méthodes statistiques au Paléolithique Supérieur. *Premiers Résultats. Bulletin de la Société Préhistorique Française* 50:323-333.

Dibble, H.L. 1987 The interpretation of Middle Paleolithic scraper morphology. *American Antiquity* 52:109-117.

Dibble, H.L. 1995 Middle Paleolithic scraper reduction: background, clarification, and review of the evidence to date. *Journal of Archaeological Method and Theory* 2:299-368.

Dibble, H.L. and A.W. Pelcin 1995 The effect of hammer mass and velocity on flake mass. *Journal of Archaeological Science* 22:429-439.

Elston, R.G. 1992 Modeling the economics and organization of lithic procurement. In Elston, R. (ed.) *Archaeological Investigations at Tosawihi, a Great Basin Quarry (Vol.1)*. Pp.31-47. Silver City, NV: Intermountain Research.

Frison, G.C. 1968 A functional analysis of certain chipped stone tools. *American Antiquity* 33:149-155.

Goodyear, A.C. 1974 *The Brand Site: A Techno-Functional Study of a Dalton Site in Northeast Arkansas*. Fayetteville: Arkansas Archeological Survey, Research Series 7.

Goring-Morris, N. 1996 Square pegs into round holes: a critique of Neeley & Barton. *Antiquity* 70:130-147.

Gould, R.A., Koster, D.A. and A.H. Sontz 1971 The lithic assemblage of the Western Desert Aborigines of Australia. *American Antiquity* 36:149-169.

Granger, J. 1978 Meadowood Phase Settlement Pattern in the Niagara Frontier Region of Western New York State. University of Michigan Museum of Anthropology, Anthropological Papers 65. Ann Arbor.

Greaves, R.D. 1997 Hunting and multifunctional uses of bows and arrows: ethnoarchaeology of technological organization among Pumée Hunters of Venezuela. In Knecht, H. (ed.) *Projectile Technology*. Pp.287-320. New York: Plenum Press.

Grimes, J.R. and B.G. Grimes 1985 Flakeshavers: morphometric, functional and life-cycle analyses of a Paleoindian unifacial tool class. *Archaeology of Eastern North America* 13:35-57.

Hayden, B. 1977 Stone tool functions in the Western Desert. In Wright, R.V.S. (ed.) *Stone Tools as Cultural Markers: Change, Evolution, and Complexity*. Pp 178-188. Australian Institute of Aboriginal Studies, Canberra.

Henry, D.O. 1996 Functional minimalism versus ethnicity in explaining lithic patterns in the Levantine Epipalaeolithic. *Antiquity* 70:135-136.

Hiscock, P. 1988 A Cache of Tulas from the Boulia District, Western Queensland. *Archaeology in Oceania* 23:60-70.

Hiscock, P. 1996 Transformations of Upper Paleolithic implements in the Dabba Industry from Haua Fteah (Libya). *Antiquity* 70:657-664.

Hiscock, P. and Attenbrow, V. 2003 Early Australian implement variation: a reduction model. *Journal of Archaeological Science* 30:239-249.

Hoffman, C.M. 1985 Projectile point maintenance and typology: assessment with factor analysis and canonical correlation. In Carr, C. (ed.), *For Concordance in Archaeological Analysis: Bridging Data Structure, Quantitative Technique, and Theory*. Pp.566-612. Kansas City, MO: Westport Press.

Holdaway, S. 1995 Stone artefacts and the transition. *Antiquity* 69:784-797.

Kuhn, S.L. 1990 A geometric index of reduction for unifacial stone tools. *Journal of Archaeological Science* 17:583-593.

Kuhn, S.L. 1994 A formal approach to the design and assembly of mobile toolkits. *American Antiquity* 59:426-442.

Lancashire, S. 2000 End scraper variability among early Paleoindians. Paper presented at the 65th Annual Meeting of the Society for American Archaeology, Philadelphia.

Lekberg, P. 2000 The lives and lengths of shaft-hole axes. In Olausson, D. and H. Vandkilde (eds) *Material Culture Studies in Scandinavian Archaeology*. Pp.155-161. Lund, Sweden: Institute of Archaeology.

Meindl, R.S., Lovejoy, C. O. and R.P. Mensforth 1982 Skeletal age at death: accuracy of determination and implications for human demography. *Human Biology*

55:73-87.

Morrow, J.E. 1997 End scraper morphology and use-life: an approach for studying Paleoindian lithic technology and mobility. *Lithic Technology* 22:70-85.

Neeley, M. and C. M. Barton 1994 A new approach to interpreting late Pleistocene microlith industries in Southwest Asia. *Antiquity* 68:275-288.

Odell, G.H. 1981 The morphological express at function junction: searching for meaning in lithic tool types. *Journal of Anthropological Research* 37:319-342.

Schiffer, M.B. 1976 *Behavioral Archeology*. New York: Academic.

Shott, M.J. 1986 Technological organization and settlement mobility: an ethnographic examination. *Journal of Anthropological Research* 42:15-51.

Shott, M.J. 1989 On tool class use lives and the formation of archaeological assemblages. *American Antiquity* 54:9-30.

Shott, M.J. 1995 How much is a scraper? Curation, use rates and the formation of scraper assemblages. *Lithic Technology* 20:53-72.

Shott, M.J. 1996a An exegesis of the curation concept. *Journal of Anthropological Research* 52:259-280.

Shott, M.J. 1996b Stage versus continuum in the debris assemblage from production of a fluted biface. *Lithic Technology* 21:6-22.

Shott, M.J. 1997 Lithic reduction at 13HA365, a middle woodland occupation in Hardin County. *Journal of the Iowa Archaeological Society* 44:109-120.

Shott, M.J. 2003 Size as a factor in Middle Paleolithic assemblage variation: a North American perspective. In Moloney, N.and M. Shott (eds) *Lithic Analysis at the Millennium*. Pp.137-149. London: Institute of Archaeology, University College London.

Shott, M.J. In press Lower Paleolithic industries, time, and the meaning of assemblage variation. In Holdaway, S. and L.Wandsnider (eds) *Time in Archaeology: Time Perspectivism Twenty Years Later*. Cambridge: Cambridge University Press.

Shott, M.J., A.P. Bradbury, P.J. Carr, and G.H. Odell 2000 Flake size from platform attributes: predictive and empirical approaches. *Journal of Archaeological Science* 27:877-894.

Shott, M.J. and P. Sillitoe 2004 Modeling use-life distributions in archaeology using New Guinea Wola ethnographic data. *American Antiquity* 69:336-352.

Tindale, N. 1965 Stone implement making among the Nakako, Ngadadjara and Pitjandjara of the Great Western Desert. *Records of the South Australian Museum* 15:131-164.

Truncer, J.J. 1990 Perkiomen points: a study in variability. In Moeller, R. (ed.) *Experiments and Observations on the Terminal Archaic of the Middle Atlantic Region*. Pp.1-62. Archaeological Services, Bethlehem, CT, USA.

Weedman, K.J. 2000 *An Ethnoarchaeological Study of Stone Scrapers Among the Gamo People of Southern Ethiopia*. Unpublished Ph.D. Thesis, Department of Anthropology, University of Florida, Gainesville.

Weedman, K.J. 2002 On the spur of the moment: effects of age and experience on hafted stone scraper morphology. *American Antiquity* 67:731-744.

Wheat, Joe Be 1975 Artifact life histories: cultural templates, typology, evidence and inference. In Raymond, J., B. Loveseth and G.R. (eds) *Primitive Art and Technology*. Pp.7-15. Calgary: University of Calgary Department of Archaeology.

White, J.P. 1969 Typologies for some prehistoric flaked stone artefacts of the Australian New Guinea Highlands. *Archaeology and Physical Anthropology in Oceania* 4:18-46.

White, J.P., Modjeska, N.and I. Hipuya 1977 Group definitions and mental templates: an ethnographic experiment. In R.V. Wright (ed.) *Stone Tools as Cultural Markers: Change, Evolution and Complexity*. Pp.380-390. Australian Institute of Aboriginal Studies, Canberra.